Communications with the Future

Donald D. Stone

Communications with the Future

Matthew Arnold in Dialogue

Henry James

Charles-Augustin Sainte-Beuve

Ernest Renan

Michel Foucault

Friedrich Nietzsche

Hans-George Gadamer

William James

Richard Rorty

John Dewey

Ann Arbor

THE UNIVERSITY OF MICHIGAN PRESS

*A CIP catalog record for this book is available
from the British Library*

Library of Congress Cataloging-in-Publication Data

Stone, Donald David.
    Communications with the future : Matthew Arnold in dialogue
/ Donald D. Stone.
      p.   cm.
    Includes bibliographical references and index.
    ISBN 0-472-10801-8 (acid-free paper)
    1. Arnold, Matthew, 1822–1888—Criticism and interpretation—
History.   2. Arnold, Matthew, 1822–1888—Philosophy.   3. Arnold,
Matthew, 1822–1888—Influence.   4. Culture—Philosophy—
History—19th century.   5. Culture—Philosophy—History—20th
century.   I. Title.
PR4024.S83 1997
821'.8—dc21   97-4486
                                                                    CIP

Preface

This book pays tribute to Matthew Arnold and his dialogical temper. It is also a tribute to friends, colleagues, and students, from China and from the West, whose humane dialogue sustained me during two trying decades. The 1980s and 1990s have been a difficult time for many who entered, and who are still entering, the teaching profession because of their love for both literature and the teaching of literature. We have become more adept, perhaps, at "professing" literature—in exposing its ideological deficiencies and in advancing our own self-promoting agendas—than in writing and speaking on behalf of something bigger and nobler than our professional selves. The humanities, hence, have been starved from within no less than they have been starved from without. Yet, even "in these bad days," Arnold's voice has rarely seemed so fresh. The most dialogical-minded of the great Victorian writers, Arnold believed that we are born into a vast cultural tradition that speaks to us as living voices from the past and present and that provides us with a basis for communicating with and listening to the future.

Chief among the Arnoldians who made my work possible is the late R. H. Super, whose edition of the *Complete Prose Works* is magnificent testimony to Arnold's range, vitality, and continuing relevance. While lecturing on Arnold in 1991 at the Chinese Academy of Social Sciences (CASS) in Beijing and at various other colleges in China, I was struck by the audience's responsiveness to Arnold's words and ideas. When Professor Super learned of their interest, he kindly donated copies of the *Prose Works* to the CASS library. To my Arnoldian-minded friends in China, who are neither disdainful of the past nor fearful of the future, I dedicate this volume: to Zhu Hong, Huang Mei, and my other friends at the Institute of Foreign Literature, CASS; and to my colleagues and former students at Capital Normal University in Beijing, including Han Zhixian, Yang Chuanwei, and Wang Wei. There is one more dedicatee: my dear sister Nadine Millstine.

I am deeply grateful to Ruth apRoberts for our many years of friendship. She provided me with generous support during every stage of the writing of this book, and she read the completed manuscript with thoroughness and care. I am thankful to Miriam Allott, Bob apRoberts, Barbara Bowen, Jerome H. Buckley and Elizabeth Buckley, Robert and Vineta Colby, Morris Dickstein, Robert Ginsberg, Roy Hovey, Kay Kier, Wendy Martin, Nicole Soulé-Susbielles, Adeline R. Tintner, and Zhang Longxi for their encouragement and advice. I am indebted to Cecil Y. Lang for giving me the galleys of the first volume of his new edition of Arnold's letters, plus copies of Arnold's letters to Henry James. I thank the City University Committee on Research for the PSC-CUNY Research Award that allowed me to begin work on this book, and I thank Shirley Strum Kenny and the Queens College Presidential Research Award committee for giving me the time and means to complete a substantial portion of it. I am grateful to Robert Kiely and Sue Lonoff of the Harvard Victorians, to Wendy Martin at the Claremont Graduate School, and to the Victorian Seminar of the City University of New York Graduate Center for their invitations to read portions of the manuscript. My thanks also go to the library staffs at Queens College, Lehman College, Harvard University, and the New York Public Library, and also to my editors at the University of Michigan Press, LeAnn Fields, Kristen M. Lare, and copyeditor Leslie Barkley.

An earlier version of chapter 3 appeared in *Nineteenth-Century Literature*, 43 (December 1988): 289–318. Permission to reprint this article, in its revised and expanded form, has kindly been granted by the Regents of the University of California.

Contents

Introduction: Arnold in Dialogue

On April 5, 1879, Matthew Arnold addressed the Eton Literary Society. "Never in my life," he later recalled, "did I find a more agreeable audience."[1] Although he was preoccupied with his job as inspector of schools, as well as with a commission he had just undertaken to produce an anthology of Wordsworth's poetry, Arnold generously accepted the Eton invitation, just as, two months earlier, he had enthusiastically agreed to address the Ipswich Working Men's College. Perhaps because it is a talk directed to the young, Arnold's "A Speech at Eton" is one of his least-known compositions. Yet it is an engagingly written work that incorporates familiar Arnoldian themes: the relevance of a classical education, the relationship between a nation's cultural and social and political well-being, the necessity for an alliance between Hellenic and Hebraic values. Arnold's gifts as a speaker alert to the moods and needs of his immediate and larger audience are abundantly displayed here. In its published form, the essay provides us with an admirable and succinct introduction to Arnold as the most dialogical-minded, as well as one of the most future-oriented, of Victorian literary and social critics. After an amusing opening description (by way of Epictetus) of student life in first-century Greece, Arnold proceeds to remind his listeners that, whether at Eton or Nicopolis, "the thoughts and habits which [a student] brings with him from home and from the social order in which he moves, must necessarily affect his power of profiting by what his schoolmasters have to teach him" (*CPW*, 9:20). But how does one persuade a member of modern English society that there is a profit in reading Greek and Latin authors—in harkening to any nonmodern or non-English voices? In response to such skepticism, Arnold in the Eton talk demonstrates the value of studying a foreign culture, and he makes a dialogical argument in favor of our finding ourselves in that other world.

Arnold's dialogical temper—his openness to a variety of voices from past and present, from home and abroad, plus his recognition of the multiplicity of voices within each individual—is a testament both to his continuing modernity and to his immersion in the Platonic dialogues. Over twenty years earlier, in his inaugural lecture as Professor of Poetry at Oxford, "On the Modern Element in Literature," Arnold had spoken of England's need for "intellectual," no less than moral, "deliverance": "To know how others stand, that we may know how we ourselves stand; and to know how we ourselves stand, that we may correct our mistakes and achieve our deliverance—that is our problem" (*CPW*, 1:21). Invoking Thucydides' famous account of Pericles' eulogy of Athens, Arnold linked the flourishing of Greek culture with its " 'freedom [in Pericles' words] . . . for individual diversities of opinion and character' " (1:25). Greek culture in its prime celebrated polyphony. The Platonic dialogue itself, as Hans-Georg Gadamer asserts, depended on "a living community" of varied individuals discussing ideas in an "open-ended" manner that precluded authoritative conclusions. For Plato, hence, "dialectic is unending and infinite." Walter Pater, in *Plato and Platonism*, similarly depicts the continuing "dialectic process" as "co-extensive with life": "it does but put one into a duly receptive attitude towards such possible truths, discovery, or revelation." It does not of itself "provide a proposition, nor a system of propositions, but forms a temper." Here, Pater is echoing Joubert's view (quoted approvingly by Arnold) that Plato " 'teaches us nothing; but he prepares us, fashions us, and makes us ready to know all' " (3:203). We learn by listening and responding, by discovering that there is no such thing as an isolated ego or an isolated culture. Encountering our dialogical identity, we see (as Mikhail Bakhtin noted) that "being" is tantamount to "co-being." In Gadamer's words, we learn "to become at home in" the other.[2]

Unlike Periclean Greece, mid-Victorian England seemed to Arnold an insular nation, singularly indifferent to alternative viewpoints or dialogical interchange, whether expressed by ancient authors or foreign thinkers. When he finally published "On the Modern Element" in 1868, a decade after having given the lecture, Arnold apologized for its dogmatic style, the sign of an ambitious but novice speaker. However, by the late 1860s (the period when the "Culture and Anarchy" papers were appearing in *Cornhill*), he felt no need to apologize for its theme. For while Arnold had learned over the years to be a better auditor as well as a more experienced speaker, he had also become increasingly convinced of the perils confronting a nation that refused to listen or enter into that dialogue with the past and future that Arnold called "culture." Praising the efforts of the state-run educational systems he had inspected on the Continent, Arnold lamented the absence at home of such solidarity-making institutions. In his tribute to one such school, "A French Eton" (1864), Arnold targeted as "the great end of society . . . the perfecting of the individual, the fullest, freest, and worthiest development of the individual's activity." But for true "perfection" (a process Arnold perceived as never ceasing), he observed, the individual "must often learn to quit old habits, to adopt new, to go out for himself, to transform himself" (*CPW*, 2:312).

It is through education, Arnold believed (as did his American admirer, John Dewey), that the individual and the nation conjointly flourish. In coming to speak at the original Eton, he used the occasion to reaffirm the importance of education as that which permits one "to get to know himself and the world," and to become acquainted with such examples of "the best which has been thought and said in the world" (here, Arnold's emphasis is as much on "world" as "best") as were produced in ancient Greece and Rome (*CPW*, 9:21). For as we read the classic texts, we also learn about their world, a world with "connection with ourselves." To underscore this point, Arnold seizes upon the Greek word *eutrapelos, eutrapelia,* seeing in it "a thread which will lead you, if you follow it, to large and instructive results" (9:23). The word appears in Pericles' oration as a term expressing that "quality of flexibility" that has made Athens great. For Arnold, the critical spirit demands such flexibility as the prerequisite for "lucidity of thought, clearness and propriety of language, freedom from prejudice and freedom from stiffness, openness of mind, amiability of manners" (24). It is the quality needed alike by the critic of poetry (as Arnold had said with reference to the "*undulating and diverse* being of Montaigne" [1:174]) and by the critic of society: "a free play of mind upon all subjects" (3:268). Only with such openness and attempt at clarity of mind can one see where the world is tending and prepare oneself accordingly. Such an attitude may be found in newly powerful societies, such as Athens, or in the young. Hence, Plato and Aristotle, a generation after Pericles, employ the term *eutrapelia* to describe the "flexibility and felicity in the give-and-take of gay and light social intercourse," the sort of "happy and right mean" that is achieved, say, "when old men try to adapt themselves to the young" (9:25). An individual learns, and a nation learns, by listening and adapting.

But Greece, despite her greatness, fell; and in the wake of her fall, the term *eutrapelia* came to signify something ignoble. For Pindar and, later still, for St. Paul, the term stood for light-minded attitudes, a frivolous disregard for moral conduct. Athenian freethinking gave way to "filthiness and foolish talking" (*CPW*, 9:26). What, then, can be learned, Arnold asks his youthful audience, from the fate of a word, a word so important to "that Greek world so nearly and wonderfully connected with us" (26)? The answer is certainly not to shut one's ear to the example of Hellenism, as the English are prone to do. In the individual and in society are "certain needs, certain instincts," of a diverse nature. One's preservation and happiness depend on the satisfying of the various needs for beauty and knowledge, for "social life and manners," for righteous behavior (26–27). And Greece in her prime knew this to be so. The victorious Athenians may have supplanted the older Dorian population—a people stiff, hard, narrow, unprogressive, unamiable (like England's Puritan stock)—but they also profited from the Dorian heritage.³ "Man has to advance . . . along several lines," Arnold observes; and it was precisely the "alliance" that Periclean Athens maintained "between the old morality and the new freedom" (29, 31) that make her worthy of study. However, the balance did not last. Greece could not return to the discredited religion of her predecessors, nor would she respect the moral values that continued to inspire her best poets and philosophers. The greatest thinker of the age, who advocated *both* an intellectual free play of mind and a respect for the old "religion of righteousness," Socrates, finally, had less to say to his own time than he did to the future. His own pupil Alcibiades did not listen. And so, "Hellas as a whole, oscillated and fell away" (32–33).

Greece fell, Arnold asserts, because, in the last resort her "flexibility was really not flexible enough," because she would not heed those "moral ideas" that are an essential part of a society's diversity and health. The "moral," Arnold concludes, affects "no nation more than ours," an England that bows to Jerusalem but slights Hellas, and that listens to one political party or another, Conservatism or Liberalism, without realizing that any one line, "taken alone, is not sufficient, is not of itself saving" (*CPW*, 9:34–35). In "A Speech at Eton," Arnold drew upon convictions that had long fired his writings on literary, social, political, and religious issues. No English writer of his time was so diverse—frustratingly so, as his detractors discovered. None looked in so many directions—to fifth-century Greece and modern France and Germany, to Eastern and Celtic sources, to such disparate voices as Emerson and Burke, Goethe and George Sand, Byron and Wordsworth—in order to provide values to nourish the ongoing democratic revolution. Arnold is perhaps the preeminent example of what Stefan Collini has (in a fine recent book) called the "Public Moralists" of Victorian England.4 But if none of his contemporaries speaks to our own century with Arnold's flair and force, the reason may lie less in some of the answers he provided to his various audiences than in his dialogical frame of mind.

Arnold's mentor here was Socrates, a speaker less eloquent on the podium, perhaps, than Pericles (as Arnold concedes in *Culture and Anarchy*). Yet while "men went away from the oratory of Pericles, saying it was very fine, it was very good, and afterwards thinking no more about it [,] . . . they went away from hearing Socrates talk . . . with the point of what he had said sticking fast in their minds, and they could not get rid of it" (*CPW*, 5:228). In Arnold's time, speakers like Carlyle and Ruskin made a more flamboyant oratorical impression. The young Etonians, apparently, were more excited by Ruskin's visit than by Arnold's. But Arnold made his auditors listen not just to him but *through* him, to "the point of what he had said," and through him to the voices of other cultures, other points of view. His method is part of his theme: to encourage in us a free play of mind while not allowing us to disregard the moral responsibilities we owe to our collective identity. Arnold practices a Socratic strategy of the sort Gadamer praises when he describes language, as, ideally, an unending dialogue, one in which we discover that we are part of an extended conversation. Realizing that we belong to language, Gadamer asserts, is the first step toward recognizing that we belong to a cultural heritage that is always remaking itself. According to Gadamer, we participate in dialogue even when we are alone, in that "inner dialogue of the soul with itself, as Plato so beautifully called thought." But Arnold's immediate predecessors were apprehensive of the individual's retreat into the self; they feared the antisocial implications of what Coleridge, discussing *Hamlet*, called "inward brooding," or what Carlyle saw as the modern disease of "self-contemplation." (In an intriguing new book on Pater, Denis Donoghue has defined that retreat into the self as the beginning of modernism.)5

Arnold's career may be seen in terms of his rejection of the modernist stance of a Hamlet or Empedocles, engaged in "the dialogue of the mind with itself" (*CPW,* 1:1), and of his adoption of a different role model. He appealed instead to the "possible Socrates" within us all, to "that power of a disinterested play of consciousness upon [our] stock notions and habits, of which this wise and admirable man gave all through his lifetime the great example, and which was the secret of his incomparable influence" (5:228–29). But this same Socrates ("who," Arnold observes, "introduced a stream of thought so fresh, bold, and transforming that it frightened 'respectable' people and was the cause of his death") was also "never weary of recalling the Hellenic mind to the old-fashioned maxims of righteousness, temperance, and self-knowledge engraved on the temple at Delphi" (287).

Many of Arnold's best essays originated as lectures. His initial audiences were the Oxford students to whom he presented a variety of contrasting voices—from Theocritus and St. Francis to Maurice de Guérin and Heine, from Celtic poets to a "French Coleridge" (Joubert). At Oxford he lectured on the value of academies as an antidote to "provincial" thinking, and he hailed the progressive nature of "culture" as a deterrent to the individualistic, laissez-faire mentality of his countrymen. The proponents of culture, he memorably argued, bespeak a *"social idea";* they "are the true apostles of equality" (*CPW,* 5:113). It was at Cambridge, however—home to men of science like Darwin—that Arnold first delivered his defense of the humanities, "Literature and Science" (1882), with its contention that "Letters will call out [our] being at more points, will make [us] live more" (10:70). He subsequently included this talk among the discourses he gave, a year later, in America, his other topics being "Emerson" and "Numbers; or The Majority and the Remnant." Although he was not a prepossessing speaker (barely audible on his first attempts), Arnold learned to make himself better heard. He spoke seventy times altogether in the New World—to undergraduates at the Universities of Michigan and Wisconsin, for example, as well as to members of the Boston elite and the Washington political establishment. According to Park Honan, Arnold's greatest appeal was "to the young." But many who had been put off by the critical nature of his comments, as heard from the podium, recognized the truth of his position when the *Discourses in America* (Arnold's favorite among his books) was published.[6]

If Arnold sometimes seemed a bit hard on his auditors—challenging them to rethink positions they had come to take for granted—he was also hard on himself. At times, in Socratic manner, he humorously refers to his unattractive image, describing himself in "A Liverpool Address" (1882) as "a nearly worn-out man of letters, with one nostrum for practical application, his nostrum of public schools for the middle classes; and with a frippery of phrases about sweetness and light, seeing things as they really are, knowing the best that has been thought and said in the world, which never [according to his critics] had very much solid meaning, and have now quite lost the gloss and charm of novelty" (*CPW*, 10:74).7 An important feature of Arnold's talks is the way he combines a confrontational message with an urbane manner. Except, perhaps, in the case of some of the more appreciative Oxford or American audiences, Arnold rarely preached to the converted. It was, for example, to the privileged members of the Royal Institution ("the most aristocratic and exclusive place out," as one detractor put it) that he read his passionate denunciation of England's political inequality. "I am glad to treat [this subject, 'Equality'']," he announced at the outset, "before such an audience as this" (8:283).8 And the talk at Liverpool University College—given to a group honoring its medical students—is remarkable for its noncelebratory theme. "In no country in the world," he contends, "is so much nonsense so firmly believed" (10:87). Arnold cajoles his auditors to look about Liverpool and decide whether they should be praising the city for its scientific and industrial achievements or instead be lamenting the low "standard of life" practiced there. "Money-making is not enough by itself," he avows. "Industry is not enough by itself. Seriousness [Liverpool's Protestantism] is not enough by itself." Education should sharpen our sense of values, he urges; it should encourage a "desire for beauty" and a "social spirit"; it should point us toward a world with better architecture and more amenities (83–84).

In his talk before the Ipswich Working Men's College ("Ecce, Convertimur ad Gentes"), Arnold offered a "perfect frankness" despite the possibility that he might "offend some of those who hear me" (*CPW*, 9:6). But the cause of public education was very dear to him, and the reforms he advocated (as he told his sister soon after he gave the talk) were "the first practicable of those great democratic reforms to which we must, I believe, one day come" (see 9:327). Hence, he repeated his charge that England's inequalities have resulted in a "*materialised*" upper class, a "*vulgarised*" middle class, and a "*brutalised*" lower class (9);

and he reasserted his conviction that only the intervention of the state can provide for a fair and equitable order. Only state-run schools, such as those in France and Germany, can foster a feeling of social "co-operation" and encourage meaningful individual growth. Middle-class opponents of the principle of solidarity may have taken the political lead, Arnold declares, but they do not deserve it, as "they have lived in a narrow world of their own, without openness and flexibility of mind, without any notion of the variety of powers and possibilities in human life. They know neither man nor the world" (16–17). They are, thus, unfit to wield power, and it is in your own best interests, Arnold tells his audience, to support "middle class education." As you carry the work "forward yourselves," he concludes, rather daringly, ". . . insist on taking the middle class with you" (19).

It is a mistake, I think, to accuse Arnold of looking down on his audiences. The truth is that, whether he is addressing Eton school-boys or Ipswich working men, Americans or Liverpudlians, he is looking forward *with* them. To whomever he spoke, he urged an "openness and flexibility of mind" (the "first of virtues" [*CPW*, 2:29]) as the best way to confront the future. And to look forward is to look outward. Here, Arnold showed himself to be the heir to German thinkers such as Herder, Goethe, and Humboldt for whom exposure to life's polyphony—the recognition and celebration of multiple voices and perspectives—was necessary for the development (*Bildung*) of the individual and society. This key tenet of German Romanticism lies behind Bakhtin's "dialogical principle." In his study of Dostoev-sky, Bakhtin hailed that novelist's creation of "*a plurality of indepen-dent and unmerged voices and consciousnesses, a genuine polyphony of fully valid voices*," and he hailed Dostoevsky's depiction of a world still being made, a world "*open and free*, [in which] *everything is still in the future and will always be in the future.*" Friedrich Schlegel had already suggested that "Novels are the Socratic dialogues of our day"; but Bakhtin's interest lay not only in the novel as a dialogical form but also in the novel as a way of life, as a metaphor for "a world whose unity [in the words of Gary Saul Morson and Caryl Emerson] is essentially one of multiple voices, whose conversations never reach finality and cannot be transcribed in monologic form."[9]

This necessary paradox in Bakhtin's thinking, his celebration of a "unity" that is polyphonic, is one that is found in Arnold's dialogical position too. It informs Arnold's welcoming of democracy and his

championing of culture—both of them actively dialogical forces—
even as he upholds, at the same time and in Socratic fashion, the
value of collective standards and ideals. But the standards and ideals
themselves are always to be sought after and defined anew; and Arnold's practice is to look everywhere for help, even if he seems at
times to contradict himself in the process. "There is hardly a state-
ment in Arnold's prose," Morris Dickstein astutely remarks, "that
cannot be counterpointed with remarks elsewhere which qualify it.
This 'thinking against oneself' and against the prevailing prejudices
of the moment is one of his sovereign values."[10] But this allowing for
multiple inner, as well as outer, voices is made in behalf of a principle
that (for Arnold and Bakhtin) denies the right of any single voice,
Hebraic or Hellenic, Liberal or Conservative, to monopolize the truth.
The proponents of culture, from Socrates to Goethe, from Arnold to
Bakhtin and Gadamer, celebrate all that is various and meaningful
outside and within us; they champion a principle of growth and re-
newal through genuine dialogue.[11] No position, as Arnold told the
Etonians, is of itself alone "saving."

In the following chapters I will be examining Arnold's dialogical
nature. To do so, I place him in the company of a varied group of major
figures, some of whom directly influenced or were influenced by him,
others with whom he shared a common critical task. Two of the latter,
Friedrich Nietzsche and Michel Foucault, might be considered Arnoldian to some degree in spite of themselves, given their positions as
revaluators of past traditions and as proponents of the idea of *Bildung*.
(Nietzsche's and Foucault's rejection of Arnoldian humanism is not, I
think, to their credit.) In the first chapter, I show how Arnold's "largeness of horizon" (in Henry James's phrase) inspired James's critical and
creative energies. The Arnold of the *Essays in Criticism* (which James
rapturously reviewed as a fledgling critic) and *On the Study of Celtic
Literature* is an advocate of multiculturalism, in the widest sense of the
word. Arnold's ties with French criticism are the focus of chapter 2; and
here I survey the obvious connection between him and Sainte-Beuve
(who called Arnold "un étranger qui nous connait mieux que personne"), but also the connections between him and Ernest Renan,
Edmond Scherer, and Foucault. My middle chapter pairs Arnold with
his greatest nineteenth-century counterpart, Nietzsche, as advocates
of the idea of culture, an idea deriving from Greek and German Romantic sources. But while Arnold's Nietzschean side is one that questions

the customs and dogmas of the past (*"is* it so?" this Goethean voice asks; "is it so to *me?"* [*CPW,* 3:110]), his hermeneutic side, the topic of chapter 4, endeavors to see what remains of living value among the canonical texts. Arnold's heir in this enterprise is the German philosopher Gadamer: for both of them, a classic author is necessarily one whose voice is always fresh and thus always worth heeding. We never stop conversing with the classics, according to Sainte-Beuve, who trenchantly wondered, "What would they say of us?"[12] By studying Arnold's religious writings alongside Gadamer's hermeneutical texts, especially *Truth and Method* and his studies of Plato, I highlight their position as humanists.

In the last chapter, I return to Arnold's dialogue with America, as seen in his affinities with American pragmatists such as William James, Richard Rorty, and, above all, John Dewey. In their shared faith in the power of education, and in their liberal values, Arnold and Dewey saw culture as a process necessary to a flourishing democracy. Both men possessed a "lucidity of mind and largeness of temper," as well as a formidable idealism, which often put them (as Arnold says of Falkland) in opposition to their times. But by taking a "stand against the inadequate ideals dominant in their time, [they] kept open their communications with the future, lived with the future" (*CPW,* 8:204). If, along the way, I focus on Arnoldian texts that have not always received their due—works like "A Speech at Eton," *On the Study of Celtic Literature, Literature and Dogma,* or the *Mixed Essays* (among which the essay on Falkland appears)—I do so in the belief that these examples of Arnold's dialogism, together with the better-known *Essays in Criticism* and *Culture and Anarchy,* will enrich our sense of Arnold's "openness and flexibility of mind." They reinforce our sense of Arnold's intellectual range and his social commitments, as well as increase our appreciation of his stylistic gifts, and they reinforce our sense of the continued modernity and relevance of Arnold's voice.

Chapter One

Arnold and Henry James: Crossing Cultures

My brother Saxons have, as is well known, a terrible way with them of wanting to improve everything but themselves off the face of the earth; I have no such passion for finding nothing but myself everywhere.

Arnold, *On the Study of Celtic Literature*

In art there are no countries.

James, "Collaboration"

Among Arnold's many nineteenth-century American admirers, none was more receptive than Henry James. Praising Arnold on the occasion of his visit to America in 1883–84, James called particular attention to the English writer's "largeness of horizon," which took in not only Europe but America as well. "To an American in England," he said, ". . . the author of the *Essays in Criticism*, of *Friendship's Garland*, of *Culture and Anarchy*, . . . speaks more directly than any other contemporary English writer"; and, in a paraphrase of one of Arnold's most widely quoted remarks, James declared, "It is Mr. Arnold . . . that we think of when we figure to ourselves the best knowledge of what is being done in the world, the best appreciation of literature and life."[1] Arnold had been, "in prose and verse, the idol" of James's young manhood, a role model for James and his New England friends, whose desire it was, as the Civil War ended, to vindicate and strengthen the claims of civilization in the New World.[2] James's introduction to Arnold's *Essays* was a milestone, as he later recalled, in his literary career. It is fitting, then, that James should be the subject of the first of the Arnoldian dialogues in this book: he was initially a disciple, later a friend (whose work Arnold enjoyed reading), and eventually himself an influence on Arnold. James was deeply indebted to the author of the *Essays* and *On the Study of Celtic Literature* (Arnold's key multicultural texts), both for his example as an English-speaking critic who was at home in many cultures and for his critical

11

ideas—ideas that proved fruitful in James's fiction, his own criticism, and in such travel writings as *The American Scene*.

Privileged Arnoldian terms such as *civilization, culture, perfection,* and *the critical spirit* can be found not only throughout James's writings, but in those of his family too. Henry James, Sr., for example, expressing his love for and pride in his author-son in 1873, commended "what Mr. Arnold calls your 'sweet reasonableness.' " In *A Little Tour in France* (1882), James recalled appropriate passages from Arnold's poetry on several occasions: while visiting the town of Sète, the fountain at Vaucluse, and the church at Brou. James's novels, tales, essays teem with Arnoldian phrases, of which the following are a representative sampling: Mrs. Brookenham, in *The Awkward Age* (1899), facing an opportunity for her family, "saw it steadily and saw it whole"; the Moreen family, in "The Pupil" (1891), constitute "a household of Bohemians who wanted tremendously to be Philistines"; "we are all Philistines to the core," complains Nick Dormer, in *The Tragic Muse* (1890), "with about as much aesthetic sense as that hat"; the American Philistine Dr. Jackson Lemon, beguiled by "the look of race" in a young aristocrat ("a daughter of the highest civilization"), discovers too late that his fiancée, "Lady Barberina" (1883), is an Arnoldian Barbarian without "the least curiosity"; Isabel Archer, the too-curious heroine of *The Portrait of a Lady* (1881), "was always planning out her own development [the gospel of *Culture and Anarchy*], desiring her own perfection, observing her own progress."[3] Some of James's many allusions to Arnold's terms *Hellenism* and *Hebraism* will be discussed in due course. However, I want to call particular attention to his receptiveness to the Arnoldian appeal for the "free play of the mind," a phrase applied to many of James's preferred sensibilities, such as Isabel with her "vagabond mind"; or Merton Densher, from *The Wings of the Dove* (1902), whose "play of . . . mind" must compensate for the inability to act; or Adam Verver, from *The Golden Bowl* (1904), with his "play of vision." The play of mind is a favorite resource for Lambert Strether as he strolls to the Luxembourg Gardens, in *The Ambassadors* (1903), enjoying the "plenitude of his consciousness" and "finding himself so free" in the process.[4]

Arnold's initial use of the expression, in "The Function of Criticism at the Present Time" (1864), deserves quotation in full:

The notion of the free play of the mind upon all subjects being a pleasure in itself, being an object of desire, being an essential provider of elements without which a nation's spirit, whatever compensations it may have for them, must, in the long run, die of inanition, hardly enters into an Englishman's thoughts. It is noticeable that the word *curiosity*, which in other languages is used in a good sense, to mean, as a high and fine quality of man's nature, just this disinterested love of a free play of the mind on all subjects, for its own sake,—it is noticeable, I say, that this word has in our language no sense of the kind, no sense but a rather bad and disparaging one. But criticism, real criticism, is essentially the exercise of this very quality. It obeys an instinct prompting it to try to know the best that is known and thought in the world, irrespective of practice, politics, and everything of the kind; and to value knowledge and thought as they approach this best, without the intrusion of any other considerations whatever. (*CPW*, 3:268)

In our time, these words (or a brief portion, invariably wrenched out of context) are often cited as if they were a defense of elitist and reactionary standards set in stone at some point in the Mesolithic Age and passed down from one generation of Mesocentric cavemen to another until they ended up as the repressive protocols of modern-day English departments.[5] For James, however, the words meant the liberation and justification of his critical and creative energies. The "free play of the mind" would become the vocation of the Jamesian character and author alike; and what the mind played over was, in James's case, a variegated terrain, a map of competing ideas, truths, cultures.

In his autobiography, James chronicles his discovery, at the age of about eleven, that a baffled consciousness and restless curiosity such as his had a value that could be put to expressive use. Attending a professional staging of *Uncle Tom's Cabin* (earlier, he had seen a less sophisticated adaptation), James recalls "the thrill of an aesthetic adventure": watching the playing and also critically *watching* himself watching, receiving "his first glimpse of that possibility of a 'free play of mind' over a subject which was to throw him with force at a later stage of culture, when subjects had considerably multiplied, into the critical

arms of Matthew Arnold."[6] That decisive moment came in the summer
of 1865 when James, at twenty-two, a new contributor to the *North
American Review,* was assigned Arnold's *Essays in Criticism,* "with the
classicism of its future awaiting it." So important was this event that
fifty years later James imbued it "with the color of romance" as he
remembered "the rapture with which, then suffering under the effects
of a bad accident [the back injury that had disqualified him from potential service in the war], I lay all day on a sofa in Ashburton Place" (the
James family home in Boston), reading the ink-stained proofsheets,
"and was somehow transported, as in a shining silvery dream, to London, to Oxford, to the French Academy, to Languedoc, to Brittany, to
ancient Greece."[7] As a multitude of Arnoldian worlds opened up to the
ambitious invalid so too did a world of literary possibilities. For Arnold
had demonstrated how criticism satisfies a moral, aesthetic, and civic
claim; he had shown that the critic's function, in large part, is "to exalt
the importance of the ideal" ("poetic feeling subserving the ends of
criticism") while also revealing his powers of acute "observation" and
"sympathy" in the form of a "charming style."[8]

James was not alone in embracing Arnold. Indeed, a cultured
remnant in America was ready for the author of the *Essays,* some of
them already, like James, admirers of this poetry. A new generation of
dedicated editors, including Charles Eliot Norton, Edwin L. Godkin,
and James T. Fields (and, later, William Dean Howells), were seeking
clever young talent with Arnoldian predilections for their journals, the
North American Review, the *Nation,* the *Atlantic.* Norton in particular,
with whom (and with his sister Grace) James would maintain a deep
friendship, was New England's "representative of culture," in James's
phrase, preaching as his "mission" no less than "the matter of
civilization—the particular civilization that a young roaring and money-
getting democracy, inevitably but almost exclusively occupied with
'business success,' most needed to have brought home to it." With his
seemingly contradictory goals—addressing "the moral conscience
while speaking as by his office for our imagination and our free
curiosity"[9]—Norton readily saw an ally in Arnold. Norton and James
were attempting to balance what Arnold called (first in the essay on
Heine, later in *Culture and Anarchy*) their "Hebraic" and "Hellenic"
instincts. In much of his criticism from the 1860s to the 1870s, and in
much of the fiction of this (but not only this) period, a Jamesian version
of Hebraism and Hellenism, the New England conscience and the free

play of the mind, provides two of the points of influence between which the Jamesian world moves.[10]

In 1865 Arnold provided James with a needful assurance that his "disinterested" sensibility, uninterested in the conventional male world of "doing" (of "downtown," in New York parlance), was valuable. The "business" of criticism, he notes in his review of Arnold's *Essays*, "is to make truth generally accessible, and not to apply it. It is only on condition of having its hands free, that it can make truth generally accessible." Criticism, moreover, is a form of doing—showing to the public, in Arnold's words (cited by James), examples of the "best that is known and thought in the world, and, by in its turn making this known, to create a current of true and fresh ideas" (*CPW*, 3:270)—but its activity has nothing to do with the Philistine preoccupation with what is "almost exclusively practical," with politics and business. Among the *Essays*, James singles out for special praise "The Function of Criticism" and "The Literary Influence of Academies." The first he admired for addressing issues "perhaps more directly pertinent" in America than in England, given his countrymen's obsession with the practical and their accompanying disregard for the "ideal." The second piece, with its appeal to "a recognized authority, imposing on us a high standard in matters of intellect and taste" (3:235), bolstered James's sense of the need for critical safeguards and his distaste for things "provincial." James's subsequent fear about declining American "vocal tone" standards echoes Arnold's concern with the lack of English writing standards. Both Arnold and James loved the theater and regarded the stage as a potential national Academy for the dissemination of civilizing standards. A visit by the Comédie Française to London in 1879 inspired Arnold to write in behalf of a similar institution in England, a nationally organized theater containing a repertory of classic works and the "modern English drama, when it comes," whose mission it would be to raise English taste to higher standards.[11]

Arnold and James jointly called attention to the superiority of French critical and literary standards, and both were accordingly castigated by their nations' reviewers. Not surprisingly, the two often admired and wrote about the same French author. In the case of Joubert and the two Guérins, Arnold took the lead, but James was first to discuss Edmond Scherer's work on Goethe. Perhaps inevitably, the early James reviews suffer in comparison with Arnold's. They lack, all too often, the quality James praises in Arnold: "having a *subject*," being *"about* something." With Eugenie de Guérin, for example, James does not have Arnold's grasp of what constitutes her special "distinction," her mixture of Catholic piety and personal struggle. For James, it is enough to call her a "saint": "What is a saint? the reader may ask. A saint, we hasten to reply, is—Mlle. de Guérin."[12] Arnold's portrait is more complex: "Mdlle. de Guérin is not one of those saints arrived at perfect sweetness and calm, steeped in ecstacy; there is something primitive, indomitable in her, which she governs, indeed, but which chafes, which revolts" (*CPW,* 3:88).

What the youthful James lacked as a seasoned critic, he attempted to make up for through the appearance of authority; and here Arnold's influence was not always beneficial. One thinks of the condescending reviews of Dickens, dismissed for his vulgarity and lack of "philosophy," and of Trollope. Such *"monstrous"* novels as *Miss Mackenzie* are "anomalies," he charges. "Mr. Matthew Arnold, however, has recently told us that a large class of Englishmen consider it no objection to a thing that it is an anomaly. Mr. Trollope is doubtless one of the number." Even authors James admired were criticized on Arnoldian grounds. The complaint that *"Middlemarch* is a treasure-house of details, but . . . an indifferent whole," restates Arnold's position, in the 1853 preface to *Poems,* that while Keats's "Isabella" is a "perfect treasure-house of graceful and felicitous words and images," it lacks form, coherence, *"Architectonicé"* (*CPW,* 1:9–10). Above all, one remembers James's 1865 review of *Drum Taps,* which slashes away at Whitman's "prosaic mind," vatic pretensions, "anomalous style." "To be positive one must have something to say," James declares; "to be positive requires reason, labor, and art; and art requires, above all things, a suppression of one's self, a subordination of one's self to an idea."[13] James's source here is Arnold's criticism of the Romantic poets for their lack of ideas and cohesiveness. James would eventually change his mind about Whitman, but for Arnold the author of *Leaves of Grass* appeared (in Lionel Trilling's words) "the perfect Philistine." Whatever his admirers might say of his being "so unlike anyone else, to me," Arnold avowed, "this seems to be his demerit; no one can afford in literature to trade merely on his own bottom and to take no account of what the other ages and nations have acquired."[14] For Arnold, art and criticism required crossing cultures. What are the *Essays in Criticism* if not essays in multicul-turalism? (And for those who discern only a single "Eurocentric" voice, Arnold deftly shows how complex and varied the European polyphony is: he underscores how each voice—Heine's for example, "a juncture between the French spirit and German ideas and German culture," who founds something new [3:120]—is a mass of verities and contradictions.)

Elsewhere among his reviews of the 1860s and early 1870s, James offers glimpses of the mature themes to come. Three months after the review of Arnold, he saluted the tolerance and wide-ranging sympa-thy, the "liberal" temper, of Scherer, whom he calls "a solid embodi-ment of Mr. Matthew Arnold's ideal critic."[15] More impressive still is the 1867 essay on "The Works of Epictetus," the Stoic slave who helped "prop, . . . in these bad days," Arnold's mind, and whom James com-pares to the hero of one of Arnold's *Essays*, Marcus Aurelius. The essay is significant as an attempt to meet Arnold on his own ground, to write seriously about something (an exploration of the "best"), and to detach an interesting figure from (for James) an unattractive philosophy. A Stoicism such as Epictetus's, James maintains, is unsuited for modern times. Arnold, having characterized Eugénie de Guérin's Catholicism as beautiful but "sterile," placed a higher importance on the Protestant allowance for "freedom" (*CPW*, 3:98). James, similarly, dismisses Sto-icism as an outworn doctrine, given "that the true condition of happi-ness is freedom." The temptation of Stoicism, as Arnold and James jointly realize, is that "It declares a man's happiness to be wholly in his own hands, to be identical with the strength of his will." But such a form of detached "self-control" is ultimately (like New England Puritan-ism) life-denying.[16] A number of James's fictional protagonists will struggle with this Stoical predisposition—Strether, of course, as well as Rowland Mallett in *Roderick Hudson* (1875), and both Basil Ransom and Olive Chancellor in *The Bostonians* (1886). However, as early as 1867, James was aware that another, more life-enhancing, point of view was needed.

James's movement toward Hellenism was accomplished, as was Ar-nold's (and, before him, Heine's), by way of an extended detour through France. France seemed the most intellectually alive of na-tions, the modern successor to Periclean Athens. The leading French critics—Sainte-Beuve, Renan, Taine, Scherer—were artists in their different ways, apostles of culture, acute observers, memorable delineators, and (aside from Taine) opponents of formula and theory. To Sainte-Beuve, whom in 1875 he called "the acutest critic the world has seen," James ascribed an Arnoldian temper: "He only cared to look freely—to look all round." Sainte-Beuve may have displaced Arnold as James's ideal critic (he was Arnold's ideal critic too), but James often praised Sainte-Beuve in Arnoldian terms. "He valued life and literature equally for the light they threw upon each other," James said of him, and as James would say of Arnold a few years later; "to his mind one implied the other." But the Frenchman's devotion to culture was even more complete than Arnold's, by Jamesian standards, since he "was not even married; his literary consciousness was never complicated with the sense of an unliterary function."[17] James embraced the notion of the critic as priest, a fitting role for one carrying out the civilizing mission advocated by Norton; but James's mission involved taking in a wider range of artistic territory than that deemed necessary by Norton.

As early as September 1867, in a letter to his childhood friend Thomas Sargeant Perry, James hoped "to do as Ste. Beuve has done," to "acquire something of his intelligence and his patience and vigour." His ambition, at age twenty-four, was to be an American Sainte-Beuve, just as in the field of fiction he aimed at being an American Balzac. But where, he wondered, could an American artist-critic be expected to find the materials to nourish his dream? In the letter to Perry, James expressed the view that Americans like himself are naturally predisposed to cosmopolitanism:

> to be an American is an excellent preparation for culture. We have exquisite qualities as a race, and it seems to me that we are ahead of the European races in the fact that more than either of them we can deal freely with forms of civilization not our own, can pick and choose and assimilate and in short (aesthetically etc.) claim our property wherever we find it. To have no national stamp has hitherto been a defect and a drawback, but I think it not unlikely that American writers may yet indicate that a vast intellectual fusion and synthesis of the various National tendencies of the world is the condition of more important achievements than any we have seen.

Hence, to enrich American culture, to help in its development, one must look elsewhere, everywhere—taking (he assures Perry) the one distinctly American property that is "distinctive and homogeneous . . . (,) our moral consciousness."[18]

A year before James's letter to Perry, Arnold's "My Countrymen," his response to the attacks on "The Function of Criticism," had appeared in the *Cornhill*. To those assailing him for pointing out English defects (inaptitude for ideas, acceptance of anomalies, and so on), Arnold urged, "But look at America," which, with all its transported Anglo-Saxon stock, nevertheless shows "a feeling for ideas, a vivacity and play of mind, which our middle class has not, and which comes to the Americans, probably, from their democratic life, with its ardent hope, its forward stride, its gaze fixed on the future" (*CPW*, 5:30). America's "culture" is accordingly better because, as the future author of *Culture and Anarchy* affirms, Americans believe in the principle of development. James assuredly read "My Countrymen" as well as its sequel, "Culture and Its Enemies," which appeared in *Cornhill* for July 1867. By the late 1860s, he and his friends were applying Arnoldian themes to the American scene. In 1869, the year before she died, James's cousin Minny Temple (the prototype of Isabel Archer and Milly Theale) wrote him expressing her interest in "that culture which Matthew Arnold thinks the most desirable thing in the world." To Perry, thus, James affirmed that "we young Americans are (without cant) men of the future." One must, as Americans and for America, appropriate the cultures of Arnold and Sainte-Beuve, but go beyond them, creating a "fusion and synthesis."[19]

Arnold deserves a good deal of credit for James's development into both a seasoned literary critic and a storyteller drawing upon cross-cultural (or "international," in James's phrase) themes and subjects. From the late 1860s to the end of the 1870s, the period of James's apprenticeship, Arnold's influence took a variety of forms. One sees it, for example, in the "passionate pilgrimage" of Jamesian characters, and James himself, to Oxford, "Queen of Romance," as James deemed her upon reading the Preface to Arnold's *Essays in Criticism*, with its famous tribute to Oxford ("home of lost causes"). "An American of course," James states in an 1877 travel sketch, "with his fondness for antiquity, his relish for picturesqueness, his 'emotional' attitude at historic shrines, takes Oxford much more seriously than its sometimes unwilling familars can be expected to do." Jamesian Americans bring higher aesthetic and moral standards to bear upon the Old World. In the fine early story "The Madonna of the Future" (1873), an expatriate laments all that has been denied American artists: "The soil of American perception is a poor little barren, artificial deposit. . . . [We] are wedded to imperfection." Once in Europe, however, they are torn between opposing poles, "the critical and the ideal," the one showing things as they (often unpleasantly) are, the other pointing to an unreachable perfection. And Americans abroad are caught between the desire to enjoy life in its variety and the moral impulse restraining that desire. The fourth chapter of *Culture and Anarchy* provided James with terms applicable to these contending forces, *Hellenism and Hebraism*. Here, Arnold argues that both components are necessary—the capacity "to see things as they really are," plus the need for "strictness of conscience" (*CPW*, 5:165). In practice, however, the one generally thrives at the expense of the other. If ancient Greece and modern France were, for Arnold, preeminent in the free play of ideas, both countries nevertheless fell (as he says in 1871, apropos of France's recent debacle) for "want of a serious conception of righteousness."[20] Yet the triumph of Hebraism, taking in England the form of Puritanism, has been a major obstacle, he argues, lying in the way of England's development.

The conflict between Hellenism and Hebraism often takes the fictional form, in James, of a struggle between an invariably European husband and his (usually) American wife. Thus, we have the struggles between the pagan-minded Count Valerii and his wife ("The Last of the Valerii," 1874), the Baron and Euphemia in "Madame de Mauves" (1874), Mark Ambient and his Philistine (British) spouse in "The Author of 'Beltraffio' " (1884), and Prince Amerigo and Maggie Verver in *The Golden Bowl*. In the early stories, American morality overcomes "pagan" predispositions. In "Beltraffio," however, James's sympathy is with the Hellenic-minded husband, Mark Ambient, whose goal as an author is to "give an impression of life itself"—an aesthetic version of the Arnoldian injunction "to see the object as in itself it really is" (*CPW*, 3:258). To the sympathetic narrator of the tale, Ambient describes the "difference between" himself and Mrs. Ambient as "simply the opposition between two distinct ways of looking at the world, which have never succeeded in getting on together. . . . They have borne all sorts of names, and my wife would tell you it's the difference between Christian and Pagan. . . . She thinks me, at any rate, no better than an ancient Greek. It's the difference between making the most of life and making the least—so that you'll get another better one in some other time and place. Will it be a sin to make the most of that one too, I wonder?"[21]

Following *Culture and Anarchy,* Arnold devoted much of the 1870s to a study of the Hebraic legacy and its importance. (That he did not abandon his Hellenizing impulse, even while writing on the Scriptures, is a point I argue in the fourth chapter.) In the same decade, James applied a Hebraic brake to his studies of French authors, collected as *French Poets and Novelists* (1878). Perhaps James felt that readers in England, where he had just settled, would demand such an approach; but there is a personal zeal in the way he charges Balzac and company with lacking a "natural sense of morality." (George Eliot and Thackeray, he notes by way of comparison, "are haunted by a moral ideal.") Baudelaire, he writes, "went in search of corruption, and the ill-conditioned jade proved a thankless muse." James does exempt two Continental writers from the charge of moral laxity. Turgenev displays an Arnoldian "criticism of life" that meets with his approval: "The great question as to a poet or a novelist is, How does he feel about life? what, in the last analysis, is his philosophy?" But of the one French writer whom James (like Arnold) credits with a moral sense, George Sand, James decrees that her failing is insufficient Hellenism: "we suspect that something even better in a novelist is that tender appreciation of actuality which makes even the application of a single coat of rose-colour seem an act of violence."[22]

In his novels of the '70s, too, James veers from one side of the Hebraic-Hellenic pole to the other. For Arnold, a balance of the two was deemed necessary for England's future, but for James an imbalance makes for dramatic (or amusing) fiction. New England is often the locus of the Hebraic spirit: it is from here that Puritan-bred Rowland Mallett proceeds and where he meets the promising sculptor Roderick Hudson, whom he takes to Italy. In Rome, however, Hudson announces, "I am a Hellenist; I am not a Hebraist!" But while Hudson is referring to his determination to create things of beauty, he is also admitting to the personal trait, his lack of self-control, that will undermine his career. *Roderick Hudson* (1875) is the only James novel, incidentally, that Arnold mentions by name in one of his essays. (Perhaps he recognized his share in that book.) In *The American* (1877) we find the Unitarian minister Mr. Babcock touring Europe in pursuit of "culture" and put off by Christopher Newman's lack of "high tone." Newman is bemused by the way he seems Hellenic to Babcock, but Hebraic to a traveling Englishman. And in *The Europeans* (1878), Europeanized Americans visit New England and comment on the incapacity for enjoyment that they find there. It is the "failure to enjoy," of course, that characterizes Woollett, Massachusetts, from whence Strether embarks in a much later James novel, *The Ambassadors*—one of the Jamesian late trio of masterpieces in which Hebraism and Hellenism do come together in the "wonderful impressions" of its hero.[23]

By the end of the '70s, James had derived a measure of success from his tales drawing on the "international theme," among them "Daisy Miller" and "An International Episode" (1878 for both). But he was coming to dislike having his name linked with works that simplified national characteristics for literary effect. In the Preface to volume eleven of the New York edition, which contains many of these tales, James points to the superiority of his later work in which "a new scale of relations" was created, "a state of things from which *emphasised* internationalism" seemed anachronistic.[24] One can see James's refinement (and transformation) of the "international theme" if we compare two tales from this volume, noting, in both these exercises in multicultural exploration, a significant Arnoldian presence. The first story, "A Bundle of Letters" (1879), contains a number of stereotypical Americans and Europeans inhabiting the same Paris boardinghouse. Among the letter-writers is a variation on Daisy Miller, a young woman from Maine in search of "culture" (her mission, she informs her mother, is to absorb what she finds in Europe, "and keep Boston to finish up") who strikes her European fellow boarders as "vulgar," if not "evil." "A type that has lost itself before it has been fixed," pontificates a German pedagogue, "—what can you look for from this?" There is more than a hint of Arnold's epistolary *Friendship's Garland* in all of this, with its censorious Prussian visitor to England (James's Dr. Rudolph Staub stands in for Arnold's Arminius) and Arnold's amusing self-portrait as a ragged exponent of "culture," "rather a poor creature" (*CPW*, 5:43, 314). James's version of the latter (one of a number of James's literary self-parodies) is Louis Leverett, an aesthetic Bostonian who speaks continually of the need to "live" and who misappropriates Arnold's appeal for self-cultivation. "The great thing is to *live*, you know," he writes his friend Harvard Trement, "—to feel, to be conscious of one's possibilities. . . . That is the great thing—to be free, to be frank, to be *naïf.* Doesn't Matthew Arnold say that somewhere—or is it Swinburne, or Pater?" The pursuit of culture takes on a sinister dimension in the person of Gilbert Osmond (in *The Portrait of a Lady*) and a tragic dimension in the small figure of Hyacinth Robinson (in *The Princess Casamassima*, 1886). But for the moment, James is amused to laugh at the image of himself as (to anticipate a critic's description of him) a "Superfine Young Man."[25]

With the second story, "The Point of View" (1882), James directs his wit and seriousness against an Arnoldian target: Philistinism at home and abroad. This was his first tale in three years; James had devoted himself, in the interim, to a great novel about the traumas experienced in the quest for culture, *The Portrait of a Lady*. In that novel James suggested, as had Arnold before him, that culture ultimately "places human perfection in an *internal* condition" (*CPW*, 5:94). In the new story, James's method is conspicuously Arnoldian: "To try and approach truth on one side after another" (as the preface to *Essays in Criticism* has it), and to do so with "vivacity" (3:286–87). The story is made up of the letters of visitors or natives returning to America, each of whom offers a point of view about the country, a partial "truth" (just as each of Arnold's subjects in the *Essays* offers an approach to truth). A member of the French Academy (hence, a man of "standards"), M. Gustave Lejaune, sees in America what only a French intellectual would see, the presence of absence: no civilization, no manners, "no *salons*, no society, no conversation," no respect for anything but money, "no officials [in Washington], no authority, no embodiment of the State." James, here, is parodying the famous list of everything missing in the America of Hawthorne, the subject of his 1879 biography: "No sovereign, no court, no personal loyalty, no aristocracy, no church, no clergy, no army," and so on. In a delightful bit of self-parody on James's part, M. Lejaune (literally, Mr. Jaundice), complaining of the lack of "literature" in America, points to a "novelist with pretensions to literature, who writes about the chase for the husband and the adventures of the rich Americans in our corrupt old Europe, where their primeval candor puts the Europeans to shame. *C'est proprement écrit;* but it's terribly pale." "A Frenchman couldn't live here," he sniffs; "for life with us, after all, at the worst is a sort of appreciation. Here there is nothing to appreciate."[26]

A returning expatriate finds advantages in the comforts, disadvantages in the quality, of life. She sees the English language being crowded out by Americanisms, and she sees adult society crowded out by children. Louis Leverett, returning to Boston, is horrified by the low aesthetic tone, the newspapers, and "the great tepid bath of Democracy." An English M.P., by contrast, notes the freedom of American women, the overall "freedom of development," the flourishing "educational system" (thanks to which "the children in this country are better educated than the adults"), the triumph of "equality" but also the curious persistence of "inequality." (In 1878, James had recommended to his father Arnold's "very charming" article on "Equality.") In all these letters, James writes about America with greater authority and good humor than Arnold was shortly to do in his essays on America of the 1880s. But when he assumes the persona of Marcellus Cockerel, an American patriot returning home from a visit to Europe, James provides both a roaring defense of his native land and a résumé of many Arnoldian targets (including the attack on English politics in "The Function of Criticism") of the past two decades. "They revile us for our party politics," Cockerel retorts,

> but what are all the European jealousies and rivalries, their armaments and their wars, their rapacities and their mutual lies, but the intensity of the spirit of party? what question, what interest, what idea, what need of mankind, is involved in any of these things? Their big pompous armies, drawn up in great silly rows, their gold lace, their salaams, their hierarchies, seem a pastime for children; there's a sense of humor and of reality over here that laughs at all that. Yes, we are nearer the reality—we are nearer what they will all have to come to. The questions of the future are social questions.

Americans are "men of the future," James had told Perry in 1867; and in 1882, Cockerel maintains, "The future is here." Pointing to the preoccupation of English politicians with "the Deceased Wife's Sister" (a favorite Arnoldian thrust against Liberal Dissenters), Cockerel asks, *which* country is the more genuinely "provincial"?[27]

Yet even as he wrote these words, James was unequivocally casting his lot with the "old world—my choice, my life." "My work lies there," he wrote in his notebook in 1881, during a return visit. But an American writer in Europe has a double "burden," he declares, since he must write of both cultures, "whereas no European is obliged to deal in the least with America." James had discovered, as first he traveled and then he settled in Europe, that "provincialism" was not exclusive to Hawthorne's America. His letters home from the 1870s reiterate the theme of French "narrowness," of English incapacity for "ideas" and "their mortal mistrust of anything like criticism." And there were personal disappointments. To Grace Norton, in 1877, he described himself as "more of a cosmopolitan (thanks to that combination of the continent and the U.S.A. which has formed my lot) than the average Briton of culture; and to be—to have become by force of circumstances—a cosmopolitan, is of necessity to be a good deal alone." But he was gradually making friends; and in the year of the letter to Grace, James could boast to his brother William that he was often in the company, courtesy of the Athenaeum Club, of many objects of their mutual admiration, including Matthew Arnold.[28]

James first met his longtime "idol" in the spring of 1873, in what should have been the most "privileged" of circumstances, at the Palazzo Barberini in Rome, where Arnold was the dinner guest of William Wentworth Story and his family. To his parents, to William and Alice, to Norton and other friends, James wrote first of the anticipation, then of the "disappointment," of the actual meeting. Alas, the free play of mind James had hoped for did not materialize. ("When I met him again, later on, in London," James reminisced in his biography of Story, "*then* it had free play.") The great Victorian was charming; he displayed "an easy, mundane, somewhat gushing manner"; but he appeared no more Arnoldian than, on another occasion, Tennyson would prove "Tennysonian."[29] In a story written two decades later, "The Private Life" (1892), James would indicate that what makes for greatness is not always on show. By 1881 James and Arnold had assumed a warm, if not overly close, relationship. "Yes, I know Matthew Arnold very well," James wrote Perry in that year, "and like him much. I was pleased to hear that he told a friend of mine the other day that 'Henry James is a de-ah!' " (Arnold, during his visit to America, complained to Howells that James had never accepted his invitation to visit him at his Surrey retreat.) James's *Hawthorne* first appeared on Arnold's reading list for 1880. "That is a man I don't much care for," Arnold admitted to James, "but I am sure to like what you say of him."[30]

It was during the stay in Rome that James picked up background material needed for his novel about a Hellenic-minded American sculptor, *Roderick Hudson*. Arnold refers to this novel in "A Word about America" (1882), the first of his essays devoted to America, which appeared in the same year as "The Point of View." He cites it to rebut the argument of Thomas Wentworth Higginson and others that he has been unfair to America. Colonel Higginson, reviewing Arnold's *Mixed Essays* in the *North American Review* in 1879, had written that while "no man in England says things that seem nearer to an American point of view, . . . no man in England seems more absolutely indifferent to results obtained in America." For example, in speaking of "Equality" (one of the great essays included in the new volume), Arnold looked to France rather than America, ignoring the triumphs of civilization to be found in the New World. Before responding to Higginson, Arnold checked with James for advice as to how to reply; and when "A Word" appeared (three years later), he was gratified by the knowledge that James, when asked "to write a reply to it, said after reading it that he could not write a reply to it, it was so true, and carried him so along with it."[31] Yet Arnold's essay and its sequels, despite much discerning commentary, are not among his happiest achievements. To understand why, it is necessary to backtrack and consider Arnold's attitude to America before the 1880s, the decade when he finally decided to write about and visit America. If Arnold was unable to see America steadily and see it whole, this was largely owing to his habit of viewing America as symbol of what he felt England dare not turn into. Arnold liked Americans (he would gain an American son-in-law as a result of his first visit there), but he feared a dim effigy that, bolstered by readings in Renan and Alexis de Tocqueville, he called "America."

Arnold's enthusiasm for democracy at work in France was strengthened by that country's possession of a strong state-run educational system. In a country governed by the masses, the difficulty (he stated in 1861, apropos of America, in "Democracy") is in finding and keeping "high ideals" (*CPW*, 2:17). For Arnold, democracy was inevitable, the happy legacy of the French Revolution whose ideas he cherished. (It was, after all, a *French* revolution.) Seeing the enlightened attitude of the French "people" (the "*idea-moved masses*," as he had called them, years earlier, in 1848), in the midst of researching *The Popular Education of France*, Arnold felt no hesitation in supporting the right of "Democracy . . . *to affirm its own essence*" (2:7). But it is only with the aid of some agency from above representing our "best self," only from the state and a government-sponsored educational system (nonexistent in the England of 1861), that "the English people [can be prevented] from becoming, with the growth of democracy, *Americanised*" (16). Arnold cites the authority of Renan, in his Preface to *Culture and Anarchy* (1869), to counter John Bright's enthusiastic view that America has "offered to the world more valuable information during the last forty years, than all Europe put together" (5:241).[32] For Renan (like James's fictional M. Lejaune in "The Point of View"), Americans are notable only for "*their intellectual mediocrity, their vulgarity of manners, their superficial spirit, their lack of general intelligence*" (5:241) to which a lack of intellectual standards has condemned them. Renan's view was enough to convince Arnold of the American deficiency in culture—despite the favorable comments expressed earlier in "My Countrymen." How, Arnold reasons, can America *not* be deficient when they are "just ourselves, with the Barbarians [upper classes] quite left out, and the Populace nearly [?]." This leaves the Philistines for the great bulk of the nation;—a livelier sort of Philistine than ours, and with the pressure and false ideal of the Barbarians taken away, but left all the more to himself and to have his full swing" (243). ("They are the English *minus* the conventions," M. Lejaune similarly contends. "You can fancy what remains.") The worst that Arnold knew about England he presumed to be in America too—an England, as he had complained in "My Countrymen," "drugged with business" and stimulated only by "a religion, narrow, unintelligent, repulsive" (19). "From Maine to Florida, and back again," Arnold shuddered, "all America Hebraises" (243). Over a decade later—despite Colonel Higginson's protest that "modern Boston" has nothing "to do with that dungeon of Puritanism held up by Mr. Arnold"[33]—Arnold persisted in this view: "Our Dissenting ministers think themselves in Paradise when they visit America" (10:11).

In his occasional snobbishness toward America, Arnold resembles a character in a James story—Winterbourne, say, of "Daisy Miller"—and like Winterbourne, he was appalled by the poor upbringing of Americans ("a nation *mal elevée*") he saw on display in the Coliseum, "and by moonlight too." James, to be sure, was even more severe to his touring compatriots. "There is but one word to use in regard to them," he wrote his mother from Florence in 1869, "—vulgar, vulgar, vulgar . . . It's the absolute and incredible lack of *culture* that strikes you."

Nevertheless, there were also readers in America cultured enough to appreciate Arnold's work. Arnold was pleased by an 1863 review of his poetry in the *North American Review,* and he was delighted by that same journal's 1865 review of *Essays in Criticism.* The latter review inspired him to write his sister about the "intellectual liveliness and ardour" of some visiting Americans (this was said a few months after the experience in the Coliseum), an intelligence that is "one of the good results of their democratic régime's emancipating them from the blinking and hushing-up system induced by our circumstances here." There might be something to learn from America after all, Arnold concedes, even though that which satisfies John Bright "will never satisfy me."[34]

Did Arnold ever discover that the admiring American reviewer of the *Essays* was Henry James? Perhaps not, but by the late 1870s James was strongly identified in his mind as one of the "remnant," one who had demonstrated his cultural credentials by satirizing American Philistinism in his work and by drawing upon English and French sources. ("A nation is really civilized by acquiring the qualities it by nature is wanting in," Arnold had noted in 1865.) It is fitting that since James had learned so much from Arnold for so long, it was now time for Arnold to learn from James. In fact, "A Word about America" may be read as Arnold's dialogue with James, about whose opinion of the piece he was so anxious. Arnold is responding to the view of Higginson and others that there *is* "civilization" in the United States, and that it is exemplified in the " 'highly civilized individuals' " that one finds in James's fiction. (One Boston critic snidely described them as "people who spend more than half their life in Europe, and return only to scold their agents for the smallness of their remittances.") His thrust in "A Word about America" is that it is insufficient to speak of American civilization if it is confined only to a handful of "lovers of perfection" (*CPW,* 10:9). Arnold considers the blight caused to America by its importation of the English Philistine, the true American in his view; and to illustrate his belief in the predominance of this species, he holds up the character of Striker from James's *Roderick Hudson.* In 1879 Arnold had written James of his admiration for the book: its "writing . . . so good and so *fin* that it bears being taken slowly." But three years later he had forgotten the profession of Striker (he mistakes the attorney for an "auctioneer" [10:7]), a minor character, in any case, who drops out of the narrative early on. Arnold further cites, as examples of American Philistinism, the great popularity of

Mark Twain—"so attractive to the Philistine of the more gay and light type"—and the description by an English traveler of the " 'hard, narrow life' " practiced by a Denver family of obviously " 'British stock' " (14, 16–17). Clearly, America could have a "higher, larger culture, a finer lucidity," Arnold concludes; and he teasingly urges the "friends of civilization" that, "instead of hopping backwards and forwards over the Atlantic," they "stay at home a while, and do their best to make the administration, the tribunals, the theatre, the arts, in each state, to make them become visible ideals to raise, purge and ennoble the public sentiment" (22).[35]

But it was Arnold who now sailed to America, in late 1883, the year that James, following the deaths of his parents, returned to England. (He would stay away for another two decades.) Among the fruits of James's visit were the story "The Point of View" and plans for novels with American or America-related themes, *The Bostonians* and *The Princess Casamassima*. (Although set in Europe, the latter book takes Renan's antidemocratic views to an extreme, pitting the forces of democracy against the vestiges of civilization. Arnold's view of democracy was far more hopeful, as I argue in chapter 5.)[36] But while James had returned to America to bid farewell to his past, Arnold had come to give a number of lectures and have a firsthand look at the country of the future. James served as his publicist, urging American friends to attend the lectures (despite his doubts concerning Arnold's performance as lecturer) and writing the appreciative essay for the *English Illustrated Magazine* that I cited at the beginning of this chapter.[37] By now James had learned to separate Arnold the speaker from Arnold the author. In the 1884 tribute, he commends the religious writings, the poetry (the work by which "I first knew and admired him"), and, of course, the critical writings. "Those who have been enjoying Mr. Arnold these twenty years," James remarks, "will remember how fresh and desirable his voice sounded at that moment; if since then the freshness has faded a little we must bear in mind that it is through him and through him only that we have grown familiar with certain ideas and terms which now form part of the common stock of allusion." Meanwhile, Arnold's American admirers—including the Nortons in New England and Andrew Carnegie in New York—awaited the arrival of the man whom another visitor, Lord Coleridge, described as "the most distinguished of living Englishmen." The trip was not a failure, despite all that buildup or the lively account by Sir Lepel Griffin, "A Visit

to Philistia," in the *Fortnightly:* "Mr. Matthew Arnold, piloted by
Mr. D'Oyley Carte, and inaudibly lecturing to New York society, too
painfully recalls Samson grinding corn for the Philistines in Gaza."[38]
Nor was it altogether a success, if one regards the writings that came
out of the visit.

Of the three "Discourses" that Arnold gave in America, the most
popular was an adaptation of the great talk "Literature and Science"
that he had given at Cambridge University in 1882. For American
audiences, he happily noted that Greek literature was being taught at
women's colleges such as Smith and Vassar (*CPW,* 10:71). In "Numbers; or the Majority and the Remnant," Arnold seconded Colonel
Higginson's encomia in behalf of American men and women of culture. It is this "remnant"—a dedicated minority mentioned by both
the Hellenic Plato and the Hebraic Isaiah—that "saves the State."
And in so big a democracy as the United States, he adds, "What a
remnant yours may be, surely!" (10:148, 163) There is something almost shameless in the way Arnold manages to flatter his audience (as
auditors, of course they qualify), while at the same time he directs his
spleen at a distant target, the English Philistine (he ignores the American version for now) for, among other things, its mistreatment of the
Irish. He also criticizes the French, whose decline in recent years he
ascribes to their worship of "the great goddess Lubricity" (10:155).
Interestingly, Renan, whose authority was enough to demolish American claims to civilization in "A Word about America," is now quoted,
disapprovingly by Arnold, as an apologist for French licentiousness.

The discourse on "Emerson" is far and away the finest of the
writings Arnold devoted to America. It reminds us of the difference
between Arnold the *social* critic, who adopts an essentially oppositional stance, and Arnold the *literary* critic, who combines clarity of
definition with sympathy toward his subject, without losing sight of
the social context of literature. True, Arnold does strip away Emerson's claims to philosophical, poetic, and literary greatness; but what
remains is considerable. Emerson stands alongside Newman and Marcus Aurelius as one of the very few trustworthy friends and aiders "of
those who would live in the spirit" (10:177). James's 1887 essay on
Emerson (which I'll come to shortly) may have been intended as a
rejoinder to Arnold's lecture, but James's Emerson is also a far less
commanding figure. Arnold does caution against the overuse of the
Emersonian invocation "Trust thyself." "It may be said," Arnold

notes, "that the common American or Englishman is more than enough disposed already to trust himself." But Emerson's emphasis on the "culture" of the self is linked, for Arnold, with Goethe's similar appeal. "Only thus could he break through the hard and fast barrier of narrow, fixed ideas" (179–80).[39] To demonstrate America's need for the Emersonian-Arnoldian regimen of "cultural transformation," he directs his audience to American novelists for proof that Philistinism is omnipresent (180).

The day before he sailed back to England, Arnold wrote James, "I hope to shake you by the hand very soon, and to communicate to you—what I have no intention at all of communicating to the public—my 'impressions of America,'—or at least some of them." What he did publish five months later, "A Word More about America," is directed at England rather than America. Arnold had been more impressed than he had anticipated.[40] He admits, at the outset of "A Word More," his incapacity for writing a speculative study on the order of Tocqueville. But he does commend the political and social "institutions" he had observed. Democracy in America has made for an equitable distribution of wealth and a leveling of classes that allows for general tolerance and social "homogeneity." Neither the enmity excited by riches in France, nor the rancor between parties and classes in England, is to be found there. In consequence, the American government "sees things straight and sees them clear" (*CPW*, 10:202–3). (This penchant for seeing things "straight and clear" is a trait Arnold admired in General Grant, whose memoirs he reviewed in early 1887.) England, by contrast, is hampered by partisan "interests . . . very different from the true interests of the community. Our very classes make us dim-seeing. In a modern time, we are living with a system of classes so intense, a society of such unnatural complication, that the whole action of our mind is hampered and falsened by it. I return to my old thesis: inequality is our bane. The great impediments in our way of progress are aristocracy and Protestant dissent. People think this is an epigram; alas, it is much rather a truism!" (213)

Something of the dire tone of "A Word More" can be found in what turned out to be Arnold's last essay, "Civilisation in the United States" (1888). Having considered France's and England's failings while in America, Arnold in England holds up America once more as an example of what to resist. His thesis is valid enough: America, having solved the "political" and "social" problems, has failed with the "human" problem. But the examples he cites to demonstrate American lack of civilization—her lack of things "interesting," her want of "awe and respect," her shoddy newspapers (*CPW*, 11:357, 360–61)—are enumerated with a disturbing shrillness of tone that undercuts his argument in behalf of civility. The essay has no sweetness and little light, and what flickering illumination he does provide comes from other sources, including James's *Hawthorne*, which he had read before leaving for America. "If we in England," Arnold says without irony, "were without the cathedrals, parish churches, and castles of the catholic and feudal ages, and without the houses of the Elizabethan age, but had only the towns and buildings which the rise of our middle class has created in the modern age, we should be in much the same case as the Americans. We should be living with much the same absence of training for the sense of beauty through the eye, from the aspect of outward things" (359). Coming from one notably deficient in an aesthetic eye, the point carries less weight than if it were being made by Ruskin or James. But whereas James had drawn on Arnold's attack on provincialism, in "The Literary Influence of Academies," to underscore the nudity of Hawthorne's America (no cathedrals, nor abbeys, nor little Norman churches, and so on), James had also leavened his commentary with Arnoldian good humor: "The American knows that a good deal remains; what it is that remains— that is his secret, his joke, as one may say."[41]

In "The Function of Criticism at the Present Time," Arnold had memorably warned his countrymen against "a self-satisfaction which is retarding and vulgarising," a complacency that hobbles one from proceeding toward "perfection" and from dwelling on "the absolute beauty and fitness of things" (*CPW*, 3:271). But in his last essay, he nearly reduces the argument for culture to a narrow formula: "What people in whom the sense of beauty and fitness was quick could have invented, or could tolerate, the hideous names ending in *ville*, the Briggsvilles, Higginsvilles, Jacksonvilles, rife from Maine to Florida?" (11:359). (One recalls "Wragg, poor thing!," whose name was the least of her and England's problems.) The nadir of Arnold's essay is the attack on Americans for glorifying their literary achievements—and here he cites Edward Payson Roe as the typical "native author" (364). In denigrating Whitman and Twain, and overlooking his devoted James, Arnold disregarded his own injunction "to try to know the best that is known and thought in the world"; he had forgotten out of what heterogeneous materials the stuff of civilization is made.[42] Still, he ended with the hope that as England "becomes more democratic," it may gain many of the good things possessed by America while not succumbing to the reign of mediocrity (and here his hope was for America too), and that both countries will move toward "a renovated and perfected society on earth" by looking to ideals inspired *"from above"* (368–69)—a position commingling American pragmatism with old world idealism.

It would be a mistake to regard the 1880s as a period of decline for Arnold. During his final decade, he published his *Irish Essays* (1882), most of his pieces on the theater (collected only in 1919 as *Letters of an Old Playgoer*), and the *Discourses in America* (1885). In 1888, the year of his death, two major literary collections appeared: Arnold's second series of *Essays in Criticism* and James's *Partial Portraits.* Each volume draws upon its author's varied work during a decade of increasing critical refinement and redefinement. But the two books can also be read as dialogues—dialogues reflecting something of the rich interchange that existed between Arnold and James, reflecting how each had listened to and learned from the other. Arnold's emphasis is repeatedly on the essentially moral nature of literature. "A poetry of revolt against moral ideas is a poetry of revolt against *life*," he says in the great essay on Wordsworth; "a poetry of indifference towards moral ideas is a poetry of indifference towards *life*" (*CPW*, 9:46). This is the volume that contains Arnold's criticism of Keats for his want of "self-control" (shades of *Roderick Hudson*?) and of Shelley for his licentiousness ("What a set!"); and it is also the volume in which Arnold makes religious and philosophical demands of poetry ("The Study of Poetry") that are perhaps none of poetry's business. But it is also here that Arnold eulogizes Byron for his warfare against English Philistinism, and here that he, belatedly, regards the novel (in the hands of Tolstoy, whose English reputation was launched as a result of this essay) as a subject of critical importance. In 1880, he had paid homage to "those charming novels of [Henry James] which we are all reading" (10:130). In an 1884 tribute to George Sand, Arnold says, "The novel is a more superficial form of literature than poetry, but on that very account more attractive" (10:189). For Arnold, the idealistic Sand was preferable to Balzac's followers, the "naturalists and realists" (187), with their reliance on art at the expense of life. "But . . . we are not to take *Anna Karénine* as a work of art," he maintains; "we are to take it as a piece of life" (11:285). And here Arnold echoes James's comment, in his 1876 review of *Daniel Deronda* (reprinted in *Partial Portraits*), that while Eliot's novel has "little art, . . . there is a vast amount of life. In life without art you can find your account; but art without life is a poor affair."[43]

James, after all, had anticipated Arnold's assault on French writers who worship "the goddess Lubricity" (*CPW*, 11:292) in his own *French Poets and Novelists;* and in *Partial Portraits* James praises Trollope at the expense of Flaubert and company. Trollope's "perception of character," he maintains, "was naturally more just and liberal than that of the naturalists." The English novelists may lack the "audacity" and concern for artistic form of the French, "But they have been more at home in the moral world." Throughout *Partial Portraits* James pays homage to his critical mentor, but he does so by means of building upon and distancing himself from Arnold. James originally intended to include among these "portraits" his 1884 essay on Arnold, as well as the 1880 piece on Sainte-Beuve and that of 1883 on Renan; but he finally devoted only one essay to a critic, and that on Emerson from 1887. In this, the first item in the volume, James takes issue with Arnold's celebratory discourse. Where for Arnold, Emerson's Back Bay and Concord are "names invested to my ear, with a sentiment akin to that which invests for me the names of [Newman's] Oxford and of [Goethe's] Weimar" (10:167), for James the New England cultural world is singularly barren. The color of "Emerson's personal history is condensed into the single word Concord," James declares, "and all the condensation in the world will not make it look rich." Despite Arnold's denial to Emerson of the title "man of letters," James maintains that Emerson's was "the very life for literature." (He had said as much of Sainte-Beuve, but the Frenchman's milieu, after all, was Paris.) James's Emerson lacks passion, a personal life, aesthetic awareness, a sense of evil. Moreover, "he rarely read a novel, even the famous ones." "I was struck," says James in memory of a stroll with Emerson through the Louvre, "by the anomaly of a man so refined and intelligent being so little spoken to by works of art." That James's Emerson may be, in part, a surrogate for Arnold is underscored by the use of the word "anomaly"; the Arnold James first met in Rome "was preoccupied with botany rather than with the fine arts."[44]

In form, the pieces in *Partial Portraits* proceed from sketches of comparatively innocent American and English writers (Emerson, Eliot, Trollope, Stevenson, Constance Woolson) to depictions of more worldly Continental figures (Daudet, Maupassant). The last individuals considered (Turgenev and George du Maurier) are of mixed cultures, Anglo-French in the case of the *Punch* caricaturist, "cosmopolite" in the case of the Russian who lived in France but was never "Gallicized." Du Maurier's forte was to satirize a nation deficient in "spontaneous artistic life." English taste, notes James, "is a matter of conscience, reflection, duty, and the writer who in our time has appealed to them most eloquently on behalf of art has rested his plea on moral standards—has talked exclusively of right and wrong." (Since James is speaking of the visual arts, he is obviously referring to Ruskin here, not Arnold.)[45] But it is Turgenev's play of mind that most appeals to James: "Our Anglo-Saxon, Protestant, moralistic, conventional standards were far away from him, and he judged things with a freedom and spontaneity in which I found a perpetual refreshment." For Turgenev there was no need to choose between art and life, Hellenism and Hebraism. He is James's model novelist in terms both of the "free play" with which he looked at life and the deeply moral quality of the "mind" which did the observing. It is Turgenev one thinks of when reading the celebrated passage in the essay that brings *Partial Portraits* to a triumphant conclusion, "The Art of Fiction": "There is one point at which the moral sense and the artistic sense lie very near together; that is in the light of the very obvious truth that the deepest quality of a work of art will always be the quality of the mind of the producer. In proportion as that intelligence is fine [James originally wrote "rich and noble"] will the novel, the picture, the statue partake of the substance of beauty and truth." For a quarter century Arnold had lambasted the Puritan establishment for imprisoning English sensibility. In "The Art of Fiction" James builds upon Arnold's thesis (early in the essay, he laments the state of " 'art' in our Protestant countries, where so many things have got so strangely twisted about"), and he brings it to the logical conclusion with which the Arnold of the 1860s would have agreed: "The essence of moral energy is to survey the whole field."[46]

Two decades earlier, immediately before writing the articles that became *Culture and Anarchy*, Arnold had cautioned American admirers of Whitman and Theodore Parker that "At this time of day it is not enough to be an American voice, or an English voice, or a French voice; for a real spiritual lead it is necessary to be a European voice." At the same time, he looked forward to the time "When American intellect," having "broken . . . the leading strings of England, but also [having] learnt to assimilate independently the intellect of France and Germany and the ancient world as well as England," should *then* become, in Parker's words, " 'a many-gated temple, with a dome wide and lofty enough to include all earnest minds' " (*CPW*, 5:81). During his literary apprenticeship, with Arnold as mentor, James had pursued this goal, and by the late 1880s the author of *Partial Portraits* had traveled far beyond the American provincialism described in the Hawthorne biography, had gone beyond the "international" mode of his stories (which had restricted him to making simplified contrast between two nations), had even transcended the cosmopolitanism of Turgenev and Arnold. (Each of them, as James realized, had kept his standingpoint in Russia or England.) He had become a "many-sided temple" in which the old oppositions, America and Europe, Hebraism and Hellenism, art and life, merged. "I can't look at the English and American worlds, or feel about them, any more," he wrote William in 1888, "save as a big Anglo-Saxon total, destined to such an amount of melting together that an insistence on their differences becomes more and more pedantic." His goal now, he continued, was "to write in such a way that it would be impossible to an outsider to say whether I am, at a given moment, an American writing about England or an Englishman writing about America (dealing as I do with both countries), and so far from being ashamed of such an ambiguity I should be exceedingly proud of it, for it would be highly civilized." In an essay in dialogue, "An Animated Conversation," published the next year, James remarks that it is up to the "children of light" (Arnold's term for the enemies of the Philistines) to encourage Americans and Britons to "cultivate with talent, a common destiny, to tackle the world together, to unite in the arts of peace—by which I mean of course in the arts of life."[47]

With this new perspective, James no longer saw himself as isolated because of his cosmopolitanism. Secure in his Anglo-Saxon, multicultured position, he could now reexamine America with a fresher and freer play of mind than ever. James's series of "American Letters," written in 1898, begins as an Arnoldian meditation on his native land in light of the "question of numbers," the question of whether "a variety of races and idioms" will retain that "homogeneity" that Arnold admired or whether, under the "multiplication of possibilities," the country will change. In "the great mill of the language," for example, what new "forms, what colours, what sounds" will emerge, and what will be lost in the process? The "critic" in James admits to a sense of "bliss" (as well as possible "misery") in the observing of this "endless play." He differs, thus, from Theodore Roosevelt, who speaks of the " 'American' name" as something fixed forever, "revealed once for all in some book of Mormon dug up under a tree." On the contrary, James replies, "We are all making it"—what it means to be an American—" in truth, as hard as we can, and few of us will subscribe to any invitation to forego the privilege." Like Arnold, James sees in education the means by which a democracy attains solidarity; but while James accepts the fact of a culture that is "multiform," he admits to an anxiety as to how that will affect the language.[48]

James's concern for the future of "our predominant and triumphant English" language becomes a minor theme in *The American Scene* (1907), James's collected impressions of America taken during his 1904–5 return trip, and a major theme in the speech he delivered at Bryn Mawr, "The Question of Our Speech." As much as he enjoyed the spectacle of change and development (Arnold's principle of "culture" vigorously at work), he worried that the loss of a "common language," and of vocal standards within that language, might thwart mutual interests and needful relationships. Like Arnold, James respected a version of multiculturalism, a respect for different cultures, that promoted unity, not divisiveness. Extending Arnold's defense of Academies (or something like Academies) for the fostering of enlightened solidarity through written language, James argues, "All life therefore comes back to the question of our speech, the medium through which we communicate with each other." But James's homecoming was not an occasion for nostalgia or regret. In *The American Scene,* James writes with fascination of his response to an America different from the land of his childhood and young manhood, but not less "interesting" on that account. He was now in the same position he described in his autobiography, that of the sophisticated child enjoying his own reactions (his "free play of mind") while watching

Uncle Tom's Cabin. Initial worries about "the monstrous form of Democracy" awaiting him soon gave way to wonder at the spectacle of the variety of cultures that make up "our huge national *pot au feu.*"[49]

He saw new arrivals everywhere—an Armenian among the hills of New Hampshire, Italian workmen on the Jersey shore, Jews on the Lower East Side of New York. At Ellis Island he was struck by the "claim of the alien, however immeasurably alien, to share in one's supreme relation." But, he finally reflected, "Who or what is an alien, when it comes to that, in a country peopled from the first under the jealous eye of history?"—peopled by immigrants who were "urgently required" before and are still "urgently required." James's reflections on American multiculturalism proceed from Arnold's description of democracy's triumphant crusade *"to affirm its own essence; to live, to enjoy, to possess the world"* (*CPW*, 2:7); in *The American Scene* he reversed the negative image of Demos that underlay *The Princess Casamassima.* His description of New York's thriving Jewish population is particularly noteworthy, and reminds one of Goethe's sympathetic account (a sympathy as rare in James's time as it was in Goethe's) of the Jews in the Frankfurt ghetto. It is here that the American triumph seems most evident, in the assimilation of a people made "alien" everywhere else, but at home and prospering in "the New Jerusalem on earth." The American South, by contrast, with its dreams of bygone glory, seems nothing if not "provincial." "We talk of the provincial," he says of Richmond, "but the provinciality projected by the Confederate dream, and in which it proposed to steep the whole helpless social mass, looks to our present eyes as artlessly perverse, as untouched by any intellectual tradition of beauty or wit, as some exhibited array of the odd utensils or divinities of lone and primitive islanders."[50] Forty years after absorbing Arnold's message in "The Literary Influence of Academies," James remained opposed to "provinciality" in all its forms.

With one aspect of his American background James had little interest, his Celtic origins. "His vision of a greater Anglo-Saxon community," Fred Kaplan notes, kept him from sympathizing with Irish demands for Home Rule; and his Scotch-Irish ancestry notwithstanding, he had only negative opinions about Irish culture. In this respect he differed from Arnold, whose lectures *On the Study of Celtic Literature* (1867) constitute its author's pioneering contribution to multicultural studies. I have deferred consideration of this important work until it could be seen alongside James's own major contribution, *The American Scene*. Based on lectures at Oxford that he gave soon after writing "The Function of Criticism at the Present Time," Arnold's *Celtic Literature* is his first concrete example of "criticism" in operation. His target is the prevailing English Philistinism, as expressed in the English press's position that the only culture worth knowing is that of "the old Anglo-Saxon breed." The London *Times* thought that Arnold's sympathetic descriptions of Welsh customs and festivals were "arrant nonsense."[51] Why can't the Welsh or the Irish or the Scots be more like *us*? the *Times* demanded. Once again, Arnold thought of the difference between the French and the English: the citizens of Alsace consider themselves a part of France despite their difference in language, while the Irish detest the English. And why should the Irish like the English?, Arnold asks in the lecture. The Englishman "employs simply material interests for his work of fusion; and, beyond these, nothing except scorn and rebuke. Accordingly there is no vital union between him and the races he has annexed" (*CPW*, 3:392). (Interestingly, James's reason for finally supporting Home Rule was that it would lift a burden from England's shoulders; Arnold, more idealistic and less practical, opposed Home Rule because he felt that both countries would benefit from the fusion of their best qualities.) If the Englishman expects to be friends with the Irish, Arnold asserts in the Preface to *Irish Essays*, he not only has to "*do* something different"; he has "to *be* something different" (9:312). "He must transform himself," as he says in *Celtic Literature* (3:394); and this can be done only by appreciating the perspectives that coexist alongside Anglo-Saxon attitudes, those of the Celtic and (Latin-derived) Norman races that are also part of England's heritage.

In the first lecture, Arnold deplores the popular English wish for only a single, dominant Anglo-Saxon culture:

> They will have nothing to do with the Welsh language and literature on any terms; they would gladly make a clean sweep of it from the face of the earth. I, on certain terms, wish to make a great deal more of it than is made now; and I regard the Welsh literature—or rather, dropping the distinction between Welsh and Irish, Gaels and Cymris, let me say Celtic literature;—as an object of very great interest. My brother Saxons have, as is well

known, a terrible way with them of wanting to improve everything but themselves off the face of the earth; I have no such
passion for finding nothing but myself everywhere; I like variety
to exist and to show itself to me, and I would not for the world
have the lineaments of the Celtic genius lost (3:297–98).

In a deeply felt personal aside, Arnold tells of how, when he was
young, "I was taught to think of Celt as separated by an impassable
gulf from Teuton; my father, in particular, was never weary of contrasting them; he insisted much oftener on the separation between us and
them than on the separation between us and any other race in the
world; in the same way Lord Lyndhurst, in words long famous, called
the Irish, 'aliens in speech, in religion, in blood.' This naturally created a profound sense of estrangement; it doubled the estrangement
which political and religious differences already made between us
and the Irish: it seemed to make this estrangement immense, incur-
able, fatal" (299–300). Personal as well as critical motives lay behind
Arnold's decision to examine this culture: these included the scientific
and critical bent of his time "towards knowing things as they are"
(298), demonstrating "that there is no such original chasm between
the Celt and the Saxon as we once popularly imagined" (302); the
literary impulse provoked by his reading of Renan's "beautiful essay
on the poetry of the Celtic races" (342);[52] and the autobiographical
desire to know something of his own partly Celtic nature, as inherited
from his mother's Cornish ancestry.
    To know the Celtic people, Arnold says at the outset, "one must
know that by which a people best express themselves—their literature" (CPW, 3:303); and here he proceeds to discriminate, as a critic,
between what is "precious and genuine" and what is "rubbish" or
forgery (313–15). Drawing on his literary perspicacity, as well as the
ethnological and philological findings of the day,[53] Arnold examines
various works of Celtic literature, seeking to highlight what is characteristic of the Celtic race. In doing so, he comes to the conclusion "that
there is a Celtic element in the English nature, as well as a Germanic
element" (341). But whereas the Germanic temperament is stolid,
hard-working, impervious to beauty, the Celtic spirit is sentimental,
impressionable, "always ready to react against the despotism of fact" (344).
The Celts are, for Arnold, archetypal romantics; and he sees the Celtic
spirit, with "its turn for style, its turn for melancholy, and its turn for

natural magic," as the source of much that is great in English poetry (361). Unable to bend the world to its will, the Celt, in his poetry, compensates "by throwing all its force into style, by bending language at any rate to its will, and expressing the ideas it has with unsurpassable intensity, elevation, and effect" (366). Celtic melancholy, with its mixture of "piercing regret and passion" (370), Arnold finds articulated in James Macpherson's *Ossian*. The feeling for the magical qualities in nature he finds eloquently displayed in Keats. But it is Byron (along with Milton's Satan) who best sounds "the Celtic passion of revolt" (373). In the recent essay on Heine, Arnold had just paid tribute to Byron as "the greatest natural force, the greatest elemental power . . . which has appeared in our literature since Shakespeare"—Byron, who "shattered himself to pieces against the huge, black, cloud-topped, interminable precipice of British Philistinism" (132). And even in the midst of his crusade against lubricity in the 1880s, Arnold nonetheless bracketed Byron with Wordsworth as one of England's two "poetic glories" of the past century (9:237).

If England is to thrive, Arnold contends, it must accept the fact of its multicultured heritage; it must indulge in a crosscultural dialogue. To the Germanic genius for order and steadiness must be added the Norman genius for "strenuousness, clearness, and rapidity" and the Celtic genius for sentiment with its "love of beauty, charm, and spirituality" (*CPW*, 3:350–51). These are exaggerations, as Arnold knows, but exaggerations for effect. Arnold adds that each of the races has defects too, which interaction with the others can temper: "we have Germanism enough to make us Philistines, and Normanism enough to make us imperious, and Celtism enough to make us self-conscious and awkward; but German fidelity to nature, and Latin precision and clear reason, and Celtic quick-wittedness and spirituality, we fall short of" (382). There are, Arnold notes near the end of the last lecture, those who might say that England would do better by becoming more homogeneous, becoming "all of a piece. Our want of sureness of taste, our eccentricity, come in great measure, no doubt, from . . . our having no fixed, fatal, spiritual centre of gravity" (381–82). But Arnold rejects this tantalizing option. It is from variety, he contends, that a nation has strengths (James would imply the same in *The American Scene*), just as it is variety that has marked the greatest of poets, Shakespeare and Goethe (358). As long as we are possessed by contending natures that we do not recognize, we are at the mercy of our ingrained frailties; but as "soon as we have clearly discerned what they are, and begun to apply to them a law of measure, control, and guidance, they may be made to work for our good and to carry us forward" (383). In any case, the reigning Anglo-Saxon voice cannot continue to drown out the others; it must recognize its kinship with the others. Arnold ends by urging that a chair in Celtic studies be set up at Oxford. "The hard unintelligence, which is just now our bane, cannot be conquered by storm," he concludes; "it must be suppled and reduced by culture, by a growth in the variety, fullness, and sweetness of our spiritual life; and this end can only be reached by studying things that are outside of ourselves, and by studying them disinterestedly" (386).

On the Study of Celtic Literature is perhaps best read today if we regard the ethnological scaffolding as so much metaphorical playfulness, a "poet's flight," as James says of Arnold in another context. But his call for a multicultured perspective is serious indeed. It was Arnold, after all, and only Arnold among major Victorian critics, who pointed his countrymen to the cultures of Germany and France, ancient Greece and Israel, China and India, the Middle East and the Celtic world.[54] And Arnold also pointed to the multiple voices existing within a single culture. James's description of Arnold's "largeness of horizon" was fully justified. In his defense of its poetry, Arnold "paid the Celtic world," John Kelleher has stated, "the first valuable compliment it had received from an English source in several hundred years"; and despite its simplifications, the lectures "can never be unconsidered by anyone dealing with the subject, or be taken lightly, or—in the end—be read with anything but recurrent admiration." Despite the scorn from the Times, Arnold's book served to inspire Yeats and other members of the Celtic Revival.[55]

So it is only right to conclude this chapter with a reminder of the effect on the arts, including the art of criticism, of Arnold's multicultured position. Arnold's call for improved theatrical standards in England produced responsive chords in James and other would-be playwrights.[56] Here was another example of how England could learn from France. James's question in The American Scene—"Who or what is an alien, when it comes to that?"—is one that artists have traditionally understood better than politicians or businessmen. In his essay on Wordsworth, Arnold imagined nations becoming, "for intellectual and spiritual [not political] purposes, one great confederation, bound to a joint action and working towards a common result; a confederation whose members have a due knowledge both of the past, out of which they all proceed, and of one another" (*CPW*, 9:38). This Arnoldian dream is beautifully illustrated in a little-known James story of 1892, "Collaboration," which describes how a cluster of artists from rival nations, through the interchange of ideas and talents and cultural dialogue, prove that "In art there are no countries—no idiotic nationalities, no frontiers, nor *douanes*, nor still more idiotic fortresses and bayonets. It has the unspeakable beauty of being the region in which these abominations cease, the medium in which such vulgarities simply can't live."[57]

In that half-parody of, half-tribute to, the Arnoldian program, "The Critic as Artist," Oscar Wilde ascribes to criticism the temper "that makes us cosmopolitan." Savior of the English stage and exemplar of Arnold's Celtic spirit, forever fighting the "despotism of fact," Wilde in this essay is indulging his own "free play of mind" in dialogical fashion. While nations contend with nations, Arnoldian critics want only to bring cultures together. "Criticism," Wilde affirms, "will annihilate race-prejudices, by insisting upon the unity of the human mind in the variety of its forms. If we are tempted to make war upon another nation, we shall remember that we are seeking to destroy an element of our own culture, and possibly its most important element."[58]

Chapter Two

"Flutterings of Curiosity":
Arnold and the French Critics

Flutterings of curiosity, in the foreign sense of the word, appear
amongst us, and it is in these that criticism must look to find
its account.
     Arnold, "The Function of Criticism at the Present Time"

The essence of criticism is to be able to understand states very
different from those in which we live.
     Renan, *Souvenirs d'enfance et de jeunesse*

I can't help but dream about a kind of criticism that would not try
to judge, but to bring an oeuvre, a book, a sentence, an idea to
life; it would light fires, watch the grass grow, listen to the wind,
and catch the sea-foam in the breeze and scatter it . . . I'd like a
criticism of scintillating leaps of the imagination.
     Foucault, interview

For the lover of the arts of living, no less than the practitioner of art
and criticism, no country seemed so desirable to Arnold (or to James)
as France. "Life is so good and agreeable a thing there," he marveled,
"and for so many" (*CPW*, 8:362). The comment appears in an essay of
1878 ("Porro Unum Est Necessarium") in which he compares France's
superior secondary schools to those of England. And why, he asks,
shouldn't France have better schools? Its middle class enjoys a greater
"homogeneity," a more acute sense of social solidarity, better standards of living, and a higher and more widely shared level of civilization than does its English counterpart. In no other country are ideas
so widespread or standards so high. The British, with their faith in
mindless action, are as often "for suppressing" the "world of ideas,"
Arnold had wryly observed in "The Function of Criticism," as the
French are for suppressing the "world of practice" (3:265). French
intellectuals, disenchanted by the turn of nineteenth-century politics,
tend to harp on the need "de ne pas être dupe, of not being taken in"
(8:348). But ideas and practice need not be opposed to each other. For
Arnold, some of the best ideas were to be found in the most notable

French critics of the day; and it would be his object as a cultural critic
to bring France and England—the worlds of ideas and practice—into
dialogue with each other. He would indicate, in his own criticism,
how England would benefit from ideas imported from abroad; but he
would also suggest to his French colleagues that criticism, whose
originating force is "curiosity," is incomplete without a commitment
to application.

In "The Study of Poetry," Arnold cites Sainte-Beuve for confirma-
tion of the need for high poetic standards. In the political world, Sainte-
Beuve declares, "charlatanism" is widespread. "But in the order of
thought, in art, the glory, the eternal honour is that charlatanism shall
find no entrance; herein lies the inviolableness of that noble portion of
man's being" (*CPW*, 9:162). French enthusiasm for the arts and the
intellect is nourished by their ingrained sense of curiosity—that desire,
as Arnold describes it in *Culture and Anarchy*, "after the things of the
mind simply for their own sakes and for the pleasure of seeing them as
they are" (5:91). But the French possess a related habit: what Arnold
calls, apropos of Voltaire, "negative lucidity" or "the perception of the
want of truth and validness in notions long current" (10:85). This
"horreur d'être dupe" (a phrase ascribed to Ernest Renan, among others)[1] is an attitude that links Montaigne, La Rochefoucauld, and Voltaire with Sainte-Beuve, Renan, Edmond Scherer, and their twentieth-
century descendant, Michel Foucault. But culture, Arnold contends,
entails more than the play of curiosity and skepticism; it also entails a
"social" sensibility, a determination to make reason "prevail" (5:91).[2]

"We have more to learn from France than from any other nation,"
Arnold wrote his mother in 1863, "mainly because she is so unlike
ourselves." Fifteen years earlier, in the revolutionary year of 1848,
Arnold directed his friend Arthur Hugh Clough's attention to the *"wide
& deepspread intelligence* that makes the French seem to themselves in
the van of Europe." The French do not resist or ignore the *Zeitgeist*, as
do the English; and in their best journals, such as the *Revue des Deux
Mondes*, one finds the circulation of "ideas on all points:—of litterature,
of politics." Both Arnold and James saw France as the country in which
the "critical spirit," the guiding spirit of the age, was practiced to best
advantage. Preoccupied as he was with the problem of "modernity"—
the sense of living at a time when so many received values and traditional beliefs were vanishing—Arnold readily accepted Renan's view
that theirs was a century of "universal criticism." "Nôtre siècle est celui

de la critique," Arnold wrote Sainte-Beuve. "An intellectual deliverance is the particular demand of those ages which are called modern," Arnold declared in the first of his lectures at Oxford (*CPW*, 1:19); and in the lectures he subsequently devoted to Homer (1860–61), Arnold urged his audience to compare the meager intellectual response in England to the challenge of modernism with that *"critical* effort" widespread in France and Germany, "the endeavour, in all branches of knowledge,—theology, philosophy, history, art, science,—to see the object as in itself it really is" (1:140). Whereas English literary critics like Macaulay and Ruskin are content (in Arnold's view) with uttering sentimental platitudes, French and German critics take an objective look at what they are surveying, be it Homer or the Bible or contemporary literature. It is precisely this kind of clearheadedness in surveying political and social reality that England also needs, Arnold felt, if England is to thrive as a nation. Arnold turned to many non-French sources as he developed his individual form of criticism: he drew on the literary elegance of the age of Addison, for example; he was deeply influenced by Heinrich Heine's use of irony and his ideas relating to Hebraism and Hellenism; and in his fondness for the role of critic-sage, he emulated the examples of Goethe, Johnson, and Carlyle. ("What work nobler," Carlyle had asked in *Sartor Resartus,* "than transplanting foreign Thought into the barren domestic soil?")[3] But it was above all in France that he found a form of criticism (*la critique*) that combined what might seem to be contradictory impulses. It made an appeal to authority, on the one hand, while, on the other, it sanctioned an unlimited expenditure of curiosity, a "free play of mind" (Montaigne's "free, flexible, and elastic spirit" [1:174]) which not infrequently nibbled away at the claims of authority.

The finest, most various of French critics, for Arnold, was Charles-Augustin Sainte-Beuve, the defender of tradition and truth (*"la vraie vérité,"* as opposed to what sometimes passes for truth), as well as the possessor of astonishing powers of sympathy, tolerance, and curiosity. Very early in the lectures on Homer, Arnold refers to Sainte-Beuve as "the most delicate of living critics," an enemy of *"le faux"* (*CPW*, 1:102). In the later lecture (and subsequent essay) on "The Literary Influence of Academies," Arnold approvingly cites Sainte-Beuve's remark that "the first consideration" for the French "is not whether we are amused and pleased by a work of art or mind, nor is it whether we are touched by it. What we seek above all to learn is, whether *we were right* in being amused with it, and in applauding it, and in being moved by it" (3:236). Arnold's turn to Sainte-Beuve came just as his critical energies began to supplement, eventually to supplant, his poetical impulses. Their friendship began in early 1854 when Arnold, just turned thirty and a hard-working inspector of schools, sent him a copy of his 1853 volume of *Poems*, with its important Preface (Arnold's first critical effort). "Since the death of Goethe," he wrote, "you have remained, in my opinion, the sole guide and the sole hope of those who love above all else the truth in the arts and in literature, and who yet wish to find a criticism that is true, unaffected, and serious, a criticism . . . imbued with an essentially philosophical and European intelligence."[4]

By 1863, Arnold, now embarked on the *Essays in Criticism*, was assuring Sainte-Beuve (himself a poet manqué) that great critics are rarer than great poets. A great critic, moreover, is invariably "un grand poëte un peu supprimé." And if the present age has nurtured nothing but second-rate poets, it has at least brought forth one first-rate critic: "c'est vous." Protesting, in his reply to Arnold, that there were greater critics—Carlyle, for example, or the eminent literary historian François Villemain, or his own protégé, Renan—Sainte-Beuve received Arnold's assurance that he alone had the versatility, the delicacy, the disinterested curiosity (*la curiosité désinteressée*) of the master critic. During the fifteen years of their friendship, they continued to exchange compliments and copies of their books, to dine together when Arnold was in Paris ("his conversation is about the best to be heard in France," Arnold wrote his wife in 1859), and to promote each other's reputations at every opportunity. In an 1868 essay, Sainte-Beuve described his English friend as "un étranger qui nous connaît mieux que personne."[5]

Arnold's prediction to his mother that his published Oxford lectures *On Translating Homer* would "be attacked in the *Saturday Review* as too French in style" proved accurate. He was accused by Fitzjames Stephen of writing in "a dialect as like French as pure English can be," of having, "like his French models, . . . quick sympathies and a great gift of making telling remarks; but, also like them, . . . hardly any power of argument." For F. T. Marzials, in a *Quarterly Review* piece on Sainte-Beuve, Arnold was described as the French critic's "disciple," writing "graceful but perfectly unsatisfactory essays" on the importance of criticism. But if England were really in such dire need of a critical overhaul, the *Quarterly* wondered how the "feuilletons of

M. Sainte-Beuve" recommended by Arnold ("the most French of the English writers of the present day") were supposed to do the job. More recently, John Gross has questioned Arnold's choice of hero: "With all his merits, how many members of the human race would really be willing to adopt that rather chilly figure as their spokesman?"[6] But the selection of a hero lies as much in the perceived needs of the one admiring as in the merits of the adored. "Enthusiastic admirers," as Sainte-Beuve himself notes, "are a little like accomplices: they worship themselves, with all their own qualities and defects, in their great representatives." Yet Arnold was perfectly sincere when, three years after Sainte-Beuve's death, he named him as one of the four individuals (the others being Goethe, Wordsworth, and Newman) from whom he had learned most,[7] or when, for the 1886 *Encyclopaedia Britannica* entry he contributed on Sainte-Beuve, he listed him alongside Homer, Plato, Shakespeare, and Voltaire as one of the individuals "perfect" in his particular line (*CPW,* 11:119).

In this chapter I will be considering Arnold's dialogue with the French critics who most strongly influenced or appealed to him, with those whose views he often cited as a way of expressing, or of discovering, his own views on literature, religion, or contemporary social issues. Sainte-Beuve was, for him, "by far the best and most edifying critic whom we have had amongst our contemporaries" (*CPW,* 11:542). In his *Causeries* and other writings, Arnold found a rich source of material on figures and topics he also chose to write on. But Arnold was also drawn to Renan, whose writings on Celtic poetry and religious history influenced his own treatment of these topics. Arnold was particularly impressed with Renan's attack on the vulgar materialism and botched liberalism that resulted from the French Revolution. Renan's engaging style, and his sense that one wins over opponents by style as well as arguments, also appealed to Arnold, even though, in the wake of the French debacle of 1870, Arnold's feelings for Renan cooled slightly. Sainte-Beuve and Renan, for their part, deferred to Arnold's critical acuity, and they were grateful for his tributes to them. In the case of another French eminence, Hippolyte Taine, however, Arnold held back, declining Taine's suggestion that he review his *History of English Literature.*[8] Instead, he singled out for praise Edmond Scherer, whose devaluations of Milton and Goethe seem overly harsh nowadays, but who did write (unusual for a French critic) enthusiastically of English authors such as Wordsworth, George Eliot, and Arnold himself.

In the last part of the chapter I will be pairing Arnold with a French writer who, with the passing of time since his death in 1984, seems less an anomaly than a member of a certain iconoclastic French critical tradition, Michel Foucault. It would be preposterous to suggest that Arnold anticipates Foucault in any way, and it is unlikely that Foucault ever read or would have appreciated Arnold. (In my view Arnold is vastly greater than Foucault in his intellectual range and sympathies, his substance and style.) But Foucault's "negative lucidity," his campaign against his own ingrained romanticism, and his eventual turn, in late career, to the exponents of Hellenism and Stoicism suggest that Foucault may belong, in part, as much among the critics I am examining here as with the philosophers, historians, or various political radicals with whom he is customarily placed. Foucault would have hated the idea of being treated as a Sainte-Beuveian "subject"—seen in terms of his historical period and his individual reaction to or against it. But Arnold's comment on Sainte-Beuve, in a canceled passage of *Culture and Anarchy*, might well be read with Foucault in mind: "Monsieur Sainte-Beuve's critical activity belongs chiefly to a time of no great faith and ardour. . . . No man can resist the influences of his time, and Monsieur Sainte-Beuve's criticism and culture, coming at such a time, inevitably took the character of a criticism and culture founded mainly in curiosity,—curiosity here meaning a generous and liberal zeal purely for knowing and knowing right,—rather than of a criticism and culture founded in a study of perfection" (*CPW*, 11:542). Sainte-Beuve's "disinterestedness" prevented him from *applying* what he knew, from committing himself to certain needful judgments. Arnold reproached Sainte-Beuve for what he himself had been reproached for not doing in "The Function of Criticism"—not being "practical." (In *Culture and Anarchy*, Arnold qualified his earlier position by adding a pragmatic component to culture.) But this is similar to the charge Foucault's critics have made against him: his "singular lack of interest in the force of effective resistence" to the world he criticized.[9]

One of the difficulties in assessing Arnold fairly at the present time is that he himself encouraged that definition of criticism by which others, subsequently, have come to demand that literary critics be oppositional forces in society.[10] Foucault's "disinterestedness," thus, like Sainte-Beuve's, strikes them as perverse. But perhaps criticism remains, at best, a modest enterprise, despite the ambitions of its practitioners. In

Arnold's case, in Sainte-Beuve's case, in Foucault's case, the propelling desire was to "see the object as in itself it really is," whether that object be the Pauline Epistles, Port-Royal, or the prison system. And yet it is inevitable that the most "objective" of programs should seem subjectively motivated. The varied figures that make up Arnold's *Essays in Criticism*—Marcus Aurelius, St. Francis, Spinoza, Wordsworth, the Guérins, Heine, Byron—are an assortment of saints, searchers after truth, heroic transgressors. As such, they make an interesting contrast, in biographical terms, to Foucault's choice of anti-saints who are *also* searchers after truth and heroic transgressors: Nietzsche, Bataille, Blanchot, Roussel. Each critic may be said to have found or fabricated his own particular saving "remnant." More importantly, Arnold and Foucault each shifted the boundaries of criticism, moving from the realm of "knowing" to the realm of ethics, what Foucault called an "aesthetics of existence" and Arnold called the "study of perfection."

Arnold and Sainte-Beuve

There are many reasons why Arnold and James regarded Sainte-Beuve as the "perfect" critic, but paramount among them was his staggering abundance and variety. "The enormous scope of his work," as René Wellek nicely sums it up, "extends to some sixty volumes of criticism in a wide sense of the term. The readability and deft charm of his writings, the authoritative voice of his pronouncements, the impressive erudition and substantial knowledge he conveys, the basic sanity, good sense and good taste, a certain centrality, suspicion of the eccentric and extravagant—all these qualities have made Sainte-Beuve a major figure in European intellectual history." For an ambitious fledgling critic like James, what better model than a writer of such encyclopedic gifts, a mixture of the "poet," "moralist," "historian," "philosopher," and "romancer"?[11] Born in 1804, a generation earlier than Arnold, thirty years older than James, Sainte-Beuve was a member of the Romantic generation, a onetime intimate of Victor Hugo, and himself (in his youth) a poet whose work Baudelaire admired. But he was also a scholar who wore his learning lightly—far more the scholar than Arnold, who was often content to receive his information at secondhand, and far more various and supple in his range and criteria. Sainte-Beuve seems to have absorbed the major

critical tendencies of his period—Claude Fauriel's comparativist studies, Villemain's devotion to literary history, Désiré Nisard's vigilant
antiromanticism, Théophile Gautier's aestheticism—while also drawing on examples from the past such as the amused skepticism of
Montaigne, the moral portraiture of La Bruyère, and the concern for
rules of Boileau. In La Rochefoucauld Sainte-Beuve found a source of
tonic disenchantment that particularly appealed to him during the
shipwreck of his romantic and poetic aspirations. And from the con-
versationalists of the eighteenth century, the habitués of Madame
Geoffrin's salon, for example, he borrowed the habit of treating literary and nonliterary subjects in dialogical form. In the famous *Causerie*
"What Is a Classic?" of 1850, Sainte-Beuve imagines the great authors
of the past perpetually holding forth in conversation with each other
and, by extension, with us. Job and Solomon chatter with Confucius,
Horace with Pope and La Fontaine, Cervantes with Molière. The classic author is one "with whom we shall find ourselves in steady conversation, as with an old friend."¹² Not the least of a critic's gifts, as
Arnold soon realized, was Sainte-Beuve's seductive ability to engage
the reader in what seems an intimate dialogue.

It was as the author of verbal "portraits" that Sainte-Beuve was
particularly renowned. In a career that spanned more than four decades, he wrote hundreds of sketches of major and minor (mostly
French) figures, only a minority connected to literature. He also assembled two important volumes of group portraits, *Port-Royal* (1842),
with its sympathetic treatment of the Jansenists (like Arnold in the
"Stanzas from the Grande Chartreuse," Sainte-Beuve, a nonbeliever,
could write poignantly in behalf of abandoned creeds), and *Chateaubri-
and et son groupe littéraire sous l'Empire* (1860), with its critique of Romanticism, which was to reinforce Arnold's similar views. From 1849
on, he wrote the famous *Lundis,* weekly articles from which Arnold
found clues for his own pieces on Maurice and Eugénie de Gúerin,
Joubert, and the French Academy. (Arnold also found clues for poems
such as "Sohrab and Rustum" in Sainte-Beuve.) In the tribute Arnold
wrote immediately following Sainte-Beuve's death in 1869, Arnold
characterized his predecessor as a "naturalist" in search of data, determined that his should be the "real data" (*CPW,* 5:306). As Sainte-
Beuve himself said, his method as a critic was to study the individual
in terms of his historical milieu (*"tel arbre, tel fruit"* is the famous
formula) and his network of relationships and affiliations. But unlike

his disciples Taine and Scherer, he was also interested in the particular qualities of his subjects, in what made them exceptional and, in some cases, opposed to their times. What was his male subject's attitude toward religion, for example, or toward money or nature or women?[13] In the case of a Voltaire or Rousseau, he was determined (like La Rochefoucauld) to unmask human duplicity. But he was also capable of generosity, of praising someone like Eugénie de Guérin or F. M. Grimm, whose virtues might otherwise go unnoticed.

To a practical reader, such as the writer for the *Quarterly*, the question arose as to the purpose of all these portraits. Compared to a writer like Mill, Sainte-Beuve shrinks from passing judgment. Such later essays as the famous review of *Madame Bovary* do contain implied moral judgments (which Arnold drew on for the essay on Tolstoy);[14] but Sainte-Beuve's general attitude is one of tolerance. He accepts his subjects, saintly and duplicitous alike, as interesting because of their human foibles and complexities. Despite Arnold's reiterated demands that criticism be "disinterested," as Sainte-Beuve's criticism was disinterested, Arnold's own critical practice is, by contrast, rarely that. One need only compare their treatment of the same individual to see how Arnold is invariably more interested than Sainte-Beuve in pursuing an extraliterary theme. His eye is ultimately turned away from the text he is surveying, looking instead at the current need for educational, social, or religious reforms, whereas Sainte-Beuve's eye is on the text.

Arnold is closest to Sainte-Beuve in the 1863 essay on Maurice de Guérin, based on a *Causerie* for 1860. But even as he relates the same biographical story and uses many of the same quotations selected by Sainte-Beuve, Arnold reveals more of a personal stake in his subject than does Sainte-Beuve. The latter considers, very gracefully, this *"jeune Grec,"* in terms of his relations with friends and family, nature and religion. Arnold, however, finds in Maurice a mixture of rebel and truth-seeker, opposed "to the fixedness of a religious vocation, or of any vocation of which fixedness is an essential attribute; a temperament mobile, inconstant, eager, thirsting for new impressions, abhorring rules, aspiring to a 'renovation without end' " (*CPW*, 3:17)—someone not unlike Matthew Arnold, in short. The first of Arnold's literary portraits, Guérin, like most of the other *Essays in Criticism* subjects, faces a crisis of modernism; he is caught between a world of dissolving certainties and a threatening future. Unable to accept the stern, if heterodox, monastic way of life of Abbé Lamennais (to whose retreat in Brittany Guérin had come in search of religious guidance), Guérin, in his determination to pursue "perfection" as a poet of nature, turned to "that common but most perfidious refuge of men of letters, . . . the profession of teaching" (28)—this said by an inspector of schools! When both critics turn to Maurice's sister Eugénie, Sainte-Beuve chooses to celebrate the saintly woman whose life was devoted to her younger brother, while Arnold's purpose is to compare her devout but misplaced Catholicism—a religion "bent on widening the breach between itself and the modern spirit"—with Protestantism, which "has a future before it, a prospect of growth" (3:97). Arnold backs away from Sainte-Beuve's apotheosis of Eugénie as a "saint," and he protests Sainte-Beuve's comment (which the latter retracted, citing Arnold's reproof) that the sister was a greater genius than her brother. The brother, after all, was a poet, and with his Wordsworthian and classical affinities an Arnoldian poet at that.[15]

Arnold's tendency to use the subjects of his essays to make a point means that he occasionally exaggerates the importance of someone like Joseph Joubert, a reactionary in religion, politics, literature, and every other matter, but one whom Arnold holds up for his dogged belief in absolute standards in an age of confusion. From Sainte-Beuve's "incomparable" portrait Arnold elaborates on the suggestion that Joubert was a secondary figure who served to inspire Chateaubriand and others and who was, hence, the sort of critic whose ideas help provide the intellectual "current" required of creative artists. A "current of ideas" of this sort is what Arnold thought Wordsworth and company lacked. Arnold devotes much less space than does Sainte-Beuve to Joubert the person; he focuses instead on Joubert as symbol of that "critical power" deemed so essential in "The Function of Criticism" (CPW, 3:261–63). Whereas Sainte-Beuve's portraits can be appreciated as single works of art, Arnold's essays, by contrast, need to be read in terms of their larger context. The greatness of the Essays in Criticism can only be seen if one studies the volume as a whole, the reader noting how each of the individual subjects is set in fruitful dialogue with one another: the Stoic Marcus Aurelius set against the radical Heine; Maurice de Guérin's "elusive, undulating, impalpable nature" (23) contrasting with the doctrinaire self-assurance of Joubert.[16]

The most problematic of the Essays in Criticism, from a modern point of view, is "The Literary Influence of Academies," inspired by articles of Sainte-Beuve and Renan treating a recent history of the French Academy. Renan's influence was more decisive here than Saint-Beuve's; but Arnold's main purpose was distinct from either of theirs. He wished to highlight the sort of state-supported cultural institution devoted to standards of excellence that was lacking in England. Arnold's "Academy" is a symbolic institution; it is incapable of perhaps ever existing since it is designed for two very different ends: to ensure that there are intellectual and literary standards that would discourage such monstrosities as Francis Newman's translation of Homer; but also to ensure "openness of mind and flexibility of intelligence" (*CPW*, 3:237). Arnold cites Sainte-Beuve's comment that the French Academy was intended by its founder, Richelieu, to be a literary tribunal (*"haut jury"*), judging works that came before the public and setting a standard of correct taste.[17] But Arnold ignores Sainte-Beuve's admission that the Academy did not really fulfill its function. As likely as not—in the case of Corneille's *Le Cid*, for example—a masterpiece was unjustly criticized. But for Arnold, the questions of who will set the standards and why these standards will be the correct ones are irrelevant; he is imagining, after all, an *ideal* Academy, one that banishes the "provincial spirit" and guards against literary eccentricities. Such a "sovereign organ of the highest literary opinion, a recognized authority in matters of intellectual tone and taste, we shall hardly have" in fact, as Arnold realizes; and, he adds, "perhaps we ought not to wish to have it" (257). But, he concludes, we need to acknowledge the existence of standards that lie outside of ourselves, not resting content with the reiteration of our own, severely limited, subjective judgments.

In the end, as Sainte-Beuve reminds us, "there is no formula for producing a classic"—nor, one might add, for producing a critic. It is to Arnold's credit that he should have appreciated in Sainte-Beuve a temperament so different from his own. (In *God and the Bible*, Arnold defends a "classic" text that Sainte-Beuve saw no need for. "M. Sainte-Beuve, the finest critical spirit of our times," Arnold remarks, "conceived of the Bible so falsely, simply from not knowing it, that he could cheerfully and confidently repeat the Liberal formula: 'Unless we mean to prefer Byzantinism to progress we must say goodbye *aux vieilles Bibles,*—to the old Bibles' " [*CPW*, 7:392].) A clear sign of this difference can be seen in the title he chose for his first major prose publication, the *Essays in Criticism*. Arnold originally toyed with the idea of calling it

" 'Essays of Criticism' in the old sense of the word *Essay*—*attempt*—
specimen; but perhaps this would hardly do."[18] "Essays *of* Criticism"
implies something distinctly French, specimens of criticism that pay
homage to Montaigne's "essais" and Sainte-Beuve's "critique" and that
are tributes to the power of curiosity. (Arnold's suggestion that the
volume be issued in yellow paper wrappers underscores the French
connection.) But "Essays *in* Criticism" implies that practice, application, is also involved. Just as Arnold was anxious that "The Scholar-
Gipsy" *do* something for its reader, so was he anxious that the *Essays* get
"*at* the English public," as he wrote his mother. "Such a public as it is,
and such a work as one wants to do with it!"[19]

In this respect, a more ideal critic than Sainte-Beuve for Arnold's
purpose was Renan, a critic concerned with the pressing social problems of the day as well as with the history of Christianity. Still, when
asked to write on Sainte-Beuve for the *Encyclopaedia Britannica,* Arnold
responded with a portrait of his favorite critic that pays homage to
Sainte-Beuve's own methods. He selects the essential biographical
details, chronicles Sainte-Beuve's transformation from poet and medical student into the contributor to the *Revue des Deux Mondes,* and
gives a sound and generous assessment of Sainte-Beuve's overall
achievement. Whatever was lost in the failed poet and disillusioned
romantic was more than compensated for in the perfection of the
critic—"a critic of measure, not exuberant; of the centre, not provincial; of keen industry and curiosity, with 'Truth' (the word engraved in
English on his seal) for his motto" (*CPW,* 11:115).

Arnold, Renan, and Scherer

Arnold's view of Sainte-Beuve differs considerably from that of the
Goncourt brothers, intimate acquaintances of the French critic during
the 1860s and cofounders with him of the famous Magny dinners.
Their Sainte-Beuve is an elderly, spiteful, impotent figure, lacking in
noble thoughts or fine expressions, content to describe criticism as
"saying whatever comes into one's head," skilled in "tearing a man to
pieces in the guise of defending him." He resembles, in his old age (a
time when the Goncourts could scarcely form a fair impression, yet the
time also when Arnold knew him), something of his 1842 portrait of
Montaigne, an amusing skeptic who leads his reader playfully to a

realm of "universal doubt" and "utter darkness." In *Port-Royal*, Sainte-Beuve compares Montaigne to Pascal, the former "distracted, even entranced with his own shipwreck, while the other clings to the bit of driftwood with whose help he still can, by indomitable effort, reach the distant shore, his homeland in eternity." Another habitué of the Magny dinners may be said to have played Pascal to Sainte-Beuve's Montaigne: Renan. Although he was, like Sainte-Beuve, an "apostle of doubt," Renan was nevertheless the possessor of an unfailing idealism, the exemplar for the Goncourts of "the finest type of moral beauty."[20] Although Renan shared Sainte-Beuve's love of diversity—in his youth, Renan described criticism as "maintaining contradictory elements opposite each other, . . . not letting a single component of humanity stifle any other"[21]—he also aimed at higher moral and critical standards than those of his former mentor. Arnold soon realized that Renan's aims were not unlike his own.

Arnold noted the "considerable resemblance" between Renan's "line of endeavour" and his own as early as 1859. In a letter to his sister Jane, Arnold recommended Renan's works, especially the recently published *Essais de morale et de critique,* containing the important essay on Celtic poetry. A notable difference between the French author and himself, Arnold observed, is "that he tends to inculcate *morality,* in a high sense of the word, upon the French nation as what they most want, while I tend to inculcate *intelligence,* also in a high sense of the word, upon the English nation as what they most want— but with respect both to morality and intelligence, I think we are singularly at one on our ideas—and also with respect both to the progress and the established religion of the present day." For the next three decades, Arnold repeatedly cited Renan in his writings and in his notebooks, whether in reference to Celtic charms or American vulgarity (as noted in the previous chapter), or in regard to the values of education and religion. (Among the scores of Renan citations in the notebooks are the following that prefigure Arnold's own views: "La somme incomparable de goût pour le bien que le christianisme a inspiré!"; "La religion, c'est la part de l'ideal dans la vie humaine.")[22] Born only a year apart, each had undergone a period of religious crisis. Renan abandoned his priestly ambition as he came, like Arnold, to doubt the accepted faith of his childhood. But unlike Arnold, who never broke with the Church of England, convinced that it would adapt, was adapting, to the *Zeitgeist,* Renan left the Catholic

Church. Even so, he did not lose a core of idealistic faith, which he traced back to his native Brittany. His will to believe was rechanneled into faith in science. In the popular *Life of Jesus*, the first in a series of books dealing with the origins of Christianity, Renan detached Christ from the religion set up in his name, arguing that "Jesus is the highest of these pillars which show to man whence he comes, and whither he ought to tend. In him was condensed all that is good and elevated in our nature." Like Arnold in his religious books of the '70s, Renan found inspiration in Jesus' life for the idea that "We must create the heavenly kingdom, that is the ideal one, within ourselves."[23]

Reviewing Renan's memoirs in 1883, James (who considered Renan "the first writer in France" at the moment) declared that, as a stylist, "No one today says such things as well, though in our own language Mr. Matthew Arnold often approaches him." *Souvenirs d'enfance et de jeunesse*, an intimate *causerie* between author and reader, as James recognized (and perhaps the finest of Renan's writings), contains much that should have appealed to Arnold. It contains a nostalgia for the past coupled with an acceptance of the future, a coupling that justifies Arnolds's tendency to link Renan with Burke. But what Arnold did notice in the book, to his dismay, was Renan's ironical observation, after a glance back at his own impeccably moral life, that perhaps such libertines as Sainte-Beuve and Gautier were in the right. Ignoring the reference to his beloved Sainte-Beuve, Arnold castigates Renan for suggesting that "les frivoles ont peut-être raison" or that nature cares little for chaste behavior.[24] Arnold saw French disregard for conduct as being somehow responsible for her defeat at Germany's hand in 1870. In his only essay devoted to Renan, Arnold in 1872, in a review of *La Réforme intellectuelle et morale de la France*, chastized Renan for suggesting that France's main problem was insufficient scientific knowledge rather than a "want of faith in *conduct*." Renan's sense of French superiority to Germany because of her livelier social life is derided by Arnold as "Hellenism with a vengeance!" Yet even here Arnold avows that "to differ with M. Renan is far less natural to us than to agree with him." Arnold's dialogue with Renan is no less important than his dialogue with Sainte-Beuve: in 1872, with Sainte-Beuve dead, Arnold challenged any country "to produce a living critic to surpass M. Renan" (*CPW*, 7:44–46). And with the passing of George Sand, Arnold in 1877 singled out Renan as one of the very few French authors concerned with moral behavior. On occasion, disturbed by the occasional outbursts in late Renan (the playful style that became known as "Renan-ism"), Arnold complained that despite his "brilliancy," "Renan is not *sound*." (This was said in 1879, in response to Renan's praise of Hugo.) But in 1882, whole considering England's troubled relations with Ire-land, Arnold returned to "the most charming of French moralists" for an apt quotation: "Pour gagner l'humanité, il faut lui plaire; pour lui plaire, il faut être aimable."[25]

It was with such Renanian sentiments in mind that Arnold de-scribed his intention, in the *Essays in Criticism*, of "*getting at* the En-glish public" by means of "the power of *persuasion*, of *charm*. . . . Even in one's ridicule one must preserve a sweetness and good-humour." But Renan offered more than an appealing style: he offered what was, in effect, a new literary form, the critical essay put to the service of urgent social and religious questions. Whereas Sainte-Beuve had shown Arnold the appeal of the essay form for literary purposes, Renan demonstrated how that form could be expanded to cover larger issues without losing its stylistic charm. It was thus that Sainte-Beuve praised Renan as "le maître d'un genre nouveau." Renan defended the collection of several of his writings from reviews, *Etudes d'histoire religieuse* (1857), on the ground that this was a "new kind of literature" worthy of preservation, a form that "will some day be regarded as belonging especially to our epoch, and consequently as that in which our epoch has excelled."[26] For better and worse, Renan felt that his was an age of "universal criticism," an age of questions and reapprais-als made in the light of the scientific spirit. In his application of criti-cism to religious matters, Renan was consciously responding to and modifying the methods of the German Higher Critics.

While, as a scientific-minded critic, Renan could no longer accept the truth of the Christian story ("Nothing is supernatural," he avows), as a moralist and idealist, he felt its poetic appeal. Hence, his critical mission is twofold: to establish what is historically verifiable, on the one hand, and to affirm the reality of the "religious sentiment" (even as he undermines its validity) among the masses, on the other. Like Ar-nold over a decade later, Renan notes how mankind is likely and will-ing to be duped in its desire for the miraculous. Yet he insists, "Far from seeking to weaken the religious sentiment, I would gladly contribute something to raise and purify it." Even as he speaks of the multitude's "ignorance," he argues that "in the object of its worship it is not mis-taken. What it adores is really adorable; for what it adores in its ideal characters is the goodness and beauty it has itself put there." A remarkable achievement of Renan's religious writings is his combination of a Voltairean skepticism and desire for truth with an enthusiasm worthy of Chateaubriand. Whereas David Friedrich Strauss and other German critics had replaced the savior of theology with a merely "theoretical Christ,"[27] Renan set as his task a portrayal of the historical Jesus and an account of his influence and institutionalization throughout history.

Renan's multivolumed *Les Origines du christianisme*, which began in 1863 with the *Vie de Jésus*, is simultaneously an attack on the dogmas and institutions of Christianity and an affirmation of the power of the ideal. It was this kind of religious criticism that Arnold found lacking in England, a criticism that allowed for both an objective examination of Christianity and an affirmation of its symbolic value. "M. Renan's attempt is, for criticism, of the most real interest and importance," Arnold maintains in "The Function of Criticism at the Present Time," "since, with all its difficulty, a fresh synthesis of the New Testament *data*,—not a making war on them, in Voltaire's fashion, not leaving them out of mind, in the world's fashion [the "mass of mankind," Arnold says earlier, in another context, never have "any ardent zeal for seeing things as they are; very inadequate ideas will always satisfy them"], but the putting a new construction upon them, the taking them from under the old, traditional, conventional point of view and placing them under a new one,—is the very essence of the religious problem, as now presented; and only by efforts in this direction can it receive a solution" (*CPW*, 3:279, 274).

In this respect, Arnold saw in Renan a foil to Bishop Colenso, the feckless practitioner of Higher Criticism in the inadequate English manner, one who managed, Arnold charged, to disturb the faith of the multitude without telling the informed few anything they didn't know already. In appraising Colenso's program, and comparing it to that of the more "edifying" Spinoza, Arnold applied the methods of literary criticism to matters of religion, the very task being undertaken by Renan. But he warned that while knowledge of the historical truth of Christianity must continue to be sought after, such truth was dangerous if given out bluntly to the multitudes.[28] "The great mass of the human race," Arnold (like Renan) contends, "have to be softened and humanised before any soil can be found in them where knowledge may strike living roots" (*CPW*, 3:44). The origins of Arnold's arduous attempt to save the Scriptures may be traced, in large part, to his dialogue with Renan in the late 1850s and early 1860s; and if Arnold remained confident, in *St. Paul and Protestantism*, that St. Paul was *not* "coming to the end of his reign," as Renan no less confidently had announced, he nevertheless followed Renan's example in his effort, in *Literature and Dogma*, to "extract" from Jesus' credulous reporters something of the "true Jesus," regarding this as "one of the highest conceivable tasks of criticism."[29]

It was above all Renan's *Essais de morale et de critique* that confirmed Arnold's sense of the possibilities of criticism. One could overstate the nature of Renan's importance here, but by and large the tendency has been to understate it, to say that Renan did no more than confirm Arnold in his own views.[30] It is true that putting Renan's *Essais* alongside the *Essays in Criticism* does little more than show incidental and minor resemblances: the Renanian rhapsodic eulogy of his Breton forefathers at the end of his preface, for example, anticipates Arnold's tribute to Oxford at the end of his Preface. But what must surely have impressed Arnold with Renan's volume was the skill with which he had assembled his pieces from the *Revue des Deux Mondes* and elsewhere into a unified work that makes a case against the excesses of his age and that offers symbolic alternatives. Beginning with the preface, Renan argues in behalf of the critical spirit *("l'esprit critique")*, which seeks after the truth, and of the moral function *("la morale")* which safeguards the intangible and life-preserving values of life. Renan writes out of a disgust with his times—an age that worships mediocrity and material comforts. The spirit of the French Revolution is responsible, he contends, for France's thoughtless complacency with its liberal heritage and material well-being. But what, he asks, if the spirit of 1789 has come to mean little more than a national "fétichisme qui lui fait placer son amour-propre dans la défense de certains mots"? What, Renan charges (in anticipation of Foucault), if the bureaucratic institutions set up in the wake of 1789 to safeguard liberal values and individual comforts have ended by enslaving the individual? ("Le principe qui crée les institutions, à savoir la conquête et le droit personnel, c'était le principe même qu'elle entreprenait de supprimer.")[31]

In *Friendship's Garland*, Arnold praises Renan for his willingness to "give it to his poor countrymen when he thinks they deserve it" (*CPW*, 5:33); and in "The Function of Criticism at the Present Time," Arnold attacks English self-complacency in a Renanian manner. Liberalism may think it can dispense with traditional beliefs and nonmaterial values: it erects its modern cathedral in the form of the Paris Exhibition of

1855 with its glittering wares ("La Poésie de l'Exposition"). But, Renan contends, "si comme le pensant à bon droit les sages, la seule chose nécessaire [Arnold's "one thing needful"] est la noblesse morale et intellectuelle, ces accessoires y contribuent pour assez peu de chose." Still, if modern French society is seen at its worst flocking to the Exposition—in pursuit of what Renan calls *"la médiocrité"* or what Goethe, in a word much used by Arnold, calls *"Das Gemeine"*—France at her best can be seen in the Academy, an institution that has resisted mediocrity and upheld "la délicatesse de l'esprit français" (one of several phrases quoted by Arnold in his essay on "Academies"). As Jesus symbolizes, for Renan, the height of human dignity, and as the Celts symbolize faith in the unseen ("La Poésie des races celtiques"), so too does the Academy symbolize the power of French culture as an intellectual and spiritual "tribunal," resisting all revolutions or whims of fashion. Whoever calls the Academy outdated pays it the highest compliment, Renan declares: "L'essentiel, de nôtre temps, n'est pas de créer, mais de durer et de résister."[32]

"Périssons en résistant": the phrase is Obermann's, as quoted in "The Function of Criticism" (*CPW*, 3:276), but the idea that a critic's twin duties are to battle for the highest of standards and to resist the self-congratulatory vulgarity of one's time is Renan's, as argued in the *Essais*. It may be that Renan reinforced some of Arnold's less desirable critical habits—the occasional tendency toward critical hubris—and that he gave Arnold a misleadingly high sense of the powers of criticism (a legacy Renan transmitted to modern French critics as well). And while Renan's idealizations of the French Academy and Celtic traditions proved useful, his negative view of America as the incarnation of mediocrity colored Arnold's vision when he traveled there. (Renan saw the world "moving in the direction of . . . a kind of Americanism, which shocks our refined ideas.")[33] Yet in his review of Renan's *La Réforme intellectuelle,* Arnold criticizes Renan's elitist position, his view that civilization is the creation and property of an aristocratic few, and that "country, honour, duty, are things created and upheld by a small number of men amidst a multitude which, left to itself, lets them fall." "Yes," Arnold sardonically agrees, "because this multitude are in vise and misery outside them; and surely that they are so is in itself some condemnation of the 'aristocratic work' " (7:43).

In other matters, Arnold and Renan could temperamentally join—in their high regard for Spinoza and Marcus Aurelius ("that gospel of those who have no belief in the supernatural," as Renan calls the *Meditations*, "a gospel which only in our own days has been fully understood"), and in their lack of sympathy for Amiel, whose "sterility" is accounted for by Renan in the morbid Swiss diarist's lack of curiosity. Both critics wrote on Amiel late in their lives, Arnold in 1887 reaffirming the value of the literary critic over the theoretical philosopher, Renan in 1884 reaffirming the value of a limitless curiosity. (If his Semitic studies should ever be exhausted, Renan notes, he would then turn happily to the study of China.) One's love of the ideal need not paralyze one's appetite for reality. But unlike Renan, Amiel lacked faith in the "Ideal" and was disgusted by the "Real." Renan's credo, hence, is one that Arnold had used as title for one of his poems: "*In utrumque paratus!* To be prepared for all contingencies, this perhaps is wisdom. To abandon one's self successively to confidence, scepticism, optimism, irony,—such is the means of being sure that, at least at moments, we have been in the right."[34]

As Arnold aged, many of his views stiffened, and, as a result, some of the relativism and tolerance of the French critics become distasteful to him. Sainte-Beuve had made the profoundest impact because of the breadth and sanity of his criticism; Renan's appeal lay in the application of criticism to social and religious concerns. (Renan never considered himself to be a "literary" critic, in the manner of Sainte-Beuve.) Together, the two French authors showed English readers that much of "the best that is known and thought in the world" was to be found on foreign shores. For the principal "function of criticism," Arnold argued in 1864, is the discovery and transmission of "knowledge, and ever fresher knowledge." A secondary task for the critic is passing "judgment" (the *Quarterly* would call it the main task), but even then, Arnold cautions, one should pass judgment "insensibly, and . . . as a sort of companion and clue, not as an abstract lawgiver"—for the sake, perhaps, of "establishing an author's place in literature" (*CPW*, 3:282–83). A year following the lecture version of "The Function of Criticism," Arnold met another member of the Magny dinners, who had no compunction at all when it came to passing out judgments. "The only thing that counts is judgment," Edmond Scherer (the future editor of Amiel) declared in 1863. "One should possess judgment before all else."[35]

Reviewing the second of an eventual ten volumes of his collected criticism, James, in 1863, described Scherer as "a solid embodiment of

Mr. Matthew Arnold's ideal critic," one writing out of his individual "moral sense" rather than in the service of party or other vested interest. A former Protestant theologian of French-Swiss-English background, Scherer, having, in middle age, lost his faith, had turned his hand to literary criticism. However, he retained in his work a "moral distinction between good and evil" that appealed to both James and Arnold.[36] A disciple, like Renan and Taine, of Sainte-Beuve, Scherer shared his master's interest in a wide range of authors and his historical methodology, the habit of relating (in Arnold's phrase) "the power of the man" to the "power of the moment" (*CPW*, 3:261). But, unlike Sainte-Beuve, Scherer was thoroughly at home with English literature, past and present, and as such he embodied Arnold's injunction that the critic "possess one great literature, at least, besides his own" (3:284). Arnold admired Scherer's shrewdness when assessing an author like Byron—the subject of one of Taine's panegyrics, but to Scherer "one of our French superstitions"—or Milton. Scherer's fondness for passing negative judgments on the great, finding weaknesses in Goethe or Molière, can grate on modern ears. He refuses not only to be duped but also to be charmed. Although he shared Renan's intermittent fear that the future was tending toward barbarism ("Nous allons à l'américanisme"), he lacked Renan's sense of humor or his belief that in the past or in other cultures a poetic idealism could still be found. ("Les vrais poètes de nôtre temps," Renan declared, "sont le critique et l'historien qui vont l'y chercher.") With Amiel, Scherer shared a disgust for the things of the world. He might have been describing himself in the words he applied to Amiel in 1882: neither optimist nor pessimist, nor for that matter resigned to fate because he repudiated the empire of things ("la souveraineté des choses").[37]

Arnold by 1865 thought Scherer "one of the most interesting men in France." He was touched by Scherer's admiration for Thomas Arnold, after whom he had named his youngest son.[38] By the 1870s, with Sainte-Beuve dead and Renan exhibiting disconcerting signs of Renanism, Scherer became increasingly close to Arnold. He drew upon Scherer for two of his major literary essays of that decade, "A French Critic on Milton" (1877) and "A French Critic on Goethe" (1878). In addition to providing Arnold with an incentive to return to literature after a decade of religious studies, Scherer also gave Arnold an excuse to discuss two central literary figures, the first of whom he admired with grave reservations, the second of whom had shaped so much of his thinking that he could scarcely write directly about him at all. The Milton essay permitted Arnold to hit at a favorite target, Macaulay ("the great apostle of the Philistines," Arnold had called him in the Joubert essay [*CPW*, 3:310]), whose famous laudatory essay on Milton struck him as mere "rhetoric" rather than sound criticism. Neither Scherer nor Arnold can forgive or forget Milton's Puritan temper—"*unamiable*," in Arnold's view, "grotesque," in Scherer's assessment of *Paradise Lost*. Although Arnold has reservations about Scherer's "method of historical criticism," he approves of Scherer's tendency to see *Paradise Lost* in terms of beautiful passages cut loose from a repellent theology (8:169, 181, 175, 182). Scherer's treatment of Goethe is even harsher than his treatment of Milton. The date of the essay, 1872, the aftermath of the Franco-Prussian War, has been cited in partial explanation. The apotheosis of Goethe by the victorious Germans annoyed Scherer to such a degree that he felt compelled to draw up a litany of complaints about Goethe's lack of inventiveness, his many dull patches, his tiresome use of allegory.[39] Scherer seems determined, in the case of a poet whom he claims to admire, to demonstrate that whom he loveth, he chasteneth. Trying to maintain a critical objectivity to match Scherer's, Arnold is reduced to detaching Goethe the thinker from Goethe the author, and to conclude that "in his width, depth, and richness of his criticism of life" (8:275), Goethe achieved something better than mere poetic greatness.

While confirming Arnold in his drift toward increasingly judgmental standards in his later criticism (and by anticipating, in the Milton essay, something of the famous "touchstone" theory of poetry), Scherer also confirmed Arnold's sense that a critic must look outside his native borders in search of literary excellence. Scherer is at his best, perhaps, not when he is denouncing famous writers but when he is bringing to the attention of French readers English writers such as Sterne, Wordsworth, and George Eliot. James was shocked to find Flaubert's circle unacquainted with the author of *Daniel Deronda*, but Scherer, decrying French provinciality ("Which of us has any notion of the intellectual activity that occupies our neighbours?"), reviewed Eliot's novel as the latest "masterpiece" to come from her pen. And when Arnold sent Scherer his anthology of Wordsworth (its introductory essay reflecting Arnold at his best as literary critic and moralist), Scherer inserted into his review of the volume a glowing tribute to Arnold. "He presents," says Scherer, "a singular example of that modern curiosity which explores all paths, touches all subjects, and tries all ways of expression." Noting also Arnold's skill as theologian and poet, Scherer affirms that from a "marriage" of the two "sprang a critic—the liveliest, the most delicate, the most elegant of critics, the critic who has given out most ideas, has conferred upon them the most piquant expression, and has most thoroughly shocked the sluggishness of British thought by wholesome audacities"—a critic, moreover, thoroughly at home and in sympathy with the literature, culture, and institutions of France, and yet whose works (Scherer adds in amazement) have been ignored in France.[40]

Arnold and Foucault

That the "liveliest" English critic of the nineteenth century has remained virtually unknown in France while French criticism has conquered the academic bastions of England and America says at least as much about French provincialism as about Anglo-American fears of not being in tune with the latest intellectual fashions. For Arnold, warring with English provincialism, the appeal of nineteenth-century French critics lay in their encyclopedic breadth, their objectivity, their determination not to be duped by popular conventions or credulities. Even so, he acknowledged the point of Addison's sarcasm "that 'a few general words extracted out of the French authors, with a certain cant of words, has sometimes set up an illiterate heavy writer for a most judicious and formidable critic' " (CPW, 8:187). One can only wonder what Arnold, with his mixture of irony and high seriousness, would have made of the recent French supplanters of the critical tradition of Sainte-Beuve and Renan, among them the doctrinaire deconstructionists and playful pontificators whose goal, it often appears, is to leak meaning out of texts and world alike. The most influential of post–World War II French philosophers, Jean-Paul Sartre, seems to have lacked, for all his earnest political engagements, an objective awareness of self or of history; and the generation born after him has felt compelled to reject his Marxism and his existential humanism as inadequate responses to the late twentieth century's crisis of modernism. Out of the post-Sartrean generation that includes Roland Barthes, Jacques Lacan, Louis Althusser, and Jacques Derrida, it may be that only Foucault will survive as a major intellectual force.

Foucault is the philosopher and diagnostician of our time (in Jürgen Habermas's words) who has "most lastingly influenced the *Zeitgeist*, not least of all because of the seriousness with which he perseveres under productive contradictions."[41]

The tribute to Foucault's "productive contradictions" is a reflection of Habermas's own humanistic background, his allegiance to the Enlightenment faith in the efficacy of "communicative reason"; but Foucault himself, for much of his life, resisted terms such as *Enlightenment, reason,* or *humanism.* In his most intensely political-activist phase, Foucault in 1971 dismissed humanism as "everything in Western civilization that restricts *the desire for power*" on the part of the individual, as the insidious social force that denies genuine freedom even as it claims to be safeguarding freedom. (By *humanism,* Foucault meant the modern Marxist-existential-Sartrean variety as much as the version espoused by nineteenth-century social scientists.) But Habermas is right to speak of Foucault's contradictions—the fact that he can be seen as, for example, historian and antihistorian, philosopher and antiphilosopher, Marxist and anti-Marxist, humanitarian and antihumanist. "Do not ask who I am and do not ask me to remain the same," taunts Foucault in a much-cited passage from *The Archeology of Knowledge.* "The authority of Foucault's discourses," Allan Megill contends, "lies in the fact that it is *not* understood—that for all its apparent concern with changing the present, the content of that change remains enigmatic. Thus, his texts can be many things to many people, appealing to all who perceive a defectiveness in the existing order"[42]

The fate of Foucault's first major work, *Madness and Civilization* (1961), is a case in point. Originally regarded as an academic treatise (albeit written with great poetic flair), a history of the changing treatment and perception of so-called mad people, the book subsequently became cited as a pioneering text of the antipsychiatry movement. It was perceived as a gospel for those of the May 1968 generation protesting all forms of authoritarian repression (in prisons, in factories, in schools); and by the mid-1970s, Foucault's description of the "great confinement" was seen as an indictment of the Soviet gulags as described by Solzhenitsyn. In the America of the 1980s and 1990s, Foucault's study could also be seen as a Bakhtinian enterprise, whose theme is the interrogation and welcoming of "Otherness." (One might add here that Foucault's romanticizing of madness has a long French tradition behind it. Renan, in his *Souvenirs d'enfance et de*

jeunesse, nostalgically recalls the days when the lunatics of his native
Brittany were allowed to roam free, not confined to the "cruelty" of
asylums.)[43] It is not for nothing that Foucault's British biographer,
David Macey, speaks of his subject's many "lives"; nor that his
French biographer, Didier Erebon, marvels at Foucault's simulta-
neous ability to maintain the habits of a dedicated academic scholar
at the Collège de France while also marching in the streets for a
variety of causes; nor that his American biographer, James Miller,
should have such difficulty reconciling the image of Foucault as
philosophical and sexual heretic with that of a monklike seeker after
truth.[44]

   These three biographies of Foucault appeared within a few years
of his death. By contrast, nearly a century passed before the first com-
prehensive biography of Arnold, by Park Honan, was published. (In
1996, Nicholas Murray's sensitively and agreeably written *Life of Matthew Arnold* appeared in England.) What indeed would Arnold, who
bristled at Renan's frivolous asides, have made of Foucault? True, Foucault might be said to combine Sainte-Beuve's erudition, Renan's impu-
dent stoicism, and Scherer's icy rigorousness, along with Taine's
determinism—but to what end? Elected to the prestigious Collège de
France (Renan's academic home), Foucault in 1970 delivered as his
inaugural address *L'Ordre du discours*—a "subversive" attack on language itself as a means of control—"in a voice that was simultaneously
Beckettian in its gnomic ellipses and Renanian in its portentous sonor-
ity." From 1970 until his untimely death in 1984, Foucault taught and
conducted research there in subjects ranging from the prison system to
sexual mores. Among the topics he explored with his students was the
case of Pierre Rivière, a nineteenth-century Norman peasant who bru-
tally murdered his mother and siblings and then, when caught, presented a written account of his crime. Foucault was enchanted by "the
beauty of Rivière's memoir" and by the parricide himself, one of those
outlaw-heroes (for Foucault) who "rise against power, traverse the law,
and expose themselves to death through death." Given Arnold's an-
tipathy toward Victor Hugo and for the kind of romanticism that celebrates the exploits of self, one can easily imagine his disgust with
Foucault's choice of hero. Five years after publishing the dossier on
Rivière, Foucault announced a series for the publisher Gallimard, "Les
Vies Parallèles," which would be anti-Plutarchian in intent. Its subjects
would not be "exemplary ghosts speaking through the centuries," but

rather figures whose trajectories "diverge indefinitely. No meeting point, no place to take them in. . . . One should grasp them in the force of the impulse that drives them apart."[45] The series (if carried out) would have been an ultimate achievement for Foucault, a celebration of the unknowable and infamous, and as such a fitting epilogue to his literary tributes to the Marquis de Sade, Friedrich Nietzsche, Antonin Artaud, Georges Bataille, and others who either transgress or preach transgression.

Arnold, in 1864, remarked of his essay "A French Eton," "People say it is *revolutionary*, but all unconstrained thinking tends, perhaps, to be a little revolutionary." The novelty of Arnold's description of two French secondary schools, a state-run lycée in Toulouse and the private school at Sorèze run by Lacordaire, lay in his conclusion that it is through a system of state-supported institutions open to the middle classes that the individual can hope to be perfected, to quit narrow old habits and "adopt new, to go out for himself, to transform himself" (*CPW*, 2:312). Arnold's belief in the potential of a state-run educational system (a novel idea in the England of 1864) to cultivate the individual was resisted by Foucault for reasons similar to Renan's. For them, the state was the enemy of the truth-seeking individual, whereas for Arnold, living (as he felt) in a Philistine culture that promoted narrow religious and individual goals over social goals, only the state could save England from intellectual decay. For all his admiration of France, Arnold had no desire that English liberalism be replaced by French authoritarianism; and when he came to define his ideal "State" in *Culture and Anarchy*, he ended up speaking of an ideal body that represents the "best self" of each member of the community (5:134). For Foucault, the state is part of the problem, not by any means the solution. As Simon During observes, "He works against a firmer background of absolutism and statism. France is still in many ways more repressive as well as a more centralized or *dirigiste* society than Britain or America." That both Arnold and Foucault came out of elitist backgrounds (far more elitist in Foucault's case than Arnold's) and attended the best schools did not prevent them from attacking the very different social systems that had nurtured and rewarded them. Each looked to a model different from their own, even as each took advantage of what their system had to offer. In Foucault's case, a network of family patronage and academic alliances got him from the Ecole Normale Supérieure to the Collège de France. A rather more

limited kind of support provided Arnold with his position as inspector of schools.[46]

In describing the remnant of dedicated individuals who "save the
State" in his lecture "Numbers" (given in another antistatist country),
Arnold was speaking in behalf of a very different elite from that
selected by Foucault to embody his own counter-remnant. Whatever
their differences, such figures in the *Essays in Criticism* as Marcus
Aurelius, Spinoza, Heine, and the Guérins are all truth-seekers, looking for that which will provide intellectual or spiritual sustenance in
an age of dissolving values. Perhaps the finest tribute to these truth-
seekers is found in the late essay on Wordsworth (1879) in which
Arnold praises those poets who get us "home," who are preoccupied
not with incidentals such as "style" but rather with "the best and
master thing." (Arnold's image of mankind's true object in life being a
voyage home, rather than a resting in inns along the way, comes from
Epictetus [*CPW*, 9:46–47].) With Foucault's literary heroes, by contrast, their journey is not homeward but into the "labyrinth," into an
experience that partakes of the authenticity (for Foucault) of madness
and emptiness. For them, transgression is the only norm and death
and sexuality (the two interlinked) the only givens. Such authors are
not Wordsworthian preservers of past and present, upholders of mankind and of language, but instead anonymous speakers whose language, "a formless rumbling," affirms nothing and ensures no "mastery over time." In his essay on Nietzsche, Foucault celebrates the
philosopher who undermined the nineteenth century's faith in history and mankind as replacements for the loss of eternity and God.
With the death of God, on the contrary, history (like language) loses
all meaning and the individual loses his or her identity. Nietzsche's
"geneology," which replaces history, does "not seek to define our
unique threshold of emergence, the homeland to which metaphysi-
cians promise a return," writes Foucault; "it seems to make visible all
of those discontinuities that cross us."[47] Granted that there are no
truths but only interpretations or perspectives (as Nietzsche claims);
nonetheless, for Foucault some perspectives, such as Nietzsche's,
carry more weight than others.

Foucault has described his literary essays of the 1960s as providing "ways of escaping from philosophy," with Nietzsche as the philosophical "outsider" who showed what lay beyond the limits of the
academic curriculum. "I belong to that generation," Foucault said in a

late interview with the translator of his longest literary study, *Raymond Roussel* (1963), "who as students had before their eyes, and were limited by, a horizon consisting of Marxism, phenomenology, and existentialism." In the wake of the horrors of World War II, pieties such as the need to release mankind from "alienation" seemed absurd. Alienation, rather, was the reality one recognized and embraced, whether in the form of Samuel Beckett's *Waiting for Godot* or the work of Bataille, Roussel, and Maurice Blanchot. Such writers feel no desire to glorify mankind or reproduce reality. Roussel (like Amiel) feels only distaste for reality, yet he hopes to overcome his sense of the "absolute emptiness of being" with a language that allows him to "*discover* an unexpected space, and to *cover* it with things never said before." Roussel's fictions are verbal games, machines (very often) made up of plays on words, which allow their author to "disappear behind his work." A literary martyr of sorts, unable to communicate despite his wish to do so and despite his desire to be recognized, Roussel "solemnly transmits the genesis of works [in his *How I Wrote Certain of My Books*] whose kinship he defines with madness and suffering . . . , which must be its stigmata of legitimacy."[48] Foucault's essay on Bataille, which appeared in the same year as the *Roussel*, pays tribute to the philosopher-poet of "transgression," a theme Foucault sees as "decisive for our culture, . . . a part of its soil." In a world that no longer reveres the sacred, Bataille makes an erotics out of the killing of God, thereby providing through transgression a means of not only "discovering the sacred in its unmediated substance, but also a way of recomposing its empty form, its absence, through which it becomes all the more scintillating." As God dies, Sade arises to mark out a new "kingdom"; he "gives voice," Foucault intones in his essay on Blanchot, "to the nakedness of desire as the lawless law of the world."[49]

Despite the critical clichés that appear in Foucault's literary essays—the fashionable 1960s habit of describing books as being about books, of treating language as purely self-referential, of adopting the jargon of dadaism (Roussel's "ready-mades"), plus the romantic idealizing of the outcast-hero—and despite the purplish rhetoric of his style, there is much of interest in these literary antiportraits, these euologies of authors who lack or who eschew authorial identity. Unlike the subjects of Sainte-Beuve's or Arnold's portraits, Foucault's remnant seems miraculously detached from self and historical context alike. In the essay on Blanchot ("La Pensée du dehors," 1966) and the famous "What Is an Author?" (1969), Foucault carries the antiliterature tendencies of the Structuralists and the *Tel Quel* circle to such lengths that these pieces are perhaps best read as parodies or self-parodies. The subject of Blanchot's fictions is language escaping the "dynasty of representation," "language getting as far away from itself as possible," reaching out to an "outside" and becoming something "from which the subject is excluded." Thus, fiction enters into the "void"—"must" do so (Foucault is categorical about this)—articulating, in Blanchot's words, "the fullness of the void." Foucault's praise of the richness of emptiness in Blanchot reads like a parody of James's famous description of all the things Hawthorne found lacking in America, absences out of which James felt no literary substance could be made: "a discourse appearing with no conclusion and no image, with no truth and no theater, with no proof, no mask, no affirmation, free of any center, unfettered to any native soil"—with language thereby "addressing the very being of language," becoming "the outside of all language, speech about the invisible side of words," "a discourse on the non-discourse of all language; the fiction of the invisible space in which it appears."[50] After these lucubrations, "What Is an Author?" seems fairly straightforward in its attempt to deny the author-hero theory of Sainte-Beuve, Carlyle, or other benighted Victorians. Structuralist doctrines and modernist fictions such as Blanchot's having established the nonexistence of the subject, the only thing that remains is to examine "the empty space left by the author's disappearance." Foucault's customary erudition might well have left his audience (the essay was originally delivered at the Collège) wondering how one could speak with so much authority on the death of the author.[51]

The rhetorical coerciveness that accompanies Foucault's denials of authority in the essays—his reiterated stance, almost Arnoldian, that the modern *Zeitgeist* dictates that we "must " accept this point or other—is particularly noteworthy in his books of the 1960s and 1970s, works that purport to deal with no less than the history of madness, the genealogy of the human sciences, the archaeology of knowledge, the birth of the clinic and prison system, and the history of sexuality. But whereas Arnold applied the methods of literary criticism, as described in the *Essays in Criticism,* to the study of culture and religion, Foucault draws upon literature itself in the writing of his books. He has none of Arnold's or Sainte-Beuve's respect for the objective truth of his data.

Admitting that his scholarly studies were related to his own experience, that they constitute "fragments of autobiography," he also intimated that he never wrote "anything but fictions"—this said, perhaps, in response to the charge that some of the evidence he cites was fabricated. (The famous image of the ship of fools that opens *Madness and Civilization* corresponds, apparently, to no historical occurrence.)[52]

Looking at the most influential of these studies, *Madness and Civilization, The Order of Things* (1966), *Discipline and Punish* (1975), and the first volume of *The History of Sexuality (La Volonté de savoir,* 1976), one is struck not only by the extent to which Foucault draws upon literary texts, from Hölderlin to Lawrence, as *data,* but also by the degree to which these studies resemble Gothic novels in their form. Each of them deals with institutional and social forms of coercion and confinement, but Foucault exerts his own authorial coercion over his readers even as he protests the "carcereal network" that he sees everywhere in place. Critics of Foucault have been disturbed by both the "morbid glee" (in Megill's words) with which he presents these examples of ubiquitous victimization, and the fatalism that allows for no removal of the repressive structures. Refusing to be duped does not lead to change: "to imagine another system," he declared in 1971, "is to extend our participation in the present system." The effect of *Discipline and Punish* is to provide a disturbing *frisson* for the reader as Foucault relates the details of the public execution of Damiens, the author suggesting that such spectacles of power offer a "truth," the naked face of power in action, denied to the modern-day public. Terry Eagleton's discomfort at Foucault's "aesthetic gratification in the motions of power" is understandable.[53] Foucault assails the world as a theater of cruelty, while at the same time he eulogizes such aesthetes of cruelty as Sade or Artaud.

The romantic-aesthetic underpinning of Foucault's thinking is particularly evident in *Madness and Civilization,* where an elite of artists (including Bosch, Goya, van Gogh, Artaud) and artistic creations (the Shakespearean fool, Rameau's nephew) are cited as witnesses to the "truth" of madness, witnesses who arraign the "world" that has attempted to stifle them. Romantic writers from the past (Carlyle, Scott, Hugo, for example) have conflated literary characters with historical realities; but Foucault, for all his contempt for "history," might have blanched at the thought that he was rewriting *Les Misérables* for the modern *Zeitgeist.* There is something heroic in his effort to reestablish a "dialogue" with madness. (Derrida, not unreasonably, wondered from what metaphysical standpoint Foucault claimed to have discovered this lost language.) Recognition of his "romanticism," a characteristic noted by his friend Gilles Deleuze, may have helped push Foucault toward repudiation of the author-hero theory (T. S. Eliot, in a similar mood of self-censorship, argued that literature requires escape from the self) and his temporary turn to "positivism" in *The Birth of the Clinic* (1963). Still, the overheated style and the obsessional nature of his preferred themes (death, madness, sexuality) ensured that Foucault would never achieve an Arnoldian disinterestedness. (Neither, of course, did Arnold, who had begun his critical career with a repudiation of the subjective impulse in poetry.) Even in *The Order of Things*, among the most "structuralist" of his works, Foucault draws on literature (Cervantes, Mallarmé) to support his romantic thesis that with the triumph of the human sciences, the old activity of mind that consisted "in *drawing things together*" gave way to the practice of discriminations and disconnections, a position with which Wordsworth would have agreed.[54]

One measure of Foucault's literary prowess is his habit, akin to Arnold's, of coming up with quotable phrases and catchwords to publicize his ideas: "the great confinement," "the death of man" (*The Order of Things*), or the perceived thesis, by the popular media, of *La Volonté de savoir*: "*sexuality has not been repressed!*"[55] The effect of such phrases, of all the rhetorical devices employed by Foucault— unforgettable graphic details, the steady accumulation of carefully doctored evidence, the grammatical coerciveness of words like "must," "in fact," or "the real reason . . . no doubt"—is to force his reader into making the proper critical response. In this respect, Foucault is performing a critical mission in *Discipline and Punish* akin to Arnold's in "The Function of Criticism at the Present Time": to remind us of all the Wraggs, ourselves included, who are "in custody." But Foucault's critical effort, in his work up to the late '70s, ends (as Arnold might note, and *did* note apropos of Sainte-Beuve) with the presentation of materials that allows us to know, but not to do anything with our knowledge. Whereas the phrase "Wragg is in custody" serves to galvanize Arnold's readers out of their false sense of complacency with themselves and their world, serves as an invitation to transform the world and ourselves, Foucault's neo-Gothic description of the world as a prison leaves the reader paralyzed in the grip of the "universal" power structure and the author's rhetorical overkill:

> The judges of normality are present everywhere. We are in the society of the teacher-judge, the doctor-judge, the educator-judge, the "social worker"-judge; it is on them that the universal reign of the normative is based; and each individual, wherever he may find himself, subjects to it his body, his gestures, his behavior, his aptitudes, his achievements. The carcereal network, in its compact or disseminated forms, with its systems of insertion, distribution, surveillance, observation, has been the greatest support, in modern society, of the normalizing power.[56]

This is the rhetoric of Gothic fiction or the sensation novel, a world of inquisition courts and secret judges.

In this context, Foucault's famous description of Jeremy Bentham's Panopticon, in *Discipline and Punish*, works as an inspired (if paranoid) trope taken from Ann Radcliffe rather than a coherent reality. Bentham's conception of a model prison in which everything could be surveyed at all times is a fantasy (the idea was never carried into practice) that Foucault accepts as fact. And note the coercive rhetoric Foucault uses here: "the Panopticon must not be understood (ne doit pas être compris) as a dream building: it is the diagram of a mechanism of power reduced to its ideal form; its functioning, abstracted from any obstacle, resistance or friction, must be represented as a pure architectural and optical system: it is in fact a figure of political technology that may and must be detached from any specific use (c'est en fait une figure de technologie politique qu'on peut et qu'on doit détacher de tout usage spécifique)." Against this, one might cite Arnold's use of Bentham in the Preface to *Essays in Criticism*. Having been stung by the *Saturday Review*'s treatment of "The Function of Criticism" (Fitzjames Stephen's attack of his "French" style and his "transcendental" way of dealing with practical matters), Arnold looked at Stephen's model benefactor, Bentham, who had "persuaded the English nation that the greatest happiness of the greatest number was the true rule for legislation."[57]

Pretending, then, to be consoled by the *Saturday Review*'s discovery of Benthamism as the one philosophy needful, of Bentham as the perfect "anchorage for the spirit," Arnold muses, while riding on the English railway (site of a recent, much-publicized murder), on the fearful attitude of his fellow traveler. Armed by the *Review*'s wisdom, Arnold decides that what he has taken

> for the ignoble clinging to life of a comfortable worldling, was, perhaps, only the ardent longing of a faithful Benthamite, travers- ing an age still dimmed by the last mists of transcendentalism, to be spared long enough to see his religion in the full and final blaze of its triumph. This respectable man, whom I imagined to be going up to London to serve his shop, or to buy shares, or to attend an Exeter Hall [fundamentalist] meeting, or to assist at the delibera- tions of the Marylebone Vestry, was even, perhaps, in real truth, on a pious pilgrimage, to obtain from Mr. Bentham's executors a sacred bone of his great, dissected master. (*CPW,* 3:289)

Arnold uses irony to make his indictment of those who appeal to England's unparalleled comforts ("I ask you whether, the world over or in past history, there is anything like it?" [3:272]), forgetting the plight of Wragg and company. Arnold's "vivacity" and his humanism combine to make of Wragg a person in need, not an aesthetic trope. After the above-cited passage from the Preface comes the Renanian invocation to Oxford, "home of lost causes, and forsaken beliefs," the antithesis to Benthamism (290). "There is profit for the spirit in such contrasts as this," Arnold notes; "criticism serves the cause of perfec- tion by establishing them" (272, 274).

Among the figures in the *Essays in Criticism* there is one who slightly resembles Foucault, a philosopher-poet whom Mill had memo- rably contrasted to Bentham: Coleridge. Arnold (in "Joubert") de- scribes Coleridge as a truth-seeker with a hatred of liberal politics and with a knack of attracting and inspiring others, as "a stimulus to all minds capable of profiting from it" (*CPW,* 3:190). The nature of Cole- ridge's effort—"not a moral effort," Arnold adds, "for he had no mor- als" (one can imagine Arnold's reaction to descriptions of Foucault's California lifestyle)—was a "continual instinctive effort, crowned often with rich success, to get at and to lay bare the real truth of his matter at hand" (189). Coleridge, for all his personal flaws, was a practitioner of the critical enterprise, one whose work (like Joubert's) constitutes a "criticism of life" (209). Not the least of the similarities between Cole- ridge and Foucault was their readiness to announce publications that never materialized. But in Foucault's case, the critical enterprise was cut off just as it reached maturity, with Foucault having ended the first phase of his literary career—the writing of texts that indict the ubiquitous repressive structures—and having begun a new phase, one in which major Arnoldian concerns such as "criticism" and "transformation" were now major Foucauldian concerns.

With the first volume of *The History of Sexuality* published, Foucault suddenly changed direction. Having argued that the repressive forms of society are inscribed upon the language we use, the institutions we occupy, our very bodies, Foucault may have felt that he had come to a dead end. In 1978, with the lecture "Qu'est-ce que la critique?" Foucault suddenly turned to the concept of "critique" as articulated on Kant's great essay of 1784, "What is Enlightenment?" He draws in Kant's definition of Enlightenment (*Aufklärung*) as mankind's departure from his "self-caused immaturity" in order to argue that criticism itself—an attitude of mind, for Foucault, not a doctrine—is the "art of not being governed" ("l'art de ne pas être gouverné"), and that the individual who practices criticism is questioning the powers-that-be and thereby enacting "an art of voluntary insubordination, of thoughtful disobedience." (Foucault, interestingly, traces this critical habit of questioning authority back to the religious hermeneutics of the Renaissance, to the examination of Scriptural authority.) The individual, thus, has a responsibility to know the truth (Foucault cites the Kantian *"sapere aude"*) and he has the right to make his own history, as if one's life were not something preordained but something to be fashioned by oneself ("de se faire sa propre histoire, de fabriquer comme par fiction").[58]

Foucault elaborated on this theme in the text "What Is Enlightenment?" which he read at the University of California, Berkeley, in 1983. Here, he stresses the link between "critique" and "modernity," the Kantian injunction transformed into an attitude of "permanent critique of ourselves" and of "our historical era." Moreover, Foucault now declares, from out of this critical attitude comes the possibility, however limited and localized, of making changes in the self and in society. From Kant's faith in critical reason as the prerequisite for human maturity and freedom, Foucault turns to Baudelaire and the modern possibility of self-invention. (He insists, as before, that he has not become an advocate of "humanism," that term being so vague that it has served Christians and atheists, Marxists and Stalinists

alike. Unlike Habermas and Hans-Georg Gadamer, who see the Enlightenment and humanism as related, Foucault views the two "in a
state of tension rather than identity.") To two of his Berkeley hosts in
1983, Foucault stressed the aesthetic aspect of his new thinking:
"couldn't everyone's life become a work of art? Why should the lamp
or the house be an art object, but not our life?"[59]

In "What Is Enlightenment?" Foucault stressed the ascetic side of
his aestheticism. Baudelaire's dandy practiced a discipline upon himself, he says, just as the Greeks and Greco-Romans practiced the "arts
of existence." Foucault defines this phrase, in *The Use of Pleasure* (1984,
the second volume of his "History of Sexuality"), as "those intentional
and voluntary actions by which men not only set themselves rules of
conduct, but also seek to transform themselves, to change themselves
in their singular being, and to make their life into an *oeuvre* that carries
certain aesthetic values and meets certain stylistic criteria." Although
Foucault cautions, elsewhere, that one cannot return to the Greeks, as
Nietzsche once thought possible, he does suddenly draw on a
vocabulary—"transformation," "rules of conduct," "adult education,"
"cultivation of the self"—that is related to the German idea of *Bildung*,
a term crucial to thinkers from Goethe to Nietzsche to Gadamer, and to
Goethe's Victorian disciples, Arnold and Walter Pater. For Arnold, the
Hellenic experience, involving the will to know, necessitates the transformation of the self; and for Pater, the "Renaissance" is not so much a
historical period as a rebirth of the Greek idea. (The Greeks, Pater says,
"created themselves out of themselves.") The making of one's life a
work of art is a culminating Victorian idea that Foucault, ironically,
discovered late in his own life.[60] He doesn't use the word *Bildung* in
either *The Use of Pleasure* or its sequel, *The Care of the Self* (1984), but he
does draw upon the Socratic regard for the self, a knowledge of self that
is the necessary prerequisite for the transformation of self, and he
argues that this regimen of "training, an *askesis*," becomes important to
the Cynics, like Diogenes, whose very lifestyle combines transgression
with truth-seeking.[61]

For Foucault, there is much to be learned from these ancient truth-
seekers (the topic of his final lectures at the Collège), not least their
articulation of an ethics that combines self-mastery with freedom, and
that links care of the self with care for others. Learning of one's responsibilities to one's self, one discovers (Foucault affirms) that he has

"relationships" with and responsibilities toward others. The Foucault of the late 1970s and early 1980s was very much the advocate of human rights, whether that of Soviet dissidents or Vietnamese boat people. (The Foucault of the '60s, by contrast, was intoxicated by the romance of rebellion, however futile or misplaced.) "There exists," he declared in a 1981 manifesto, "an international citizenry that has its rights, that has its duties, and that is committed to rise up against every abuse of power, no matter who the author, no matter who the victims. After all, we are all ruled, and as such, we are in solidarity."[62] Foucault's arrival at such key Arnoldian concepts as "transformation" and "solidarity" proceeds from his discovery of the positive workings of "criticism." In this sense, he was making the transition from the idea of criticism-as-knowing to the idea of criticism-as-perfection, the move Arnold had found lacking in Sainte-Beuve.

In his last works, Foucault turned from Sade and Bataille to Arnold's Stoic mentors Marcus Aurelius and Epictetus, as well as to Seneca, as he evolved an ethics of self-transformation. At the same time, he expressed dissatisfaction at the decline of the "critical function." Like Arnold in "The Function of Criticism," he complained of a political-minded or "cliquish" mentality at work. But he also deplored the criticism that makes "judgment" rather than "curiosity" its aim. "I can't help but dream" he told a *Le Monde* interviewer in 1980, "about a kind of criticism that would not try to judge, but to bring an oeuvre, a book, a sentence, an idea to life. . . . I'd like a criticism of scintillating leaps of the imagination." Such a criticism, with "curiosity" as its motivation, had once been practiced by Arnold and James, Sainte-Beuve and Renan. In his memoirs, Renan defined the "essence of criticism" as the ability "to understand states very different from those in which we live."[63]

For Arnold, in "The Function of Criticism," it was from "flutterings of curiosity, in the foreign sense of the word, . . . that criticism must look to find its account"—curiosity being the instinct that prompts criticism "to try to know the best that is known and thought in the world, irrespectively of practice, politics, and everything of the kind" (*CPW*, 3:268–69). And thus, in the introduction to *The Use of Pleasure*, in a passage that Deleuze read at his funeral in 1984, Foucault tentatively joins hands with Arnold in speaking of the value of criticism at the present time:

As for what motivated me, it is quite simple. . . . It was curiosity—
the only kind of curiosity, in any case, that is worth acting upon
with a degree of obstinacy; not the curiosity that seeks to assimilate
what is proper for one to know, but that which enables one to get
free of oneself. After all, what would be the value of the passion for
knowledge if it resulted only in a certain amount of knowledgeable-
ness and not, in one way or another and to the extent possible, in
the knower's straying afield of himself? There are times in life
when the question of knowing if one can think differently than one
thinks, and perceive differently than one sees, is absolutely necessary if one is to go on looking and reflecting at all.[64]

But if Foucault, near the end of his life, approached the Arnold of
"The Function of Criticism," Arnold himself had gone on to replace
"criticism" (the exertion of curiosity) with "culture" (the application of
curiosity). In his intellectual development, Arnold resembles Foucault's mentor Nietzsche more than he resembles Foucault. But Arnold moved on from Nietzsche too.

Chapter Three

Arnold, Nietzsche, and the "Revaluation of Values"

What we want is a fuller harmonious development of our humanity, a free play of thought upon our routine notions, spontaneity of consciousness, sweetness and light; and these are just what culture generates and fosters.

Arnold, *Culture and Anarchy*

We negate and must negate because something in us wants to live and affirm—something that we perhaps do not know or see as yet.—This is said in favor of criticism.

Nietzsche, *The Gay Science*

In September 1865, Matthew Arnold, on an official inspection tour of the secondary schools and universities on the Continent, stopped at "the famous establishment of Schulpforta," Prussia's equivalent to Rugby. Alumni of the school, which specialized in Greek and Latin literature, in the German classics, and, to a lesser extent, in science and mathematics, included Klopstock, Fichte, Friedrich Schlegel, and Ranke. Just a year prior to Arnold's arrival its "best pupil,"[1] Friedrich Nietzsche, had graduated; and so a chance encounter between the two greatest exponents of culture in the late nineteenth century was avoided. While Arnold looked to France (as did Heine and Nietzsche) for examples of the best criticism, he looked to Germany for the "idea of culture, culture of the only true sort" (*CPW*, 4:288). In spite of a tendency in some quarters to see Arnold and Nietzsche as antithetical figures—with the latter being somehow more "contemporary," more agreeably "disturbing" (more Foucauldian) than the former—there are strong affinities between them. The subversive, Nietzschean side of Arnold is no less important than the humanistic, Arnoldian side of Nietzsche. Van Wyck Brooks, eighty years ago, recognized their kinship as exhilarating critics of society, bringing "not peace, but a sword"; and a chronicler of Nietzsche's early reputation has noted how readily the German philosopher entered a mainstream of English thought that extended from Byron to Meredith and Shaw by way of Ruskin and Arnold.[2] Like Heine, whom both admired, they are (in

Arnold's phrase) "dissolvents of the old European system of dominant ideas and facts" (3:109–10).

Arnold and Nietzsche aimed at common targets: the cultural Philistinism of England and Germany, the mind-numbing and life-denying
legacy of Puritanism and Lutheranism. Descendants of Protestant cler-
gymen, both were nevertheless committed to a revaluation of their
respective heritages. Arnold's sense that, in his time, "there is not a
creed which is not shaken, not an accredited dogma which is not
shown to be questionable, not a received tradition which does not
threaten to dissolve," anticipates Nietzsche's view that with the death
of God and the resultant rise of egoism, materialism, and the modern
state, mankind must embrace an "ecumenical" idea of true culture if it
is "not to destroy itself."[3] Sharing an alarm at the drift of modern
history, each trusted to culture and to their subjective abilities, and
found in man's creative potential something, in Arnold's phrase, we
"can rest upon" (*CPW*, 9:177). "Art raises its head where the religions
relax their hold," Nietzsche observes (*HH*, 81); and Arnold maintains,
"more and more mankind will discover that we have to turn to poetry
to interpret life for us, to console us, to sustain us" (*CPW*, 9:161).
Speaking of the inadequacy of most popular values, each addresses the
need to transmit and create genuine values. Despite Nietzsche's description of himself as "something decisive and doom-laden standing
between two millennia" and Arnold's of "wandering between two
worlds, one dead / The other powerless to be born," both can be seen
as continuators of one tradition and fabricators of another, as heirs to
German views of culture, on the one hand, while on the other as the
prophets and (in Henry James's phrase for Arnold) the "poet[s] of . . .
our 'modernity.' "[4]

The two are alike in their breadth and openness of mind. "I hate
all over-preponderance of single elements," Arnold wrote his mother,
explaining the comparativist rationale behind the *Essays in Criticism*
(1865), "and all my efforts are directed to enlarge and complete us by
bringing in as much as possible of Greek, Latin, and Celtic [not to
mention French and German] authors." Each underwent a strenuous
apprenticeship in the German tradition of self-cultivation (*Bildung*),
seeking more than Rugby or Schulpforta, Oxford or Bonn and Leipzig
Universities could offer. Each aimed at becoming "a cultured being,"
at home in ancient Greece ("the only place in which one would want
to be at home," Nietzsche says) while also familiar with the latest

scientific discoveries.⁵ They shared several mentors from the past: among them, Socrates for his questioning spirit and dialectic method, Thucydides for his *"courage in the face of reality,"* Spinoza for his rigorous and calming intellect (what Goethe celebrated as Spinoza's "utter disinterestedness," his view that virtue is its own reward), Wilhelm von Humboldt for his advocacy of self-perfection, Goethe for his Olympian and manifold nature, Byron for his rebelliousness, the Stoics for their self-discipline, Heine for his liberating sarcasm, Emerson for his assault on shibboleth and for his life-affirming attitude. Arnold was not impressed by two of Nietzsche's youthful heroes: he found unsatisfying Schopenhauer's view that life is no blessing (Nietzsche would subsequently agree), and he preferred his own version of the Tristan story ("Tristram and Iseult") to Wagner's. Culture, for them both, was an ongoing process of accumulating and discarding, questioning and self-questioning. Every man carries, or should carry, in his own breast, Arnold declares in *Culture and Anarchy* (1869), "a possible Socrates, in that power of a disinterested play of consciousness upon his stock notions and habits" (*CPW*, 5:228). Arnold defines the aim of culture as "not a having and a resting, but a growing and a becoming" (94); and Nietzsche, in the first of his *Untimely Meditations* (1873), assaults the Philistines for believing that "all seeking is at an end."⁶

Another point of similarity is their Socratic impudence in tone and manner. One might cite Nietzsche's description of Socrates' ability "to be serious cheerfully" and his *"wisdom full of roguishness* that constitutes the finest state of the human mind" to account for the presence of "Merry Matt" in some of Arnold's most serious work. Both offended their contemporary readers, and consciously sought to offend. They needed (as Sidney Coulling says of Arnold) an opposition to respond to. Of his first major work, *The Birth of Tragedy* (1872), Nietzsche gleefully confided, "Oh! It is naughty and offensive."⁷ His devastating attack on David Strauss in his second book reveals an Arnoldian impatience with complacency, but also an Arnoldian pleasure in finding a prime target. Poor Strauss reveals his cultural limitations when he speaks of Beethoven as "confectionary" or Haydn as "honest soup," and in his misreading of Darwin's troubling implications he offers a "universal soothing oil" to his Philistine readers (*UM*, 22, 32). For his part, Arnold's assault on Francis Newman's grotesque translation of Homer or on Bishop Colenso's heavy-handed treatment of the Bible brings out a Nietzschean delight in demolition. What Nietzsche calls Heine's "divine" sarcasm surfaces in Arnold's characterization of the Trinity, in *Literature and Dogma* (1873), as being the equivalent of three Lord Shaftesburys—a notion that provoked a furor among readers. Fitzjames Stephen deplored the "outrageous self-conceit" of the lectures on Homer; but Arnold enjoyed poking fun not only at others but at his own image. When his sister Jane complained that he "was becoming as dogmatic as Ruskin," he replied, "I told her the difference was that Ruskin was 'dogmatic and *wrong*.' "[8] One might be put off by Arnold's and Nietzsche's egotism—the latter's belief, "Why I am a Destiny," in *Ecce Homo* (1888), for example—if one missed the irony directed against themselves. (The use of irony did not preclude their thinking very highly of their roles as reformers.) Whether pontificating that Puritanism has no "reason for existing," or that criticism denies to Colenso's book "the right of existing," or that the imagination bids the modern-day aristocrat "to take himself out of the way, and to leave us to the Norfolks and Warwicks of history,"[9] Arnold demonstrates a pride and cheekiness worthy of Zarathustra's creator.

Both are Romanticists scorning Romanticism and both are religious poets of the death of God. Admirers of the Greek world, critics of their own, and champions of a time when one's "best self" will triumph, Arnold and Nietzsche are as "elusive" as they are seemingly all-inclusive.[10] Yet while each considers Goethe to be the greatest of moderns for his comprehensiveness ("Existing blithely amid antitheses," in Nietzsche's phrase [*WP*, 471]), each also follows Goethe in seeking principles of authority, coherence, wholeness. They celebrate the "unity" existing in genuine culture and accordingly look to the Hellenic example wherein "chaos" (in Nietzsche's term), or "anarchy" (in Arnold's), is overcome. Nietzsche's desire for "some counterweight to my changeable and restless inclinations" also leads him toward science. He insists that his belief in the "eternal return" is scientifically grounded, just as Arnold, in his religious writing, maintains that true Christianity is validated by scientific "experience." Arnold's declaration to Clough, that poets "must begin with an Idea of the world in order not to be prevailed over by the world's multitudinousness," is as much an expression of his desire for a unifying principle as the afterthought is a reminder of his pluralism: "or if they cannot get that, at least with isolated ideas."[11]

Arnold aptly describes himself as "facing in every direction,"[12] and this corresponds to Nietzsche's mention of "a tremendous multiplicity [in himself] which is nonetheless the opposite of chaos" (*EH*, 65). For each, the individual is a cultural microcosm, capable of maintaining unity and diversity. "It is my sagacity," Nietzsche boasts, "to have been many things and in many places so as to be able to become *one person*" (*EH*, 88). "The finest discoveries concerning culture," he proclaims, "are made by the individual man within himself when he finds two heterogeneous powers ruling there." Culture itself consists of the "harmony" achieved through the interaction (not reconciliation) of "contending powers" (*HH*, 130). For the grand "task ," which was to be Arnold's and Nietzsche's lifelong work, for the "*revaluation of values* more capacities perhaps were required than have dwelt together in one individual, above all antithetical capacities which however are not allowed to disturb or destroy one another" (*EH*, 65). One could dwell on many of Arnold's and Nietzsche's comparable capacities as definers and revaluators of culture, but I will limit myself here to four of particular significance: their roles as educators, as students of Greek culture, as commentators on religion, and, finally, as subscribers to the Goethean ideal of creative individualism.

Taking up his duties as professor of philology at the University of Basel, Nietzsche in 1869 contemplated the new limits to his ambitious program of self-cultivation: "now I must be a philistine too." In this he resembles the burdened inspector of schools, Arnold, complaining how absurd it is "that all the best of my days should be taken up with matters which thousands of other people could do just as well as I, and that what I have a special turn for doing I should have no time for."[13] Yet each, without losing his particular sense of his own mission, made use of a career in education to define education's role in the creation of culture on a large scale. Arnold praised Humboldt's view that one should first "perfect one's self by all the means in one's power," preparatory to helping "create in the world around one an aristocracy, the most numerous that one possibly could, of talents and characters" (*CPW*, 5:161). However, Arnold diverged from the Prussian minister of education in his developing belief that culture and education belong to the masses as well as to an elite. To Clough, the young Arnold acknowledged that as "the world tends to become more comfortable for the mass," it becomes "more uncomfortable for those of any natural gift or distinction—and it is as well perhaps that it should be so."[14] His definition of culture has an egalitarian thrust to it: "so all our fellow-men, in the East of London and elsewhere, we must take along with us in the progress towards perfection" (216). But if Nietzsche and Arnold diverge in their opinions of who should receive an education, they come together on the subject of what education should focus on.

In his 1886 address at the University of Pennsylvania, Arnold does approach Nietzsche's view of education as something "higher" than the masses are capable of attaining. He cites one of his favorite quotations—"that in our education and culture it is precisely the slough of 'the common and average and inferior thing,' *das Gemeine,* as Goethe calls it, which we have to cast off and rise out from." Instead of being impressed by the large number of popular educational establishments in America, he is critical of the scarcity of quality institutions of higher learning and of the lack of "connexion" between Harvard and the public schools. Where Nietzsche sees education as necessarily elitist, reenforcing the "sacred hierarchy of nature," Arnold anticipates the time when the masses will come to power, and worries lest popular instruction not "impart . . . contempt for charlatanism and vulgarity."[15] Twenty-six years earlier, in *The Popular Education of France* (with his great essay "Democracy"), Arnold affirmed the right of English populace *"to affirm its own essence;* to live, to enjoy, to possess the world." But he feared the bad example set by America: "the difficulty for democracy is, how to find and keep high ideals." The upper classes were incapable of providing intellectual guidance, while the middle classes, currently in power, offered only a "narrow, harsh, unintelligent spirit and culture" (*CPW,* 2:7, 17, 26). In "A French Eton" (1863), Arnold addressed the middle classes directly, urging an end to their "clap trap" about "self-reliance" and advocating a system of state-administered schools aimed at the genuine "perfecting of the individual. . . . But that the individual may be perfected, that his activity may be worthy, he must often learn to quit old habits, to adopt new, to go out for himself, to transform himself" (*CPW,* 2:312).[16]

The theme of self-transformation, which derives from such German authorities as Humboldt and Goethe, is crucial to Nietzsche as well as Arnold. But where Arnold, inspecting the inadequate schooling provided in Victorian England, came to advocate the transforma-

tion of his entire country, Nietzsche viewed education as the preroga-
tive of the gifted few. Addressing the "children of the future," Arnold
looked to the day when they, possessing "neither the aridity of aristoc-
racies, nor the narrow-mindedness of middle classes," would mount
"the arduous ladder whereby man climbs towards his perfection"
(*CPW*, 2:324–25). Nietzsche also used the metaphor of education as
ladder in his Basel lectures, *The Future of Our Educational Institutions*,
but this is a ladder only the few will ever be capable of mounting. In
the 1882 address delivered at the opening session of Liverpool University, Arnold, after deploring the low present-day "standard of life,"
observed that "in establishing this College you are on the way to raise
it higher" (10:83–84)—and that the higher cultural standards will find
reflection not only in increased knowledge but in more pleasurable
social activities and in a more beautiful environment. By contrast,
Nietzsche, in *Twilight of the Idols*, sees " 'higher education' and huge
numbers" as a "contradiction. . . . All higher education belongs only
to the exception: one must be privileged to have a right to so high a
privilege. All great, all beautiful things can never be common property." Nietzsche attacks both the idea of extending education to the
masses and the right of the state to interfere in education. (His target,
one should note, is the Prussian state. For Arnold, the state is an ideal
entity, made up of all its citizens' "best selves" and accordingly bound
to take charge of the educational system.) Posterity, the romantically
attuned young professor avows, cares only for the handful of ge-
niuses from any given period who are capable of the rigors of self-
transformation. The curriculum for this elite should center on Greek
civilization. Once students have been exposed to the ancients, Nietzsche maintains (as Arnold's father similarly thought) they will necessarily reject the "so-called culture of the present."[17]

In "Schopenhauer as Educator" (1874)—which he later admitted
should have been entitled "Nietzsche as Educator" (*EH*, 88)—
Nietzsche describes teachers as "liberators" who encourage their students to achieve culture. For the young Nietzsche, being *"consecrated
to culture"* means both to be faithful to "the fundamental law of your
own true self," which you acquire by having "revered objects" to
look up to, and to be attached "to some great man" (*UM*, 129–30,
163)—to someone like Wagner, in his case. Arnold's respect for his
father's teaching was never so slavish as Nietzsche's youthful devotion to Schopenhauer and Wagner, nor was his reaction against

Thomas Arnold's views as extreme as Nietzsche's against his former mentors. Yet for both, education is seen as a process that entails discipline as well as liberation if one is to become what one is.

"Become the being you are": Nietzsche made this idea of Pindar the center of his educational theory. The phrase itself turns up often in his books and letters, and it serves as subtitle to the autobiographical *Ecce Homo*. But arriving at one's authentic self requires continual study and self-sacrifice: one allows for all the antithetical components of his being to flourish, while, at the same time, one must "overcome oneself," "must organize the chaos within him by thinking back to his real needs" (*UM*, 119, 123). Our fittest educators are those who point back to the ancients—Schopenhauer, Wagner, Burckhardt, Thomas Arnold—and, best of all, the Greeks themselves. "Take away the Greeks," Nietzsche asks, "together with philosophy and art, and what ladder have you still remaining by which to ascend to culture?"[18] The Greek experience, for Nietzsche and Arnold, involves the achieving of integration, "wholeness." Arnold's sense of himself existing in "fragments," as living an inauthentic and "buried life," finds poignant expression in his poetry:

> O life unlike to ours!
> Who fluctuate idly without term or scope,
>   Of whom each strive, nor knows for what he strives,
>   And each half-lives a hundred different lives;
>   ("The Scholar-Gipsy," ll. 166–69)

> And we have been on many thousand lines,
> And we have shown, on each, spirit and power;
> But hardly have we, for one little hour,
> Been on our own line, have we been ourselves—
>   ("The Buried Life," ll. 57–60)

Nietzsche too speaks of being "fragmented and in pieces" (*UM*, 119) and of "living a completely hidden life,"[19] and, in the "Untimely Meditation" devoted to Wagner, he writes of the artist falling "prey to the feeble manysidedness of modern life" (201). For Arnold, as for Nietzsche, salvation lies in a phrase that has the authority of the ancients behind it: "Resolve to be thyself; and know that he, / Who finds himself, loses his misery!" ("Self-Dependence," ll. 31–32). In

Schools and Universities on the Continent, Arnold defines the "prime direct aim" of instruction as enabling "a man *to know himself and the world.*" And, for both writers, to know "the capabilities and performances of the human spirit" there is no "more fruitful object of study than . . . the achievements of Greece in literature and the arts during the two centuries from the birth of Simonides to the death of Plato" (*CPW,* 4:290).

In a letter to his mother, Arnold refers to the "daemonic," acknowledging what Nietzsche calls the "Dionysian" impulse:

> No one has a stronger and more abiding sense than I have of the "daemonic" element—as Goethe called it—which underlies and encompasses our life; but I think, as Goethe thought, that the right thing is, while conscious of this element, and of all that there is inexplicable round one, to keep pushing on one's posts into the darkness, and to establish no post that is not perfectly in light and firm.

The Dionysian impulse is the dark, irrational, and ultimately life-threatening force that (in early Nietzsche) must join forces with its opposite, the Apollonian, to form tragic art. The Apollonian impulse, for Arnold, "belongs . . . to every prophecy resulting from a state of illumination and elevation of the human soul, and Apollo is thus the great awakener and sustainer of genius and intellect." Arnold and Nietzsche were steeped in the *idea* of Greek culture as conceived ("misconceived," some would say) by such German sages and poets as Winckelmann and Herder, Goethe and Heine. Greek literature, Arnold declares in "On the Modern Element in Literature" (1857), is "a mighty agent of intellectual deliverance" (*CPW,* 1:20). The Greeks are "our luminous guides," Nietzsche proclaims in *The Birth of Tragedy;*[20] and in a *Nachlass* entry for 1885 he avows, "we [German philosophers] are growing more Greek by the day" (*WP,* 226). Arnold in 1864 no less confidently believed that "we [English], more than any modern people, have the power of renewing, in our national life, the example of Greece" (*CPW,* 2:314). The modern turn to Greece began with Winckelmann's admiration for the *"noble simplicity and serene greatness"* of Greek art, a calm that expresses the victory of reason over the demonic passions. Gradually, Winckelmann's view gave way to

Nietzsche's countermyth of Greek art as an uneasy balance between rival gods—the illusion-bearing calm of Apollo on one side, the tragic and frenzied anguish of Dionysus on the other. Yet whether one prizes Apollo over Dionysus, as Arnold does, or Dionysus over Apollo, in Nietzsche's case, the value of Greek culture resides for both in the achievement of equilibrium. Ancient Greece was a necessary myth for Arnold and Nietzsche, both of whom required a world of order, beauty, idealism, and truth to oppose to the anarchy, vulgarity, materialism, and nihilism of their societies. Nietzsche's dictum holds true for his English counterpart: "only a horizon defined by myths completes and unifies a whole cultural movement" (*BT*, 135).[21]

Arnold's and Nietzsche's first prose publications focus on the need for a rebirth of Greek culture. In the 1853 Preface to *Poems* and in his inaugural lecture as Professor of Poetry at Oxford, Arnold contrasts the coherence, "intense significance," "noble simplicity," and "calm pathos" found in Greek literature with the lack of values and "moral grandeur" in the present (*CPW*, 1:12,14). Periclean Athens enjoyed a serenity, confidence, and freedom of activity and of intellectual pursuit (what Arnold later calls "the free play of the mind") that are sorely missed. While the Greek tragic sense of life's harshness and brevity reveals a sobering truth, the mastery of this knowledge is necessary preparation for self-mastery. In Greek tragedy, Arnold contends (echoing Winckelmann and Goethe), the "human spirit" conquers "its own stormiest agitations," and the result is "*a sentiment of sublime acquiescence in the course of fate, and in the dispensations of human life*" (1:59). Whether in his early Schopenhauerian phase or in his Zarathustran mood with its "*amor fati*," Nietzsche takes his cue for passion, or the denial of passion, from Greek sources. There is a desperate yearning in the young Nietzsche's belief that Wagner's operas mark the rebirth of Aeschylean tragedy, or that Schopenhauer's philosophy is a revival of Empedocles' heroic Stoicism; but Arnold's attempt, in *Merope* (1857), to resurrect "a specimen of the world created by the Greek imagination" is no less zealous. Both men's view of Greece deepened as they grew older. In time they turned the critical spirit they had gained from their classical training upon their former beliefs and aspirations and upon Greece itself. "Alas, my friends," Nietzsche says in *The Gay Science* (1882), "we must overcome even the Greeks" if we are to learn to accept life as something other than a "disease."[22] And Arnold, while praising the flexibility of Periclean culture in "A Speech at Eton" (1879), suggests that Athens declined because it was "really not flexible enough" (9:34). Greece was torn between serious and frivolous impulses, and the latter prevailed. Moreover, for Arnold, the Hebraic legacy must be taken into account as a counterweight to Hellenism. Even so, the study of Greece remains, for both authors, the most useful portion of an education. "A genuine humanism," Arnold asserts in "Literature and Science" (1882), "is scientific" (10:57); and a classical education, far from being opposed to a scientific training, includes immersion in letters *and* science.

The Greeks, after all, pioneered the study of science, in the broad and technical senses of the word. If Nietzsche, in *The Birth of Tragedy,* railed against the scientific spirit as a "sublime metaphysical illusion," he soon after turned to science as an antidote to Wagnerian pretensions. One legacy of Greek philosophy is dialectic, a method of inquiry that the young Nietzsche contends was used by the plebeian "mystagogue of science" Socrates as a negative instrument to undermine "a *noble* taste" (*BT,* 95–96).[23] Dialectical thinking inevitably leads, Nietzsche realizes (like Bakhtin after him), to the unraveling of myths. Arnold, who shares Nietzsche's mistrust of systematizers, approvingly quotes Heine's hit at Hegel: "How easily one can cheat oneself into thinking that one understands everything, when one has learnt only how to construct dialectical formulas!" (*CPW,* 3:182). Yet Nietzsche and Arnold are dialectical thinkers: the development of culture depends, they perceive, upon the flourishing of antithetical positions. Thus Nietzsche sees Greek tragedy as the balancing of Apollonian and Dionysian impulses, while Arnold, in the talk at Eton, sees Greek culture at its height as a balance between Dorian seriousness and Ionian free-spiritedness. And, following Heine, each balances Hellenism against Hebraism. In his description of these polarities in *Culture and Anarchy,* Arnold felt that he had made a "distinction on which more and more will turn, and on dealing wisely with it everything depends."[24]

Arnold's championing of Hellenism—of the ability to "see things as they really are"—is a plea that England may continue to develop and not be sidetracked by the Dissenting middle-class refusal to allow for enlightenment and advancement. After *Culture and Anarchy,* it is true, Arnold increases the value of the Hebraic component of culture; but for the moment he blames Puritanism for having thwarted the aim of the Renaissance: rebirth of the Greek spirit (*CPW*, 5:165, 175). Nietzsche, on his part, blames the German Reformation for having stifled the legacy of the Renaissance, with its restoration of such classical ideals as

> liberation of thought, disrespect for authorities, victory of education over the arrogance of ancestry, enthusiasm for science and the scientific past of mankind, unfettering of the individual, a passion for truthfulness and an adversion to appearance and mere effect (which passion blazed forth in a whole host of artistic characters who, in an access of moral rectitude, demanded of themselves perfection in their work and nothing but perfection). (*HH*, 113)

Arnold's motto for *Culture and Anarchy* could scarcely be more Hellenic, despite its source in Matt. 5:48: "Be ye therefore perfect."

A paradox of the Greek legacy is that out of tragic recognition comes joy. Nietzsche's Schopenhauerian position in *The Birth of Tragedy*, that only as art is life justified, resembles the stance that Arnold ascribes to Goethe in "Memorial Verses": "*Art still has truth, take refuge there!*" (l. 28). The truth for Dionysian man, Nietzsche says, is "the horror or absurdity of existence"; while Arnold, again citing Goethe, defers to Homer's position "that in our life here above ground we have, properly speaking, to enact Hell." Yet such a realization can be "tonic and fortifying," a source of pleasure when expressed in the "grand style," just as the Sophoclean awareness of "the turbid ebb and flow / Of human misery" inspires one with its steadiness and wholeness. "There is shed over this poetry," Arnold says of Sophocles, "the charm of that noble serenity which always accompanies true insight."[25] Grim though the subject of Greek tragedy may be, there is something ennobling about its depiction of man's struggle against his fate. "The individual must be consecrated to something higher than himself," Nietzsche declares, "—that is the meaning of tragedy"; and thus when a "*sense for the tragic*" is heard again (for example, in Wagner), there is "no more rapturous joy" to be found, for it implies mankind's "rejoicing . . . at the guarantee of the unity and continuance of the human as such" (*UM*, 213). "Tragedy breasts the pressure of life," Arnold maintains. "Comedy eludes it, half liberates itself from it by irony. But the tragedian, if he has the sterner labour, has also the higher prize. Shakspeare

[sic] has more joy than Molière, more assurance and peace" (*CPW*, 9:72). Arnold and Nietzsche are poets, hence, of the "eternal return"—of what in "Dover Beach" is called "the eternal note of sadness"; yet in accepting tragic recurrence, they also assent, courageously and cheerfully, to the one world we have. Their ultimate message is therefore a "saying Yes" (in Nietzsche's words) to one's right "to be *oneself* the eternal joy of becoming."[26]

There are many other areas in which Arnold's and Nietzsche's attitudes to Greece converge, but one of particular note is their common interest in the philosopher, poet, and scientist, Empedocles. In his desire to renew "the bond with the Greeks, the hitherto highest type of man" (*WP*, 225), Nietzsche frequently turns to Empedocles, one of the "royal and magnificent hermits of the spirit." In his teens, Nietzsche was attracted to Hölderlin's unfinished *Empedocles* for its "melancholy tones" and pure "Sophoclean language";[27] and although the ancient seer was, unlike Nietzsche, a democrat in his sympathies, his rejection of his age struck a responsive chord. Like Schopenhauer, Empedocles gave a negative "verdict . . . on the value of existence"; and he did so despite living "in the midst of the most vigorous and exuberant vitality of Greek culture" (*UM*, 145). What has been said of the protagonist of Arnold's *Empedocles on Etna* (1852)—that "essentially Arnold borrowed nothing but a name and a collection of miscellaneous biographical details"[28]—applies to Nietzsche's Empedocles. But where Nietzsche stresses Empedocles' (and hence his own) defiance, his *active* rejection of his time, Arnold creates a more passive figure, a version of Hamlet (and, in part, of Arnold himself), paralyzed by doubt and engaged in a "dialogue of the mind with itself" (*CPW*, 1:1). Arnold's philosopher resembles Nietzsche's "Dionysian man," whom Nietzsche also compares to Hamlet. Such figures, Nietzsche says, "have once looked truly into the essence of things, they have *gained knowledge*, and nausea inhibits action" (*BT*, 60).

Empedocles, for Nietzsche and Arnold, is seen as a Romantic figure, a projection of their own situation. Admirers of Byron, both writers draw upon the rebellious figure of Manfred. Arnold's sage owes something to Byron's Alpine wanderer, as does Nietzsche's Zarathustra; but neither author is willing to make self-negation, or any form of stasis, the goal of life.[29] Their subsequent careers, following their most important literary tributes to Greece (*The Birth of Tragedy, Empedocles on Etna*), may be seen as a turn against the negative side of their Romanticism. In suppressing *Empedocles*, Arnold avowed that poetry should "inspirit and rejoice the reader," that it should partake of the joy Schiller requires of art (*CPW*, 1:2). It is pointless to complain (as do those following T. S. Eliot's lead) that in abandoning the writing of melancholy poetry, Arnold rejected his true calling. One might just as well demand of Nietzsche that he stop with *The Birth of Tragedy*. This overlooks the counterimpulse in both writers that demands joy, the impulse that finds eloquent expression in Arnold's praise of Emerson over Carlyle (who denies man's right to happiness): "the desire for happiness is the root and ground of man's being" (10:183). Having outgrown their apprenticeship in the Romantic agony, Arnold and Nietzsche proceed to draw joy from man's creative abilities, whether expressed in one's interpretation of the Bible or in the wish to become the poet of one's own life. The death-seeking Empedocles gives way to the life-affirming Zarathustra.

With regard to religion, one might expect Arnold and Nietzsche to be completely at odds. Nietzsche's complaint against English agnostics such as George Eliot would seem to apply to Arnold, who, despite his loss of belief in a personal God, wrote several books on religion: "they are rid of the Christian God and now believe all the more firmly that they must cling to Christian morality." And yet, on the subject of religion—and of the need to forge new values now that the old creeds are shaken—Arnold and Nietzsche have an enormous amount in common. Both are children of the *Zeitgeist*, which has ruled against the old beliefs. In an unusually candid letter written in 1881, Arnold acknowledged to a French acquaintance that religion is not one of the forces "shaping the future":

> man feels himself to be a more various and richly-endowed animal than the old religious theory of human life allowed, and he is endeavouring to give satisfaction to the long suppressed and still imperfectly-understood instincts of this varied nature. I think this revolution is happening everywhere; it is certainly happening in England, where the sombreness and narrowness of the religious world, and the rigid hold it long had upon us, have done so much to provoke it. I think it is, like all inevitable revolutions, a salutary one, but it greatly requires watching and guiding.

Arnold is encouraged by the "awakening demand for beauty" on the part of the populace, a sign of the advance of Hellenism. His admission of the public right to happiness accompanies the Arnoldian belief in equality that sets him apart from Nietzsche. Many of Arnold's most radical ideas are to be found in his religious writings: his sense, for example, that "there is certainly communism in the Bible."[30] Still, Arnold's comment about the need for "watching and guiding," in the passage quoted above, suggests that he is not a passive adherent of the *Zeitgeist*. Values are needed to keep the progress of democracy from turning into an anarchic rout. In a similar spirit, Nietzsche's second book consists of "Untimely" Meditations that reflect the need to turn to culture, to art, to myth, as a way of resisting, or redirecting the flow of history.

Coming from strict Protestant backgrounds, both men, early in their lives, lost their ancestral beliefs. Nietzsche, at twenty, wrote his sister of the need to choose between the "peace of mind and happiness" that comes with "faith" and the questioning spirit that drives the "disciples of truth." He himself preferred the difficult new path: "struggling against habituation, uncertain of one's independent course, amid frequent vacillations of the heart, and even of the conscience, often comfortless, but always pursuing the eternal goal of the true, the beautiful, the good."[31] Arnold's description of his deconversion is well known:

> For rigorous teachers seized my youth,
> And purged its faith, and trimmed its fire,
> Showed me the high, white star of Truth,
> There bade me gaze, and there aspire.
> ("Stanzas from the Grande Chartreuse," ll. 67–70)

For both, Christian dogma is no longer tenable. Yet whereas Nietzsche caustically wonders "what thinker still has need of the hypothesis of a God?" (*HH*, 27), Arnold prefers to retain "God" in the form of a literary metaphor that stands for some extrasubjective sanction for righteous conduct. Both are willing to accept fictions that admit to being fictions; and it is for this reason that Hans Vaihinger contends that Nietzsche, in time, would have recognized "religious concepts" as being "useful and even . . . necessary fictions." However, while for Nietzsche art is "true" because it "treats *illusion as illusion*," religion is seen as a deception that poses as truth. Nietzsche's gibes against Christianity are familiar: the expression of the resentful "herd" instinct as codified by St. Paul, Christianity is opposed to whatever is "natural"; it denies all reality for the sake of a spurious future life. Christianity, in sum, is the triumph of "nihilism," of the worship of "nothingness." But Nietzsche admits that while he will "have nothing to do with" a religion that purports to tell true things, he adds, "but if it means simply the need for redemption, then I can value it highly."[32] On this ground, Arnold and Nietzsche meet, for Nietzsche's term "redemption," like Arnold's "transformation," is the prerequisite for culture.

Each attacks the Philistinism of his time, middle-class Protestantism (in Arnold's words), "drugged with business," with "its sense blunted for any stimulus besides, except religion; . . . a religion [that is] narrow, unintelligent, repulsive" (*CPW*, 5:19). Such people, narrow-minded and unwilling to change, are the enemies of enlightenment—are what Nietzsche calls "*cultural philistines*" (*UM*, 7)—and against these the proponents of genuine culture must address themselves. This is the thrust of *Culture and Anarchy*, Arnold's conviction that "our Puritans . . . have developed one side of their humanity at the expense of all others, and have become incomplete and mutilated men in consequence" (*CPW*, 5:235). "Interest in education," Nietzsche declares, "will become genuinely intense only from the moment when belief in a God and his loving care is abandoned" (*HH*, 115). Arnold describes his "true business at present," following publication of *Culture and Anarchy*, as sapping the authority of Protestant Dissent. In his essay on Heine (Arnold's and Nietzsche's predecessor in the war against Philistinism), he laments the fact that the English people, despite having known Shakespeare, nevertheless "entered the prison of Puritanism, and had the key turned on its spirit there for two hundred years" (*CPW*, 3:121). Nietzsche too, having blamed Christianity for having "cheated us out of the harvest of ancient culture,"[33] charges the German Reformation with having "reversed the direction in which men were going" and thus sabotaging the "great task of the Renaissance" (*HH*, 114).

In *St. Paul and Protestantism* (1870), Arnold confidently says, "the Protestantism which has so used and abused St. Paul is coming to an end"; "the progressive thought of humanity" has no room for fundamentalist distortions (*CPW*, 6:5). But as Arnold proceeds to examine the Bible, determined to place Christianity on firmer ground, he throws out the idea of a living God and all the dogmas and miraculous props holding up Christian belief. How then, the *Westminster Review* wondered, can he dispose of "supernaturalism, yet [cling] to the Bible, of which supernaturalism is the key-note"? And Christians such as F. H. Bradley scorned Arnold's attempt to make "morality" and a few vague phrases serve in place of the older faith. Yet Arnold's religious position, as Ruth apRoberts notes, is conspicuously modern in its rejection of dogma and it acceptance of the Bible as literature. ("To say that a thing is 'poetry,' " Basil Willey remarks of Arnold's Biblical criticism, "is not to diminish its importance.")[34] In treating the Bible metaphorically and seeing Jesus (as had Renan) as a symbolic figure, Arnold anticipates Nietzsche's position. To read the New Testament carefully, Arnold contends, is to be aware of how Jesus was "misunderstood." "The history of Christianity . . . ," declares Nietzsche, "is the history of the misunderstanding, growing cruder with every step, of an *original* symbolism." Nietzsche calls Jesus a "great symbolist," who accepted "only *inner* realities as realities"; Arnold similarly stresses Jesus' method as a turn "inward." "The very word 'Christianity' is a misunderstanding," according to Nietzsche: "in truth, there was only *one* Christian, and he died on the cross." Arnold's Jesus reminds us not only of the poet's misunderstood Empedocles, to whom his followers looked for miracles, but also of Nietzsche's Zarathustra. For both authors, the "kingdom of God" exists not in heaven but within the individual, and within the society that the self-transformed individual helps to transform.[35] As Arnold maintains in *Culture and Anarchy,* "Religion says: *The kingdom of God is within you;* and culture, in like manner, places human perfection in an *internal* condition, in the growth and predominance of our humanity proper" (*CPW,* 5:94).

The Bible will survive, Arnold affirms (despite the *Westminster Review*), because humanity craves "happiness." To attend to "conduct," to act righteously, as the Bible commands, is to provide oneself with joy. And despite his scorn for the New Testament, Nietzsche, who, like Arnold is imbued with the Schilleresque faith in joy, must invent a life-affirming figure who sometimes curiously resembles the misunderstood symbolist. "Again and again in *The Antichrist,*" Thomas J. J. Altizer remarks, "Nietzsche portrays Jesus as a kind of innocent forerunner of Zarathustra; he is incapable of *ressentiment,* is free of history, and is himself exactly opposed to Christianity." "This 'bringer of glad tidings,' " Nietzsche proclaims, "died . . . *not* to 'redeem men' but to show how one must live." By stressing Jesus' inward message, Nietzsche follows Arnold in making of Jesus an apostle of culture; and by allowing his Zarathustra to proclaim the gospel of the eternal return, he similarly emphasizes the need to seek for joy here on earth. "We have no wish whatever to enter into the kingdom of heaven," says Zarathustra: "we have become men—*so we want the* earth." (" 'Hath man no second life?' " Arnold asks in "The Better Part," " 'Pitch this one *high!*' ")[36] Both writers reject the postulate of a creator, and both reject the Darwinian position that man is a passive creation of natural evolution. Martin Heidegger accuses Nietzsche of repudiating the metaphysics of Being and replacing it with the "modern metaphysics" of "subjectness"; and the charge applies to Arnold too. For their position is essentially that man—not God or any other force—creates himself and his values. In being affected by the Bible, Arnold *chooses* to be affected; and in treating the Bible as literature, he concedes that its meaning will change over time as others creatively misinterpret it. "To will liberates," as Nietzsche avows, "for to will is to create: thus I teach. And you shall learn solely in order to create."[37]

As cultivated individualists, Arnold and Nietzsche subscribe to the German ideal of *Bildung:* their model is Goethe, who, in Nietzsche's phrase, "disciplined himself to wholeness, [who] *created* himself." To follow Goethe, he contends, is to cling to the "the 'things of this world':—for in this way [one] holds firmly to the great conception of man, that man becomes the transfigurer of existence when he learns to transfigure himself." Placing Nietzsche's and Arnold's comments on the individual side by side, one notices their common source in Goethe:

> The individual is something quite new which creates new things, something absolute; all his acts are entirely his own.
> Ultimately, the individual derives the values of his acts from himself; because he has to interpret in a quite individual way even the words he has inherited. His interpretation of a formula at least is personal, even if he does not create a formula; as an interpreter he is still creative. (*WP*, 403)

Goethe's profound, imperturbable naturalism is absolutely fatal to all routine thinking; he puts the standard, once for all, inside every man instead of outside him; when he is told, such a thing must be so, there is immense authority and custom in favour of its being so, it has been held to be so for a thousand years, he answers with Olympian politeness, "But *is* it so? is it so to *me*?" Nothing could be more really subversive of the foundations on which the old European order rested. (*CPW*, 3:110)

It is typical of Arnold and Nietzsche that, whether they are looking back to Greece or ahead to the triumph of culture, whether rejecting or affirming religion, whether defending the individual as a source of value or defining the standards to which the individual must submit, they invariably turn to Goethe as their great predecessor in the task of revaluation.[38]

It may be argued that each "interprets" Goethe as he has done Empedocles, making him speak for an aspect of his own personality. However, when invoking Goethe, Arnold and Nietzsche speak on behalf of their grandest ambitions and of culture's grandest potential. For the youthful and mature Arnold and Nietzsche alike, Goethe is "the clearest, the largest, the most helpful thinker of modern times." Moreover, "in the width, depth, and richness of his criticism of life, [he is] by far our greatest modern man" (*CPW*, 8:274–75). Even in his religious books, Arnold quotes Goethe on the need for something to subdue man's baser instincts (7:140, 229). Goethe, for both writers, speaks on behalf of the standards that man himself creates in order to transform himself and his world. Hence, even while formulating their most radical views of the individual, as in the quotations cited above, Arnold and Nietzsche do so within an idealistic Goethean context.

One of the more intriguing recent interpretations of Nietzsche stresses his aesthetic rather than his philosophical importance. Commentators such as Alexander Nehamas and Allan Megill have expanded on Walter Kaufmann's suggestion that "Nietzsche's philosophy is . . . a sustained celebration of creativity"—but the broader, Goethean implications of this view have been ignored. Instead, Nietzsche's own work is seen as a fiction with Nietzsche himself (in Nehamas's words) "a creature of his own texts." A similar attempt has been made to reduce Arnold to an aesthetic presence rather than a critical force. William A. Madden's argument on behalf of Arnold's aestheticism may at least be said to highlight an important characteristic ignored by those who see Arnold primarily as a Christian humanist; and Madden sees Arnold's aestheticism embracing a wider field than Pater's or Wilde's ahistorical, asocial views. But it is a mistake, surely, to speak of Nietzsche's or Arnold's criticism as being no more than (in George Levine's comment on Arnold) "a great autobiographical fiction."[39] When considering the individual, both writers emphasize the creative and not the created self. Only by putting "the standard, once for all, inside every man instead of outside him," could Goethe allow for the possibility of individual and social development.

Arnold and Nietsche are especially scornful when dealing with societies of individuals unwilling to change. Culture's goal is the unending movement of the individual toward perfection; but this will never happen if the "self-reliant" individual speaks smugly of "doing what one likes." "The idea of perfection as a *general* expansion of the human family," says the author of *Culture and Anarchy*, "is at variance with our strong individualism, our hatred of all limits to the unrestrained swing of the individual's personality, our maxim of 'every man for himself' " (*CPW*, 5:95). Nietzsche depicts the modern German state as an "atomic whirl of egoisms" (*PN*, 41). The "free spirits" to whom he turns must, therefore, be detached from "men, customs, laws and the traditional evaluations of things" (*HH*, 30). Like Arnold, Nietzsche praises the disinterested critic who hovers above society, refusing to become a "man of action" or take political sides, in order that he might see more clearly. ("To act is so easy," says Arnold, quoting Goethe; ". . . to think is so hard" [*CPW*, 3:276].) America poses a particular warning, in Arnold's view, because it lacks standards to look up to; its faults, he suggests, are those of its "German stock" (10:163). In the late essay on Amiel, Arnold finds occasion to deplore modern man's confusion of means with ends: in the country famous for its self-reliance, people pursue lives of meaningless action, making material goods serve for the lack of intellectual or spiritual values, confounding (in Amiel's words) "being with individual being" (11:279–80).

Yet America produced another of Arnold's and Nietzsche's favorite "free spirits": Emerson. Emerson, too, had considered himself to be "a fragment," but felt it sufficient to have a share in life's rich and unending variety. ("All I know is reception; I am and I have: but I do not get, and when I have fancied I had gotten anything, I found I did not.") And for Emerson, "individuality is not only not inconsistent with culture, but is the basis of it"—so long as the individual possesses "a catholicity, a power to see with a free and disengaged look every object." Both rank the American philosopher considerably higher than Carlyle, in large part, because of what Nietzsche calls his "gracious and clever cheerfulness." Emerson, he says, "simply does not know how old he is already and how young he is still going to be." Near the end of *Daybreak* (1881), Nietzsche observes, in homage to his American predecessor, "the snake that cannot [shed] its skin, perishes. Likewise spirits which are prevented from changing their opinions; they cease to be spirits." Despite the "danger" inherent in his advocacy of self-reliance, Emerson did "the right work to be done," Arnold affirms, "at the hour when he appeared. . . . Only thus could he break through the hard and fast barrier of narrow, fixed ideas which he found confronting him, and win an entrance for new ideas." Arnold's Emerson stands outside the two political parties, pointing up the weaknesses of both; yet while "no misanthropical satirist ever saw shortcomings and absurdities more clearly than he did, or exposed them more courageously," no optimist spoke more hopefully on behalf of man's potential for growth (*CPW*, 10:180–81).[40]

The Arnoldian and Nietzschean temper is a felicitous combination of Goethe's strenuous demands on the self and Emerson's exuberance. For all their individualism and aestheticism, they point away from themselves and their texts and toward Arnold's "children of the future," or what the more elitist Nietzsche labels the "*new philosophers*," who will be "strong and original enough to provide the stimuli for opposite valuations and to revalue and invert 'eternal values.' " Such men, Nietzsche declares in *Beyond Good and Evil*, will demonstrate the effectiveness of the human will and will not look to Creators, to history, or to mass taste. This appeal to the "overman" would sound alarming if we overlooked the ideal, futuristic nature of such a figure. One might as well regard Arnold's "remnant," that squadron of critics who preserve the community, as being a historical fact rather than a cultural postulate. Although, Arnold says in agreement with Goethe, it is the individual and "not the age" that "works for progress," he also adds (qualifying Goethe's view) "that the individual is not perfect, and that he works for a future larger and better than himself."[41]

Superb phrasemakers, Arnold and Nietzsche have paid the pen-
alty of being taken literally at times. It is amusing to learn that Arnold's American audience heard his lecture on "Numbers" in "good
humour, each man imagining himself to be one of the remnant."[42]
That Nietzsche's cultural Philistines should have considered themselves to be a nation of overmen tragically confirms his belief that
great symbolists are invariably misinterpreted. For both critics, the
ideals of the past and future are reasons for discontent with the present, reasons for not accepting creeds and dogmas unquestioningly.
The world, and all its individuals, "is in a course of developing, of
becoming, " Arnold avows, "towards a perfection infinitely greater
than we now can even conceive"; but we can no longer accept, he
adds with Nietzschean sarcasm, "the idea of a God who turns himself
into a sacrificial wafer or who foredooms a large proportion of the
human race to hell" (*CPW,* 5:83). Although Nietzsche goes further, in
the task of revaluation, than Arnold, both are moving in a similar
direction.

Our desire, Nietzsche says in *The Gay Science* (once more echoing
Pindar), is *"to become those we are*—human beings who are new,
unique, incomparable, who give themselves laws, who create themselves. To that end we must become the best learners and discoverers
of everything that is lawful and necessary in the world"(266). For
Arnold and Nietzsche, forever following Socrates in this respect, one
never stops learning, one never ceases developing. Yet the risk of
"tearing . . . oneself to pieces" (in Arnold's words)[43] in order to be
creators and revaluators is always present. The "philosopher rarely
turns out well," Nietzsche cautions, because, among his other qualities, "he must be inquisitive in the most various directions" and there
is a resultant "danger of going to pieces" (*WP,* 511). In 1888, the year
that Arnold (having just written on Tolstoy and American civilization)
died, Nietzsche produced "perhaps his most important works,"[44]
ranging from *The Case of Wagner* and *Twilight of the Idols* to *The Antichrist* (the first part of his projected "Revaluation of Values") and *Ecce
Homo.* Then, in January of the following year, he went mentally to
pieces.

How would they have regarded each other? One recalls Nietzsche's
disdain for English moralists like Carlyle and George Eliot for clinging
to the vestiges of "Christian morality." Yet if Arnold draws upon the

traditional English mistrust for systems (as does Nietzsche), he also seeks, like Nietzsche, to combine the German faith in culture with the French regard for ideas. The points of similarity between them are so strong that one must be careful to recognize important distinctions too. "Seeing things as similar and making things the same," Nietzsche observes, "is the sign of weak eyes" (GS, 212). While Nietzsche's revaluation of values is conceived in purely intellectual terms, Arnold's "treatment of the 'stock notions' " matters less, as Raymond Williams reminds us, than "his effort to give his revaluation a practical bearing in society."[45] Despite their belief in the importance of education, Arnold would extend the privilege to all, Nietzsche to an elite; despite their turn to ancient Greece, Arnold comes out on the side of Apollo, Nietzsche on the side of Dionysus. On the subject of religion, Arnold holds on, if only in symbolic form, to what he calls the experiential truth of Christianity, while Nietzsche, just as decisively, embraces a countermyth of eternal return. Each fought so determined a battle against anything resembling system, dogma, metaphysics that we are surely justified in applying a Nietzschean criticism to Arnold's occasional attempts to systematize or in applying an Arnoldian invective against Nietzsche's intermittent temptations to dogmatize.

No doubt Nietzsche would have rejected Arnold, accusing him, as he does Carlyle, of being an atheist without the courage of his unconvictions. Yet Arnold, ever "facing in all directions," might well have seen in the graduate of Schulpforta another of the disparate individuals (like Emerson or Byron or Heine) he loved to call attention to for having collided with their age in order to produce "the next age. . . . [To] these individuals and to their shock [the world] owes its advance" (CPW, 9:86). And he would have recognized in Nietzsche a companion in the fight against Philistinism, the fight for culture. A century after the one's death and the other's mental breakdown, they seem saner and fresher and more various in outlook than any of the critical approaches that have been linked, very tenuously for the most part, with their names.

Chapter Four

Arnold and Gadamer: The Hermeneutics of Humanism

> To know how others stand, that we may know how we ourselves stand; and to know how we ourselves stand, that we may correct our mistakes and achieve our deliverance—that is our problem.
> Arnold, "On the Modern Element in Literature"

> Hermeneutic philosophy understands itself not as an absolute position but as a way of experience. It insists that there is no higher principle than holding oneself open in a conversation.
> Gadamer, "On the Origins of Philosophical Hermeneutics"

In my pairing of Arnold with Nietzsche in the preceding chapter, I noted how these supposedly antithetical figures shared common cultural concerns. Both were adherents of the German belief in self-cultivation (*Bildung*), drawing upon the civilization of ancient Greece for particular inspiration; and both were also "dissolvent" forces within their respective societies, turning their scorn and wit against Philistinism. But Arnold's purpose was to warn the English public of the dire consequences it faced if it failed to transform itself and adapt to changing times, whereas Nietzsche's intent was to distance himself, aesthetically, from society. Nietzsche practiced what has been called (by Paul Ricoeur) a "hermeneutics of suspicion." Along with Marx and Freud, he explained human history in terms of a god that now appeared dead and of a fictive genealogy that, he felt, needed exploding. (In the process of demystifying the past, the three "masters of suspicion" offered a new set of myths, complete with new genealogical scenarios, and with human-divinities bearing new dogmas.) But there is another kind of hermeneutics according to Ricoeur, a "hermeneutics of tradition" or "restoration."[1] The individual who has done most in our time to ground hermeneutics in tradition and the humanities is a German philosopher of a decidedly Arnoldian temper: Hans-Georg Gadamer. In this chapter, hence, I will be exploring the affinities between Gadamer's and Arnold's humanistic hermeneutics, as revealed in Gadamer's view of tradition and Arnold's view of culture, and as applied to their respective studies of Plato and the Bible.

Like Arnold, Gadamer is a humanist with a difference. In his philosophical work, Gadamer has defined the humanities in terms of their open-mindedness—their respect for multiple and changing perspectives—but also in terms of their truth-bearing standards. Like Arnold, Gadamer is a pluralist who respects authority and includes it as an important component in the dialogue that constitutes culture. This has left both men open to repeated attacks: for being too radical in the eyes of foundationalists, too conservative in the eyes of antifoundationalists. Seeking to avoid both the shoals of relativism and the rocks of authoritarianism, they have offended dogmatists and (dogmatic) antidogmatists alike. At the same time, their words have been twisted out of shape to serve the agendas of various academic factions. At a time when notions like "tradition" and the "classics" have lost their appeal to the fashionably suspicious scholars who, in significant numbers, rule the academic roosts and control the curriculum—and at a time when many younger members of the teaching profession are being permitted, even encouraged, to know less and less of what is scornfully called the "canon," and who are bringing, in consequence, a diminished grasp of languages and literatures to bear upon their teaching—at such a time Arnold's and Gadamer's belief in the need for expanding the canon and maintaining high standards is very timely.

Born in the year of Nietzsche's death (1900), Gadamer is the most important contemporary exponent of hermeneutics, a discipline that extends back to ancient Greece but that is especially associated with the work of German Protestant thinkers and German Romantics. The task for Reformation theologians like Martin Luther was specifically to establish the correct interpretation of the Gospels, while the mission of Friedrich Schleiermacher and the Romantics was to bring the heritage of the past (and other cultures) nearer to hand. Hermeneutics, in the theologically-trained Schleiermacher's hands, became the attempt to understand a text in terms of its historical context and its individual creator. A successful interpretation, hence, "depends on one's linguistic competence and on one's ability for knowing people." (Arnold acknowledged Schleiermacher's influence on Thomas Arnold's theological work, especially in detecting how in Western Christianity "there was really much more of Plato and Socrates then of Joshua and

David.")[2] Gadamer describes the importance of Schleiermacher and the other major German hermeneuticists in his magnum opus, *Truth and Method:* here, he notes the danger of the interpreter claiming "superiority over his object"—a danger deriving from the Romantic claims for genius, which Gadamer opposes—but he also credits Schleiermacher with connecting interpretation with the study of language and thereby potentially freeing texts "from all dogmatic interest." For the art of understanding—which, in its simplest definition, is what hermeneutics is all about—depends for Gadamer not on finding the correct "method" of interpretation nor on privileging the author of a text over its interpreter *or* its interpreter over the author. Rather, hermeneutics is seen as a never-ending dialogue between past and present, an evolving process in which the continuing truth-claims of the discourses that make up tradition (and only those truths that continue to make claims on us can be called viable traditions) are tested and responded to anew from generation to generation. What Arnold calls "culture," Gadamer calls "tradition," which he defines not as something fixed in the past but as "an ongoing reacquisition."[3] For both humanists, what gives value to the legacy of Hellenism and Hebraism is their ability to speak afresh to the modern world. Culture and tradition are not something inflicted upon us from above (as the disciples of Marx or Foucault believe) but something we share, as we share language and history.

Arnold's career may be seen as the transformation of a detached, second-generation Romantic poet who movingly lamented, in his poetry, the fate of individuals living in island-like isolation ("We mortal millions live *alone*") and yearning to be, once more, "parts of a single continent,"[4] into a great essayist and critic whose themes are solidarity and dialogical interchange. In his first important public utterance, the Oxford lecture "On the Modern Element in Literature," Arnold draws upon Buddhist lore as well as Greek and Roman literature to make his point: that our intellectual "deliverance" depends upon knowing "how others stand, that we may know how we ourselves stand; and to know how we ourselves stand, that we may correct our mistakes and achieve our deliverance" (*CPW,* 1:21). Arnold's position in the lecture underscores his allegiance to the view that runs through German thought from Herder to Hegel to Gadamer: that we find ourselves in the study of others. "Self-understanding," as Gadamer says, "always occurs through understanding something other than the self and includes the unity and integrity of the other" (*TM*, 97). But understanding, Gadamer maintains, requires the *applica-tion* of one's understanding: finding oneself in the other means being in an active dialogue between self and other in which neither partner is silenced and in which both are enriched. That fact that we speak in a variety of languages does not cut off dialogue but promotes it: "it is completely mistaken to infer that reason is fragmented," Gadamer argues, "because there are various languages. Just the opposite is the case. Precisely through our finitude, the particularity of our being, which is evident even in the variety of languages, the infinite dialogue is opened in the direction of the truth that we are."⁵ By the time of the Oxford lecture, Arnold, having now written the bulk of his poetry, had come to perceive the world not in terms of solipsistic fragments but of multiple perspectives offering opportunities for intellectual, moral, and even political "deliverance."

A vital hermeneutic task, for Arnold and Gadamer, is to ascertain which values *are* values in a changing world. In the modern era, a diffi-culty of difficulties is finding and keeping "high ideals" (*CPW*, 2:17). For the majority, sophistry (which Gadamer associates with mono-logical thinking) is always tempting—whether in Socrates' Greece or in Nazi Germany; and the danger comes not from "authority" or "tradi-tion" (terms which Gadamer seeks to rehabilitate in *Truth and Method*) but from those who misappropriate the past for authoritarian ends, those who cut off tradition's dialogical voices. Academic members of the "School of Resentment" (Harold Bloom's phrase) are fond of citing Walter Benjamin's powerful remark, "There is no document of civiliza-tion which is not at the same time a document of barbarism." But Benjamin ardently defended tradition—he venerated the books and artworks that constituted his portable altar to culture—and Benja-min's warning against the forces of "conformism" that attempt to "overpower" tradition and turn it into the voice of totalitarianism might be cited against the new authoritarian voices of antitradition. Traditions are invariably the targets of totalitarian leaders. "One of the first things which liberated people want to know," Iris Murdoch notes, "is the truth about their past."⁶ Something is a genuine authority, says Gadamer, because our reason persuades us to respect it, not because we are forced to obey it. Similarly, Arnold, in "A French Eton," while admiring the school set up by the Catholic conservative Lacordaire, which inculcated in students a respect for "firm order" (*CPW*, 2:273), cannot bring himself to accept Lacordaire's reproach of the modern age " 'which [in Lacordaire's words] does not know how to obey.' " "In an epoch of transition," Arnold counters, "society may and must say to its governors, 'Govern me according to my spirit, if I am to obey you' " (274). Those who reproach Arnold and Gadamer for holding on to standards and traditions ignore the dialogical nature of those values as Arnold and Gadamer define them.

To practice the hermeneutics of humanism requires, above all, an openness to human experience and the willingness to appreciate human achievement. Probably no remark of Arnold's has been so perversely misread in our time as his appeal, in "The Function of Criticism at the Present Time," for a "free play of the mind upon all subjects," for an open-mindedness that seeks to "know the best that is known and thought in the world, irrespectively of practice, politics, and everything of the kind" (CPW, 3:268). Arnold's plea for cultural pluralism has been misinterpreted as a defense of elitist standards and moribund literary texts.[7] But Arnold's position is clear from the outset, in "On the Modern Element": "that the function of culture and criticism is to deliver us from a single-minded set of dogmas, and to point us toward the vast "spectacle" of "the collective life of humanity." Who but Arnold, in the England of 1857, would have begun his lecture with a quotation ascribed to Buddha? "And everywhere," he says subsequently, "there is connexion, everywhere there is illustration: no single event, no single literature, is adequately comprehended except in its relation to other events, to other literatures" (1:20–21). The role of culture, as Arnold and Gadamer see it, is to overcome the distinctly modern sense of human alienation (a condition resulting in large part, they agree, from the triumph of the scientific over the humanistic viewpoint) through this dialogue with otherness. In the hermeneutic attempt to understand, we go out of ourselves in order to come "home." Arnold cites Wordsworth, while Gadamer cites Hegel, but both arrive at the same metaphor of understanding as homecoming. The practical lesson of the hermeneutics espoused by Arnold and Gadamer is that we mortal millions are at home amid a nexus of "connections": history, language, tradition. For the remainder of this chapter I will focus, first, on Gadamer's hermeneutics, showing how it celebrates the humanistic tradition of which Arnold is the major English defender. Then I will consider Arnold's religious writings in which he applies hermeneutics to the Bible to demonstrate (in a manner resembling Gadamer's application of hermeneutics to Plato) how tradition persists despite change because allowance for change exists within tradition.

In a distinguished academic career that has taken him from Marburg to Leipzig to Frankfurt to Heidelberg, as well as to various campuses and institutes throughout Europe and America, Gadamer has long been occupied with the humanistic heritage. At an early age, he tells us, he realized that his "inclinations" were toward literature and the "human sciences," despite the opposition of his father, a chemistry teacher who was convinced "that the natural sciences were the only honest sciences." The portrait of the young Gadamer that emerges from his *Philosophische Lehrjahre* is that of an introspective and mildly rebellious student, immersing himself in the arts, ancient history, and a variety of languages and cultures, including Sanscrit and Islam. Whereas Arnold liked to see himself as his father's intellectual heir (despite their considerable differences), Gadamer was ready, even before entering Marburg University in 1919, to reject the scientific views and authoritarian methods (the two, for him, invariably conjoined) of his father. Marburg, the oldest Protestant university in Germany, was to Gadamer what Oxford had been to Arnold: a school with idealistic traditions (including the famous "Marburg school" of neo-Kantians such as Hermann Cohen and Ernst Cassirer, which was to attract or influence such diverse figures as Mikhail Bakhtin, T. S. Eliot, and José Ortega y Gasset). Its brilliant faculty were currently engaged in new forms of cultural and philosophical discourse in response to the collapse of the old Germany. At Marburg Gadamer came into contact with members of the Stefan George circle, who spoke in behalf of spiritual solidarity "at a time when society was atomizing." He met enormously cultivated minds of the order of Ernst Robert Curtius and Gerhard Krüger, the latter "an inspired reader" with whom Gadamer and other young faculty members met as a group to read and "converse" with the writers and philosophers of the past and present, and to find themselves in the process. At Marburg, too, Gadamer came to know Rudolf Bultmann, who was to revolutionize Biblical hermeneutics through his readings of the authors of the Gospel as "partners in a theological conversation"—authors whose enduring validity is attested to not by metaphysics but by existential experience. Gadamer came to work with Paul Natorp, who was reinterpreting Plato in the

context of Plato's time—emphasizing Plato's "humanism" (as Bultmann emphasized the humanism of religion) rather than his concepts
or dogmas. Hence, Gadamer discovered, thanks to Marburg, that
"Plato was no Platonist." But it was above all at Marburg that
Gadamer came under the spell of a young instructor "who beheld as
one our time and old times, the future and Greek philosophy": Martin
Heidegger.[8]

Arnold's Oxford, by contrast, was a "home of lost causes, and
forsaken beliefs, and unpopular names, and impossible loyalties"
(CPW, 3:290)—the home, above all, of John Henry Newman, pursuing a religious purity at odds with the present. In the two universities' mutual concern with the life of the mind, however, Oxford was
never (as Arnold recalled) a dwellingplace for the Philistine, nor was
Marburg (as Gadamer notes) a haven for the Sophist. Instead, the
climate of Marburg was hospitable to one like Heidegger, thinking,
like Nietzsche before him, "his way back to the beginning" and
thereby making "understandable the ways in which the course of
contemporary civilization, right up to its present technological stage
and the current struggle for world supremacy, has been the immediate result of the thinking of the Greeks, their founding of science
and their establishment of metaphysics" (PA, 50, 53). The philosophy of "Destruktion," which Heidegger would enunciate in Being and
Time, was not, Gadamer says, formulated in the service of a "hermeneutics of suspicion," but rather as a way to recover "the primordial
Greek experience of Being." The Marburg thinkers, in their reaction
against a scientific spirit that regarded human beings as distanced
objects fit only for a narrowly framed "world picture," confronted
the legacy of the secular, post-Enlightenment, modern world with an
older and more humane tradition, that of the ancient Greeks, in
which respect for dialogue confronted the dangers of dogma and in
which practical reason (phronēsis) opposed sophistry. The young
Gadamer aligned himself with a group of seemingly iconoclastic
thinkers who were, in fact, "deeply rooted" (as he admits of his own
beliefs) "in the romantic tradition of the humanities and its humanistic heritage." Gadamer spoke of his romantic orientation in the context of his 1981 encounter with Jacques Derrida—a nondebate, as it
happened, since Derrida refused Gadamer's premise that a debate
involves a willingness to participate in a dialogue, and a measure of
"good will" on the part of the debaters. In the Marburg of the 1920s

and 1930s, as Gadamer recalls, students and teachers thrived amid the intellectual give and take. They became accustomed to a life of continuing dialogue with other minds, and especially with the thinkers who were most "modern" (to borrow Arnold's term from the 1857 lecture) and most "critical," the ancient Greeks.[9] More important even than the German Romantics were these "constant companions" whom Gadamer credits for having "formed" his hermeneutics: the dialogues of Plato (PA, 184).

During the nearly three decades before the appearance of *Truth and Method* (1960), Gadamer pondered the lessons of Greece amid the moral disintegration of Germany. His two important essays of this period, "Plato and the Poets" (1934) and "Plato's Educational State" (1942), have been well described as a form of "political hermeneutics," attacks on the revival of sophistry in Nazi Germany. To the first essay, he affixed a quotation from Goethe: " 'He who philosophizes is not at one with the premises of his times.' " Plato's aim in constructing his Utopia, Gadamer argues, is pragmatic rather than dogmatic: he is holding up, to a Greek world degraded by self-interest, a more just and ethical course of action. Plato is not escaping into a fantastic myth, but presenting in his Utopia (what Gadamer elsewhere calls) "a form of suggestiveness from afar" (RAS, 80). (Arnold similarly defended George Sand's " 'sentiment of the ideal life, which is none other than man's moral life as we shall one day know it' " [CPW, 8:236]. But then, Arnold had worried about the moral lesson to be learned by Greece's fall—hence, his view of Greece is even less idealized than Gadamer's.) Gadamer's Plato is an advocate of the harmonious and full development of the self—of what Herder and other German philosophers conceived as the idea of *Bildung*—but for Plato self-cultivation must take place within the community. An "aesthetic consciousness" that detaches people from their communal responsibilities is Plato's real target when he criticizes the poets: his implication is that the Sophists then, like the Nazis in 1934, are only too ready to disconnect rhetoric from ethics, and they do so by disallowing the possibility of Socratic dialogue, the source (as Gadamer sees it) of unending critical questioning. In the essay "Plato's Educational State," Gadamer maintains that for Plato the cultivation of the ideal self is a paradigm for the creation of the "authentic community"; "there is an indissoluble tie between political and philosophical activity."[10]

Gadamer demythologizes Plato—as Bultmann demythologizes

the Gospels and Arnold demythologizes St. Paul and Jesus—in order
to demonstrate Plato's continuing practical relevance. Gadamer's
Plato promotes dialogue, thus, as a form of ethics. In a finite world,
the Platonic dialogue guarantees that no one person or set of ideas,
not even Plato's ideas, can put an end to the human process of endless questioning. In a supplement to *Truth and Method*, Gadamer supports his view of Plato's communal principles by arguing that the
Platonic definition of thought as "the interior dialogue of the soul
with itself" (*TM*, 542–43) necessarily leads to the dialogue of the soul
with others; he argues that all resorting to language (whether in
thought or personal interchange) propels us outward. Arnold's career
is proof of the validity of this proposition. Once having defined the
besetting weakness of his poetical protagonist Empedocles as that of
alienated modern man conducting a "dialogue of the mind with itself" (*CPW*, 1:1) Arnold proceeded to turn his dialogue outward, toward the dialogical and communal ideals he shares with Gadamer
and other humanists. But Arnold also shares Gadamer's Aristotelian
position that interpretation is interlinked with application, that knowledge or theory is defined in terms of conduct; hence, the "idea of the
good" (the title of a late Gadamer book)[11] can only be imagined in
terms of the practice of goodness.

In the words of a recent admirer, Gadamer's "philosophic project
can be characterized as an apologia for humanistic learning." But
Gadamer himself admits to having felt anxiety, upon the completion
of *Truth and Method* in 1959, that it was "too late" to defend "the
humanistic tradition of the romantic *Geisteswissenschaften*" in an age
dominated by science and technology (*TM*, 551).[12] Arnold's fear, expressed over a century ago in "Literature and Science," seemed to
have been realized: the fear that the humanities, which seek to satisfy
mankind's need for beauty and conduct as part of our "instinct for
self-preservation," would be supplanted by a scientific methodology
whose practitioners scoff at (among other things) Plato and his "un-
practical and impracticable" ideas (*CPW*, 10:53). Although he seems
unaware of Arnold, Gadamer's major work brings to a climax the
Arnoldian faith in culture that itself stems, in large part, from German
Romanticism. Gadamer faults the German human sciences (as practiced, for example, by Wilhelm Dilthey) for grounding themselves
upon scientific methodology and thereby deepening the split between, on the one hand, the truth-claims of human experience and

culture and, on the other, the objectivizing and alienating demands of scientific reason. In this respect, he says, the "English-speaking countries" are luckier than the Germans because they have a counterconception of the "humanities" that argues "the indissoluble unity of all human self-knowledge" (PA, 179). In his response to Jürgen Habermas's criticism of Truth and Method (Habermas promoting reason at the expense of tradition), Gadamer points to the "deep-rooted alienation" that "all modern sciences" impose, in the form of scientific method, upon "natural consciousness"; and he contends that a humanist-based hermeneutics "can bring to consciousness what the methodology of the sciences exacts in payment for the progress it makes possible."[13] In Truth and Method, Gadamer seeks to illustrate how the achievements of humanism bring us together and bring meaning into our lives.

Truth and Method is divided into three sections: part one examines the humanist tradition and the "question of truth" as it is experienced in art; part two is an account of the truth-claims manifested in the human (as opposed to the natural) sciences as determined by hermeneutic understanding; part three contains a vindication of the hermeneutics of humanism as seen in its linguistical dimension. Endeavoring to show how the humanist tradition taps a source of truth inaccessible to the methodology-minded sciences, Gadamer draws upon the "guiding concepts" of humanism, concepts that enrich the individual and strengthen his connections with others. First among them is Bildung, the process of self-cultivation that has roots in German pietism as well as in the views of Herder, Humboldt, Hegel—and Plato. For Gadamer, the Herderian goal of "rising up to humanity through culture" (TM, 10) is not an exercise that alienates the practitioner from others (a charge leveled by W. H. Bruford, who sees in Nietzsche's elitism a dangerous consequence of Bildung).[14] Instead, Gadamer contends (with Hegel as witness), Bildung provides an enlargement of knowledge and perspective: we learn to recognize ourselves in otherness, "to become at home" in the other (TM, 14). "The general characteristic of Bildung," then, is "keeping oneself open to what is other" (17), to be willing to move from a fixed to an open perspective. The other characteristics of humanism—communal habits (sensus communis), judgment, taste— are cited by Gadamer to show how a true understanding comes through our association with others, not in our distancing ourselves from others. Kant is thus criticized for detaching the aesthetic from the

moral sense, for making aesthetic judgment a matter of purely subjective (rather than communal) interest. The Kantian privileging of genius
had, Gadamer says, a negative effect upon the romantic exponents of
hermeneutics—leading to, for example, Schleiermacher's belief in the
divinatory powers of the interpreter (187). Art and the artist came
increasingly to be seen as rarified and distant, subjectively privileged
but socially inconsequential. It is Gadamer's goal, thus, to replace this
romantic view of art with an older (Greek-derived) view in which art is
once again seen to partake of the communal and the sacred.

The universality of art affords a proof, to Gadamer, of the universality of the hermeneutic experience. The experience of art, he maintains, is a form of "sharing" in the truth of art (*TM*, 97); and the truth
of art is distinguished from the truth (or rather, method) of science
because it provides for a communal experience, whereas science, like
subjectivist aesthetics, produces alienation, cutting off subject from
object. To demonstrate how art dissolves the gap between subject and
object, Gadamer proceeds, in one of the most remarkable sections of
Truth and Method, to show how art is a form of "play," a form of
perpetual representation and participation. Just as in play the focus is
on the communal game, not on the individual players, so in art the
truth-value of the artistic experience transcends the individual artist
and admirer. In our experience of art—as audience of a play or as
reader of a book or as player in a game—the truth-claim of the art-
work acts upon us even as we respond to it. Much has been made of
Gadamer's emphasis on the part played by the interpreter, the participant, in the understanding of art. (He has been claimed as the mentor
for reception-theorists like Hans-Robert Jauss and Wolfgang Iser, but
also for reader-response critics like Stanley Fish, who privilege only
the subjective part of the artistic encounter.) But Gadamer also emphasizes the role that art plays *upon* the participant. "The work of art has
its true being," he asserts, "in the fact that it becomes an experience
that changes the person who experiences it" (102). For art has a sacred
quality: we partake, when looking at a religious painting or a portrait,
of a real presence; we lose ourselves in order to gain back a sense of
universal being. Gadamer looks back with particular care to Greek
precedents to establish this point. He notes, for example, that the
word *theory* derives from the Greek *theoros*, a witness to a sacred
festival. Hence, one who theorizes is a passive participant, "to-
tally involved in and carried away by what he sees" (124–25). (This

dramatically contrasts with the modern version of the *theorist*, professionals who, in Arnold's words, use the text to advance "their personal reputation . . . by emitting . . . a new theory of their own" [*CPW*, 7:243].)[15] In Greek tragedy, similarly, the audience is involved in the meaning re-presented each time on stage: its members learn, once again, of the finite limits to human experience while at the same time sharing this message in an affirmatively communal manner. Even the reader of a book is a participant. The act by which the interpreter brings a book to life is a "miracle," akin to the raising of Lazarus: "something alien and dead [is transformed] into total contemporaneity and familiarity" (*TM*, 163).

Gadamer's ambition in *Truth and Method* is to show how understanding is accomplished in a manner that is neither wholly subjective (the romantic danger that leads to modern relativism) nor so scientifically "objective" as to cause alienation. In fact, he argues, in the second (and most important) part of the book, we must, if we are to understand, respect the claims of what is out there as well as acknowledge our personal stake in the matter. The failing of practitioners of hermeneutics before Heidegger was to rely too much either on a sense of subjective certainty (Schleiermacher) or on an Enlightenment-derived faith in scientific methodology (Dilthey). Heidegger resolved this problem by showing how human understanding is grounded in history and language. Building upon Heidegger's observation, in *Being and Time*, that our understanding includes "fore-meanings" (*TM*, 267) that we bring with us whenever we encounter something,[16] Gadamer introduces a series of key concepts that (he argues) foreground and occasion our ability to understand: prejudice, authority, tradition. It is this section of *Truth and Method* that has aroused the most criticism from antitraditionalists, all those who see in the past nothing but patterns of domination.

For Gadamer, these three concepts enable us to have that dialogue with the past or with the other that constitutes the process of understanding. As we are situated within history, we bring historically conditioned biases to bear upon our interpretations; and it is essential "to be aware of [our] own bias, so that the text can present itself in all its otherness and thus assert its own truth against [our] own fore-meanings" (*TM*, 269). However, these biases have a positive factor if they "enable" us toward understanding. Enlightenment thinkers, contends Gadamer, had a prejudice against prejudice that disabled them from a full understanding. They mistrusted authority and tradition alike, trusting instead to a form of reason that (they believed) transcended history. But nothing exists outside of history: "history does not belong to us; we belong to it." Hence, it is our historically conditioned prejudgments (prejudices), "far more than [our] judgments, [which] constitute the historical reality of [our] being" (276–77). We must examine our prejudices, test them against the text, against experience, in order to see which are valid and which are not. Authority, too, is something to accept *if* it is valid authority, something our practical reason and experience testify in behalf of. True authority is a source of reasonable values that engage us in dialogue: "Authority can rule only," Gadamer notes elsewhere, "because it is freely recognized and accepted," not because it demands slavish acquiescence (*PH*, 33–34). And what more valid kind of authority is there than "tradition"—assuming, as does Gadamer, that a genuine tradition flourishes because it is always fresh, always a living voice, amid the various changes of history? Whereas the sciences, in their various developments, turn their back on their past history, the humanities preserve their past even as they develop.[17] The sciences (Gadamer feels) seek to impose monologues; the humanities enable dialogues.

At the heart of Gadamer's hermeneutic enterprise is a tribute to the "classic," the work of past cultures whose truth-claim and communal value are always contemporary to us. (One recalls Sainte-Beuve's description of the classic authors in "conversation" with each other and with us.) Like Arnold, Gadamer sees in Greek culture the most enduringly "modern" of perspective; but like Arnold also, Gadamer draws upon his Protestant background to explain how the process of understanding leads us from self-understanding to an understanding of a not-ourselves. To be in the presence of the classical, for him, means to be in the presence of a voice to which we must give heed. ("What would they say of us?" as Sainte-Beuve wonders.) The "example of the classical," hence, shows us that there are "normative concepts" (*TM*, 285), that there are voices that question us even as we question them.[18] Understanding, Gadamer says in a splendid metaphor, is essentially a "fusing of horizons," an apprehension of the other's historically situated perspective as well as our own. With hermeneutics we become aware of the historicity of the past and present, but as we come to understand—seeing our prejudices, our horizons,

and only thereby coming "to see beyond them"—we learn to *act* upon
our understanding (TM, 302–7). Combining Aristotle and Protestantism, Gadamer insists that understanding, interpreting, and application are interconnected. Just as "the gospel does not exist in order to
be understood as a merely historical document, but to be taken in
such a way that it exercises its saving effect" (309), so too does our
process of understanding entail self-transformation. What the classic
text tells us—whether it is Aristotle, *Oedipus,* or the Bible—is that we
live in a finite world which has "limitations" that cause us suffering,
but which also affords "insight" into our historicity, our interrelated-
ness as human beings, and of our consequent need for continuing
"openness to experience" (357–58).

For Gadamer, then, we belong to the texts that we read, to the
horizons we move among and that we attempt to expand within
ourselves, to a "tradition that is a genuine partner in dialogue" (*TM,*
358). Tradition is not an assortment of inert texts but a living "language." To be able to read and understand *Truth and Method* is to
presuppose that there is a truth-claim that transcends author and
reader, and that it has found expression in a language common to
reader and author. It is upon language, accordingly, that Gadamer
justifies his hermeneutics. "The guiding idea of [the third part of *Truth
and Method*] is *that the fusion of horizons that takes place in understanding is
actually the achievement of language*" (378). Living in a century that has
come to mistrust language, and working in an academy whose digni-
taries tend to think of language as a "prison-house" rather than a field
of interrelationships, Gadamer is noteworthy for his "linguistic idealism" (as Habermas calls it). Yet, he maintains, we do think in language, we read and write in it: "language completely surrounds us
like the voice of home which prior to our every thought of it breathes
a familiarity from time out of mind."[19] Gadamer borrows Heidegger's
formulation that "it is more correct to say that language speaks us,
rather than that we speak it"; but where Heidegger speaks of language in terms of mystic etymologies, Gadamer adopts a pragmatic
and sociable tone. Our immersion in language, he repeatedly contends, is the sign of our companionable nature and our ability to
understand the world out there: "the verbal world in which we live is
not a barrier that prevents knowledge of being-in-itself but fundamen-
tally embraces everything in which our insight can be enlarged and

deepened" (447). Language thereby frees us, to the extent that as finite beings we have freedom, and it draws us together in a world of conversation.

Like his Russian contemporary Bakhtin, Gadamer believes "that language has its true being only in dialogue, in *coming to an understanding*." Hence, he concludes in a widely quoted remark, "*Being that can be understood is language*" (*TM*, 446, 474). This does not mean, however, "that that which is can . . . be completely understood." Gadamer made that distinction in the nondebate that he had with Derrida in 1981 at the Goethe Institute in Paris. The two devotees of Heidegger had been brought together for what Gadamer believed would be a dialogue, but which resulted in a refusal on Derrida's part to participate. In his reply to Derrida, Gadamer wryly suggested that Derrida had anticipated misunderstanding, that he had expected incomprehension for the sake of confirming "his own metaphysics." In this frustrating, amusing, and revealing encounter, Gadamer spoke on behalf of the possibilities of understanding through language, and Derrida reasserted his lack of faith in a common language or in the possibility of mutual comprehension. (Derrida could no more accept Gadamer's dialogical position than he could, in his essay on Emmanuel Levinas, accept the "legitimacy" of Arnold's "coupling" of Hellenism and Hebraism. Extremes do *not* meet, voices do not conjoin, in the Derridean scheme of things.)[20] But Derrida's sense of language is text-bound: there is nothing, for the reader, outside of the text, and hence nothing determinable within it. For Gadamer (again, as for Bakhtin), it is the spoken word—the word of dialogue—that is significant. In our actual use of language, whether in spoken dialogue or in the dialogue with the other that constitutes reading, we seek to break down the self-alienation inherent in writing. Hence, for Gadamer, "this transformation back [from writing to "speech and meaning"] is the real hermeneutical task" (*TM*, 394–95).

Gadamer's most notorious academic debate has been with Habermas, in response to the latter's criticism of Gadamer's defense of tradition. Drawing upon the Enlightenment faith in critical reason, Habermas questions whether a genuine dialogue emerges out of the background "of established traditions and language games"; he wonders whether there *is* a form of authority or tradition that is not in fact a form of coercion and domination. Reason, rather than allaying itself with tradition (as Gadamer proposes), is, for him, "the rock on which existing authorities split, not the one on which they were founded." In his response, Gadamer charges that Habermas's opposition between reason and tradition is false because his interpretation of both has been "prejudiced" by Enlightenment presuppositions. Habermas has (Gadamer feels) grounded his position too emphatically on a scientific worldview, and he finds it ironic that Habermas can reject, on principle, the work of tradition while trusting to the truth-claims of psychoanalysis. The dominating force in the modern world that should concern us, Gadamer retorts, is that exerted by science and technology.[21] (The "culture industry," whose coercive force Habermas's predecessor at the Frankfurt School, Theodor Adorno, complained about, had nothing to do with culture and everything to do with technology.)

Despite the harsh words on both sides of the debate (Gadamer, who interprets Plato's enterprise as having practical and political bearing, dismisses Habermas's "vision of an anarchistic utopia"), Gadamer and Habermas have remained in dialogue and hence remain friends—hermeneutic dialogue constituting, for Gadamer, a form of friendship (*TM*, 323). Despite differing political viewpoints, both men share communally oriented values: Habermas's "communicative reason," Gadamer's "tradition as conversation." Both reject the extremes of subjectivism and relativism. If the Derridean project is an endless manufacturing of texts against texts ("The labor of deconstruction," Habermas says, "lets the refuse heap of interpretations, which it wants to clear away in order to get at the buried foundations, mount ever higher"), Gadamer's is a work that respects the text and does so precisely because he values the world outside the text and sees the two as partners in dialogue. His sense of a world outside the text, containing individuals who are capable of reasonable and ethical behavior, is linked to his sense of the existence of truth-values that lie outside the self, posited in tradition, which in turn become articulated in texts. In these trying times, such faith in people and texts may seem naive. One of Gadamer's most moving defenses of his humanistic hermeneutics appears in a letter to an American admirer, the philosopher Richard Bernstein, who has expressed reservations about Gadamer's belief in the actual existence of Aristotelean *phronēsis* (practical reason: the application of humane universal ideals to everyday situations):

Clearly your decisive argument is the collapse of all principles in the modern world, and I certainly agree with you that, if this were correct, my insistence on *phronēsis* would be nothing more than pure declamation. But is this really the case? Don't we all run the risk of a terrible intellectual hubris if we equate Nietzsche's anticipations and the ideological confusions of the present with life as it is actually lived with its own forms of solidarity?[22]

In speaking in behalf of human "solidarity," Gadamer acknowledges as "fundamental" his "divergence from Heidegger," under whom he had served the most significant of his Marburg "philosophical apprenticeships." Gadamer's relationship with Heidegger parallels, in many ways, Arnold's relationship with Newman, the most "entrancing" of voices at Oxford during his student years (*CPW*, 10:165), but a mentor from whose position Arnold diverged. The links between Gadamer and Heidegger are numerous: their crusade, for example, against the domination of science and technology; their sense of the ancient Greek writers as living forces; their belief in the truth-claim of art (particularly poetry); the historicity of their hermeneutics; the religious undercurrent of their thinking. One might be tempted to call *Truth and Method* an expansion of the hermeneutics of *Being and Time* and of the religious-linguistic aesthetics of the later Heidegger, despite Gadamer's protestation that he had been "prepared" for Heidegger as a result of his previous acquaintanceship with Kierkegaard, Stefan George, and Plato (prepared also, one is tempted to say, by his rejection of his father's scientific orientation). But the differences between Gadamer and Heidegger are substantial too.[23] One need only examine the anti-humanist drift of Heidegger's "Letter on Humanism": here, Heidegger clings nostalgically to a vision of primordial humanity at home in the state of Being, while he rejects all modern variants of the human species, whom he sees as being at once overly subjective and subjugated. For Heidegger, the Greeks, with their invention of science and metaphysics, got us into this mess; for Gadamer, the Greeks, with their utilization of dialogue and reason, offer us a way out. Heidegger's sense of modern humanity as an incorrigibly self-willed yet also manipulated herd fits the Nietzschean perspective (always tempting during terms of crisis); and Heidegger spent the Nazi years ruminating on Nietzsche, while his former pupil was directing his own students toward Plato's warnings against sophistry. Ironically, while the young

Heidegger had helped Gadamer to see that the ethical and political issues discussed by Plato and Aristotle continue to make up the modern humanist dialogue, the older Heidegger retreated into a mystic pre-Socratic universe.

Arnold's affinities with Newman are also a matter of record. We see it in their respect for authority, their zeal for "perfection," their defense of a "liberal education," their criticism of the rhetoric of political liberalism, their own rhetoric with its engagingly urbane mixture of irony and high seriousness. Both share a fear of the destructiveness of human instincts: "fierce wilful human nature in its onward course," as Newman writes in the *Apologia*;[24] "the native and barbarous vigour of primitive man, which booklearning may wholesomely temper, but will never vanquish," as Arnold declares in his study of *Popular Education of France* (*CPW*, 2:162). Arnold paid special tribute to Newman in his 1883 lecture on Emerson, given during his American tour. Emerson "was your Newman," says Arnold, and he recalls how the charm of the "subtle, sweet, mournful" tones expressed in Newman's Sunday sermons at Oxford touched the "heart and imagination" (10: 165–67). A decade earlier, while Arnold was working on *Literature and Dogma*, he and Newman briefly corresponded—the latter thanking Arnold for his presentation copy of *A Bible Reading for Schools*, prepared with the hope of showing the "civilising power of letters" to schoolchildren (7:505); Arnold, in reply, crediting Newman (along with Goethe, Wordsworth, and Sainte-Beuve) for having taught him "habits, methods, ruling ideas, which are constantly with me." Yet the correspondence, while filled with mutual respect, shows their considerable differences. The Bible, for Newman, is not what it is for Arnold, primarily "literature," but is primarily "dogma." Thirty years earlier, in "The Tamworth Reading Room," Newman had cautioned that "a literary religion is . . . little to be depended upon," noting that many prefer instead to "live and die upon a dogma."[25]

Even in the case of the affinities cited above, the dissimilarities outweigh the similarities. Whereas Newman defines authority in the form of an absolutist Church, Arnold (like Gadamer) characterizes authority in a more flexible form: as education, as culture, as tradition, as a state that embodies our "best self." For Newman, "perfection" exists: the moral of his early sermon, "Be you content with nothing short of perfection," is that through self-denial and a looking away from this world ("let us not make our own hearts our home, or this world our home, or our friends our home") one may make a "perfect end" and achieve a heavenly home. For Arnold, whose motto for *Culture and Anarchy* is "Be ye perfect," perfection is an unreachable but still this-worldly goal that prods one onward, a goal that demands continuing self-transformation and transformation of the political world toward a state of "equality."[26] (Arnold's appeal to "perfection" as that which motivates us onward parallels Gadamer's appeal to "philosophy" as the endless, unobtainable but necessary, striving toward truth.) For all his defense of a liberal education, in *The Idea of a University*, Newman makes it clear that "perfection . . . of the intellect" is not the highest of goals, that the Church has a truth-claim lacking in the humanities and sciences alike. Gadamer has been credited (by Habermas) for "Urbanizing the Heideggerian Province";[27] Arnold, similarly, may be said to have secularized Newman.

For Arnold and Gadamer, truth is defined within strictly finite parameters: they are secular humanists, which Heidegger and Newman are not, since for them the primary end of instruction is not (in Arnold's words) to make "a good citizen, or a good Christian, or a gentleman," but rather "to enable a man *to know himself and the world.*" Both thereby praise the "value of the humanities" for providing "an unsurpassed source of light and stimulus" (*CPW*, 4:290). Unlike their mentors, Arnold and Gadamer speak and work in behalf of earthly solidarity. Early on in his career as school inspector, Arnold perceived how "the strong bond of a common culture" (2:89) acts to unite the community. Very crucially, they look to the future, to the improvement of mankind's lot in society, whereas Newman and Heidegger retreat into the past, into a communion with the cosmos or the saints. When Arnold and Gadamer do look back, to traditions and cultures of the past, they do so to point us forward. Arnold repeatedly includes the voices of conservative thinkers in that polyphony of contending voices that he sees as making up culture. Edmund Burke's phrase, "our antagonist is our helper," is prefixed to the *Essays in Criticism;* and Arnold joins together the names of Burke, Newman, and Joseph de Maistre in one of his late essays, but only to say of the "infallible" authority that the latter two offer as an antidote to the liberalism of the modern world: "There's no such thing!" (9:88).[28] For Arnold, the Church of England has credibility because it "has a future before it" (3:97), because it is capable (he feels) of further development and adaptation; but the retreat into a religious purity of the past, which

Arnold describes in his essay on Eugénie de Guérin, is a doomed effort in light of the workings of the *Zeitgeist*.

Arnold and Gadamer's joint appeal to the *Zeitgeist* and to the fact of human solidarity is made in the context of a hermeneutics that privileges historical experience over unchanging dogma. Both practice a hermeneutics that values both "tradition" and "development"—key terms in Newman's own version of hermeneutics. But where Arnold and Gadamer see tradition itself as something developing in time (something, in Gadamer's words, *not* "absolute and fixed"), Newman defers to a " 'strict Traditio,' " something passed down, in the case of Christian dogma, in the form of strict apostolic succession and incapable, by its very nature, of change. (Arnold, by contrast, tends to use the word *tradition* to describe something threatened—e.g., "traditional religion"—something that the *Zeitgeist* finds "unsound" in its present form [*CPW*, 8:151–52].) For Newman, the timelessness of religious truth stands in contrast to the fact of human change. In his *Essay on the Development of Christian Doctrine*, he acknowledges the fact of earthly change, but only to justify the kind of development that allows things to "remain the same." Catholic doctrine may appear to develop, but it does so only to conserve what was always implicitly there—just as Newman may be said to have changed his religious denomination only in order to remain the same. Newman practices religious hermeneutics to find what was originally set forth in the text: rather than attempt a fusion of horizons, Newman denounces any subjectivism that would translate the texts of the ancient Church to fit a modern reading. In the manner of E. D. Hirsch, Jr. (one of the severest critics of *Truth and Method*), Newman demands that we reestablish nothing less than the author's intention.[29] But for Arnold and Gadamer, that is to deny the historical and dialogical nature of human understanding.

When speaking of Arnold's hermeneutics in the company of Gadamer, one does well to remember Arnold's humorous disclaimer that he is "a mere dabbler in these great matters, and to grasp and hold a system of philosophy is a feat much beyond my strength" (*CPW*, 5:4). But Arnold's "resistance to theory"—that refusal to adhere to a logical or partisan system of thought that infuriated some of his reviewers, and which has left him open to modern charges of evasiveness or vagueness—has only strengthened his modern appeal. Gadamer rightly speaks of the "Universality of the Hermeneutical Problem" (*PH*, 3–17); and Arnold's books on religion constitute a pioneering body of work that anticipates Gadamer's achievement.[30] For Arnold shares Schleiermacher's sense that the task of hermeneutics is to overcome misunderstanding; he shares Aristotle's view that the correlative of understanding is the application of one's understanding; and, above all, he shares Gadamer's belief that the goal and method of understanding reside in the process of dialogue. Both men conduct a dialogue with the past in their works—but not, as in the case of Heidegger or Newman, to find refuge there, nor, as in the case of many modern German and English Hellenists, to ignore past failings. For Gadamer, after all, the Sophists of Plato's time were an implacable enemy to justice; and Arnold, too, sees in Greece a modern warning.[31] In his long review of Ernest Curtius's *A History of Greece*, which immediately precedes the first of his religious books, *St. Paul and Protestantism* (1870), Arnold surveys the reasons for the breakdown of Athenian political authority, and for the rise to power of sophists who offer meaningless slogans (which remind Arnold of the modern "*liberal program for salvation*") in spite of Socratic appeals for "righteousness, temperance, and self-knowledge" (*CPW*, 5:287). The Hellenic balance was broken—the critical spirit of seeing things as they are combined with the traditional "power to respect, the power to obey" (283)—and the result was a disastrous invitation to "Doing as One Likes," to anarchy.

The major impetus for Arnold's hermeneutics in *St. Paul and Protestantism* is political rather than religious: the critical spirit that Arnold praises in *Culture and Anarchy* under the name of "Hellenism" is turned upon the Puritan middle-class establishment that has refused to transform itself in order to face the needs of modern England. As an inspector of Protestant Dissenters' schools, Arnold bemoaned that community's lack of a sense of "larger existence" and of "public responsibility."[32] He decided, thus, to show the Dissenters how their reading of the New Testament, which has affected their way of life, is based on a misunderstanding of St. Paul. "No man, who knows nothing else," Arnold declares, "knows even his Bible" (*CPW*, 5:184). What begins as an application of Hellenism (a questioning of "the very ground on which we stand, . . . giving our consciousness free play" [5:181]) to the Bible results, however, in a series of books in which Arnold also sees the need to assert the value of Hebraism, whose "uppermost idea" he defines as "conduct and obedience" (5:165). One needs to remember the approximate nature of Arnold's crucial terms here. The dialogue between Hebraism and Hellenism turns out not only to be a contrasting view of Greek and Christian cultures, but also a dialogue that occurs within each culture. Hence, Arnold's Socrates speaks in behalf of "righteousness" of conduct and Arnold's Jesus embodies "sweet reasonableness."

In the hermeneutic program of *St. Paul and Protestantism*, Arnold draws on Schleiermacher as he attempts to recover the misunderstood Pauline texts through analysis of Paul's psychology and use of language. Past readers, he says, have failed to notice that Paul sometimes "Orientalises" and sometimes "Judaises"; sometimes Paul relies on figurative language to make his points, and sometimes he uses words in an "arbitrary and uncritical fashion" in the manner (Arnold avers) of the ancient Jews, but in neither case are his words meant to be understood in a scientific or literal sense (*CPW*, 6:21–22). Arnold anticipates Gadamer's stress on how education in the humanist tradition provides a reader with the "critical tact" (20) needed to understand texts adequately. It is because of his own ability to read critically, Arnold implies, that he can see what the Puritans have missed: "what Paul really thought and meant to say." But the modern horizon must also be taken into consideration: for Arnold, Paul must be "translated" to show how he adapts to the viewpoint of "us modern and Western people" (23). He can be translated without loss or distortion of meaning because of his classic stature, because his basic position is always relevant. One recalls, in this context, Gadamer's contention that the classics of literature, "the true source of the human spirit that we find in tradition," are always rewarding "precisely because they always have something more to yield than has been taken from them" (*TM*, 502). Arnold's Paul and Arnold's Jesus are thus seen as "classic" authors whose meaning and applicability develop through time. He cites Bishop Butler's view "that 'the Bible contains many truths yet undiscovered' " (*CPW*, 6:87) to underscore the fact that even newer truths may yet be uncovered. Thus, Arnold describes his own reading of Paul as "something [not] quite new nor something quite true" (6:112), as a contribution to the developing meaning of the text.[33]

In Arnold's translation of Paul, Paul's continuing appeal has nothing to do with Puritan obsessions with "election" and "justification." What truly matters is not a form of Calvinist dogma that has served, in the name of Paul, to detach Dissenters from others, but rather a universalized Christianity that Paul bases upon the facts of "reality" and the needs of human "experience" (*CPW,* 6:29). (For Gadamer, too, the case for a work's authority rests on its verifiability by "experience.") For Arnold, the key to Paul's greatness is his crusade in behalf of human righteousness: such, he adds, was also Socrates' aim, but Paul invested " 'the rule of reason and conscience' " with an emotional fervor lacking in Socrates (6:30–31).[34] The Pauline sense of being overwhelmed by a power outside of oneself is compared by Arnold (in an audacious analogy) to our "being in love," our being animated and buoyed up by an irresistible outer force (38). At the same time, however, Paul's emotional fervor occasions a sense of universal sympathy and love, not a Puritanical sense of exclusiveness, for just as Jesus "had an unfailing sense of what we have called, using a modern term, the *solidarity* of men" (43), so too does Paul's teaching relate "us to our fellowmen": to identify with Christ is to identify "with Christ's idea of the solidarity of men" (49). Even while conceding that Paul believed in miracles, such as the Resurrection, with its promise of bodily resurrection, Arnold insists that, for a modern reader, "The resurrection Paul was striving after for himself and others was a resurrection *now,* and a resurrection to *righteousness*" (52).

Arnold thus appropriates Schleiermacher's sense of the task of hermeneutics: "To understand the text at first as well as and then even better than its author."[35] This is the opposite of Newman's determination *not* to impose a modern reading upon Scriptures (although one might contend, keeping in mind Gadamer's view of the historicity of all readings, that Newman himself reads the past through the psychological needs of his historical situation). For Arnold, one cannot avoid a modern foregrounding of classic texts. He reproaches Newman, whose argument in behalf of the development of the Church is cited, in *St. Paul and Protestantism,* as drawing conclusions supporting ahistorical Catholic dogma that are "at variance with his own theory of development" (*CPW,* 6:85–88). But while Arnold has some sympathy for the (to him) misguided Catholic position, he has none for Puritanism. His intent in *St. Paul and Protestantism* is not merely to convert Dissenters away from their narrow religion, founded on the "negation of [the] idea of development" (101), and to draw them into union with other Christians. He wishes also to stop them from being "an obstacle to progress and to true civilisation" (74) because of their opposition to the educational, cultural, and political reforms that Arnold sees as necessary for England's survival. If the English are to continue into the future, Arnold repeatedly contends, they not only have to do things differently, they have to become something different.

In Arnold's major work of hermeneutics, *Literature and Dogma: An Essay Towards A Better Apprehension of the Bible* (1873), his religious, political, literary, and cultural interests all come together. This is his most ambitious book in the sense that *Truth and Method* is the work toward which Gadamer's lifelong interests were headed; and the two books share a determination to undermine the role of method and dogma while speaking in behalf of a broader, humanistic alternative. In *Literature and Dogma* Arnold has turned from arguing how a misunderstanding of St. Paul has had negative political implications to demonstrating, in a study of the Bible's language, the contemporary relevance of the Bible to each individual reader. It is the object of "criticism" to "determine what the original speakers seem to have directly meant. But," he adds, "the very nature of their language justifies *any* powerful and fruitful application of it; and every such application may be said, in the words of popular religion, to have been lodged there from the first by the spirit of God" (*CPW,* 6:222). The Bible as text demands our personal involvement because as we read it (as Gadamer or Erich Auerbach say) its message makes a claim upon us.[36] For Arnold, the message of the Bible is the substantiation of his belief in culture and *Bildung:* culture serves as the means, the "remedy," by which our "knowing the best that has been thought and known in the world" gives us *"the power, through reading, to estimate the proportion in what we read"* (153). But *Bildung* also is Jesus' message: he is the apostle of the development of the inner life, advocating as his "method" the turn "inward" that leads to self-transformation; and offering as his "secret" the need to renounce the selfish ego in favor of the altruistic, communal-directed self (288–89, 294).

For Arnold, the Bible is the greatest and most inspirational of Western literary classics. "Into the education of the people," he complained to a friend, "there comes, with us at any rate, absolutely nothing *grand.*" Hence, his *A Bible Reading for Schools* (containing Arnold's own translation of Isaiah) was prepared to remedy that "fatal omission." Moreover, as he told another correspondent, the works of Shakespeare and Milton "will be read all the better, and with more appreciation, if there is some such basis as that which this Bible reading proposes to give."[37] The Bible, one might say, with its brilliant figurative language, wonderful stories, penetrating psychology, and its social-directed theme, becomes the grand prototype of such Victorian masterpieces as *Little Dorrit* and *Middlemarch*. In their *Literary Guide to the Bible*, Robert Alter and Frank Kermode have finely argued that (in Alter's words) the "literary impulse" of its texts is so "inextricable" from the "religious impulse . . . that in order to understand the latter, you have to take full account of the former." The books of the biblical canon have survived (in Kermode's Gadamerian-inspired phrase), not because of their historical accuracy, but because of their endless "capacity to be *applied*, their applicability to historical circumstances other than those of their origin." But where Alter and Kermode have a team of Biblical specialists at their disposal, Arnold is a one-man show; and while it is tempting to point up the various weaknesses (the "thinness" of actual religious substance, as Nathan A. Scott, Jr. notes, or the fact that, in updating the Bible, Arnold "skips with a vengeance"),[38] it is more useful to point to the fruitfulness of his approach.

The first thing to note about *Literature and Dogma* is Arnold's hermeneutic sense of the Bible's language as "fluid, passing, and literary, not rigid, fixed, and scientific" (*CPW*, 6:152).[39] It is here that the "tact" acquired through a familiarity with "letters" comes in handy: "For the thing turns upon understanding the manner in which men have thought, their way of using words, and what they mean with them" (196). Jesus' words to his followers (given "the mental range of their time" [262]) went over their heads. Hence, it is not surprising that the modernity of Jesus' message was ignored. His followers wanted miracles, dreamed of a realm beyond earth; but Jesus' message that the kingdom is *on* the earth and *within* each man could only be perceived by "future" readers. To "extract" Jesus from his mythical status, is, thus, the task of "criticism" (275). Long before Bultmann or Gadamer, Arnold is arguing that the original readers of Scriptures could only grasp a portion of that inexhaustible text, and that to attest to the Bible's contemporaneity it is necessary to see through the *Aberglaube* (the poetical conceptions, or "superstitions," that the followers of Jesus confused with realities), to strip away the accretions of myth and dogma that have overlaid it over the centuries, and to rest the text "upon something which is verifiable," upon man's experience (149).

Like Gadamer and other modern hermeneuticists, Arnold links the understanding of the text with self-understanding: the awareness of our finite nature makes us respond to a "not-ourselves which makes for righteousness" (*CPW*, 6:200). But Arnold differs from such practitioners of religious hermeneutics as Bultmann and Ricoeur in that, for him, the dialogue between self and nonself is conceived in terms of the human community. Bultmann and Ricoeur demythologize the Bible in order to reveal (in the former's words) "the real intention of myth," man's dependence upon divine grace. "They alone find security who let all security go," says Bultmann, calling for a Kierkegaardian leap of faith and rejecting any attempt to define God in terms of objective verifiability.[40] (Gadamer's belief that, in seeking to understand, one loses oneself to find oneself is surely also influenced by Kierkegaard.) But Arnold allows us *only* this world, this kingdom; his demythologizing leaves us without any consoling transcendental myth. As he states in the Preface to the Popular Edition of *Literature and Dogma* (1883), "the fundamental thing for Christians is not the incarnation but the imitation of Christ!" (146). As a secular humanist, he finds it sufficient that Bible reading inspires righteous conduct because such conduct occasions "joy and peace on earth" (204). Whereas Bultmann regards mankind as overwhelmed by anxiety (Heidegger's *"sorge"*) and desirous of escaping from the nothingness of human existence, Arnold, on the contrary, stresses the human desire for joy that finds expression in our solidary and ethical behavior. Hence, mankind will always return to the Bible, "Because they cannot do without it. Because happiness is our being's end and aim,[41] and happiness belongs to righteousness, and righteousness is revealed in the Bible" (380).

Arnold regards the Bible in the light of history, past and present. The "fall" of France in 1870 and 1871, like that of the Greeks and Romans, reminded him (writing to his mother) of the fate that awaits a nation lacking in "a serious conception of righteousness." Thus, in *Literature and Dogma* he underscores the Bible's deepest "strain": the idea that with "nations and men, whoever is shipwrecked, is shipwrecked on *conduct*" (*CPW*, 386). Arnold's insistence upon the this-worldly dimensions of the Bible, in his religious writings of the 1870s, is all the more remarkable because of his personal losses around this time: three of his children (Basil and Tommy in 1868, Budge in 1872) and (in 1873) his mother, who had been the recipient of his most heartfelt letters. To his younger sister Fan, Arnold insisted upon the "entirely religious" nature of Literature and Dogma;[42] but the book's critical reception afforded proof for Arnold that Jesus and St. Paul were not the only ones to be misunderstood in their own time. To a professional theologian like John Tulloch, Arnold's appeal for "righteousness" was valueless without the existence of a personal God to enforce righteousness. Meanwhile, the secularist Westminster Review critic harped on Arnold's "unwillingness to accept the necessary consequences of his own admissions": "He would gladly be rid of supernaturalism, yet he clings to the Bible, of which supernaturalism is the key-note."[43]

The defensive tone of God and the Bible (1875) is a reaction to such criticisms. Arnold apologizes, in his Introduction, for the "perhaps mischievous" effect of Literature and Dogma; still, he maintains, "The time for that book's wide working . . . has hardly yet fully come" (CPW, 7:149). In the new book (subtitled "A Sequel to Literature and Dogma"), Arnold reiterates his earlier position that the Bible is primarily literature and as such it will always be irreplaceable. But he adds a sober warning (inspired, no doubt, by the recent events in France): the humanist heritage, which includes the Bible as its greatest literary exemplar, cannot be set aside, as the Utilitarians and other secularists would like, because it provides mankind with a refuge against barbarism. Quoting Goethe's lines, " 'What culture has won of nature we ought on no account to let go again, at no price to give up' " (229), Arnold appeals again to experience—the facts of human history—to argue the importance of the Bible. At the same time that he dismisses completely the notion of a personal God—sweeping aside the claims made by those who appeal to "miracles" and those who appeal to "metaphysics" to justify such a notion—Arnold argues powerfully in behalf of the powers of a religion responsive to imaginative and social needs. He defends, accordingly, the Fourth Gospel on the grounds of its literary merits, even as he denies the grounds for supernatural belief. Jesus, he repeats, spoke in behalf of our inner rebirth, but his words went "over the heads of all his reporters" (313); he sought "to raise [his hearers] out of their materialism" (359), but having themselves demanded concrete miracles, they only found what they were looking for (367). Jesus' hearers were bounded by their historically situated prejudices (as Gadamer would say), and they proved incapable of fusing their horizons with that of Jesus. Such a fusion of horizons could only occur in the course of time.

So while the Christian religion, for Arnold, remains historically something "that men cannot do without," it is also something that modern men "cannot do with as it is" (*CPW*, 7:378). Humankind must have something that responds to its need for happiness, but religion cannot rest on fairy tales. Without religion, however, there is the social threat posed no less by a "frivolous and materialised upper class" than by a "raw and sensual lower class" (390–91). Arnold's sense of the historicity of the Bible merges with his sense of the historical needs and developments of his own time. Thus, in the Preface to *God and the Bible*, he reaffirms his personal belief in the Bible as the supreme sourcebook for human conduct, just as ancient Greece (he avows) provides the supreme source of artistic perfection. But Arnold presents his views with the modesty of a historicist: between the writing of the first part of *Literature and Dogma* and writing *God and the Bible*, he lectured on the fascination offered by Islam ("A Persian Passion Play," 1871), and in 1873 he cautioned his readers, "All forms of religion are but *approximations* to the truth" (108). For the English, at so critical a moment in their history, the "ideas" of Christianity still apply because of their grounding in experience, rather than (as Arnold sees it, in the case of Islam) in dogma.

In his *Last Essays on Church and Religion* (1876), Arnold again invokes the *Zeitgeist* (which he sees as ruling against Bishop Butler's *Analogy*), and he repeats his theme of the need for solidarity and equality among men. He focuses, once again, on the "transformation of the present world" as "the great original idea of the Christian Gospel" (*CPW*, 8: 61). In the fascinating essay "A Psychological Parallel," he reiterates his dismissal of the supernatural—whether in the form of St. Paul's belief in the resurrection of the body or in the Cambridge Platonist John Smith's belief in the existence of witches— while holding on to the modern relevance of both men's ideas respecting our resurrection to righteousness (Paul's real intention, according to Arnold) and our need to contend with the forces of evil that plague us from within (Smith's real point). It is in this usually overlooked volume that Arnold attacks the English class system, daringly holding up the Bible for its defense of "communism." (Renan had already called Jesus a socialist.) "The truth is," he says, "the Bible enjoins endless self-sacrifice all round; and to anyone who has grasped this idea, the superstitious worship of property, the reverent devotedness to the propertied and satisfied classes, is impossible" (72). (Newman, by contrast, spoke of the "Toryism" implicit in all worshipers. "No one can dislike the democratic principle more than I," he declared, during the debate over papal infallibility.) Arnold's beloved Church of England may have an edge on other faiths (he believes) because of its openness to ideas and its willingness to change over time. But, he cautions, it will have to abandon its debilitating deference toward the propertied classes: any national church must promote "goodness" for the entire community if it is to justify its continuing existence (82–83).[44] In his Preface to the *Last Essays,* Arnold announces his return to "literature," "a field where work of the most important kind needs to be done (148); and he concludes his final venture into religious herme-neutics with the prophecy that the religion of "joy" offered by Jesus will outlast the Schopenhauerian doctrine of "pessimism" currently "in fashion" (159–60). Arnold ends, fittingly, with a dialogue between Hebraism and Hellenism, between the voice that bespeaks conduct and that which speaks for culture. "But this does but bring us," says Arnold (in a pre-Gadamerian and pre-Deweyan strain), "to the old and true Socratic thesis of the interdependence of virtue and knowl-edge" (162).

At the heart of Arnold's and Gadamer's humanism is this awareness of the interdependence of knowledge and practice. It underlies their joint faith in the combined forces of tradition and change: in tradition that exists amid change, in change that is built into tradition. For both, the danger that besets us is not the result of tradition but of the methodological scientific (or intellectual) viewpoint. It is thus that Gadamer disputes Ricoeur's calls for a reconciliation between the her-meneutics of "suspicion" and that of "restoration" (or "tradition"), Gadamer contending that hermeneutics is in its nature "a form of overcoming an awareness of suspicion." The problem with the mas-ters of suspicion, he charges, is that they are obliged to turn to "scien-tific methods" to validate their personal positions. By contrast, the "Greeks are so exemplary for us today because they resisted the dog-matism of concepts and the 'urge for system.' "[45] Nietzsche and Marx and Freud and their modern academic counterparts resort to offering new dogmas, new absolutizing systems. (Even deconstructors or

Foucauldians who denounce the authority of the text demand that *their* readings be read authoritatively.) Suspicion thrives, moreover, as does Cartesian methodology, on alienation, on a distancing of author or scientist from solidary ideals and practice. (Hence, Thomas Kuhn speaks of the typically American belief that scientific research comes only from an individualist and *"inventive* personality, a sort of person who does emphasize divergent [as opposed to "convergent" or tradition-minded] thinking but whom the United States has already produced in abundance.") For Arnoldian and Gadamerian hermeneutics, "Practice is conducting oneself and acting in solidarity," which is, Gadamer affirms, "the decisive condition and basis of all social reason. There is a saying of Heraclitus, the 'weeping' philosopher: The *logos* is common to all, but people behave as if each had a private reason. Does it have to remain this way?"[46]

Another reason for rejecting the "hermeneutics of suspicion" is that it disallows the possibility of forms of greatness existing beyond the self: works of art are mere commodities to the Marxist, or symptoms of neurosis to the Freudian, or agents of political reaction to the Foucauldians. In many of the essays written in the wake of *Truth and Method,* Gadamer has continued his defense of the humanist position, especially as embodied in the Greek artists and philosophers and in the cultural tradition that proceeds from them. "Cultural tradition," he maintains, is not "absolutized or fixed" (*PH,* 31); unlike "the object of the empirical sciences," "the object of philosophy . . . is always reconstituted anew." In the Platonic dialogues, the readers, "we ourselves are the ones (thanks to the lasting effect of Plato's artful dialogical compositions) who find ourselves addressed and who are called upon to account for what we are saying." The distinctively "literary character" of the Platonic dialogues allows for their "inherent inconclusiveness and open-endedness."[47] This corresponds to Arnold's sense of the literary character of the Bible, whose surplus of meaning demands a never-ending dialogue between text and reader. But just as the text exists as a classic by reason of its continuing ability to speak to (and be questioned by) later generations, so too does the classic text exert a continuing claim upon the reader. Gadamer sees in the intimacy of our relationship with art a notable contrast to "dogmatic objectivism," to the scientific habit of "asserting an opposition and separation between the ongoing, natural 'tradition' and the reflective appropriation of it" (*PH,* 28). Tradition is by no means an objective, detached other; it is part of the historical experience that we belong to: "as finite beings, we already find ourselves within certain traditions, irrespective of whether we are aware of them or whether we deceive ourselves into believing that we can start anew." And thus, for Gadamer as for Arnold, it is in art and not in science that we find the means of being changed and revitalized. The work of art not only addresses us, telling us with a "joyous and frightening shock" what as finite beings we are; "it also says to us," in the manner of Rilke's Greek torso, "you must change your life" (*PH*, 104).[48]

Much of Gadamer's position in defense of humanism is prefigured in Arnold's classic essay "Literature and Science," based on a lecture given at Cambridge in 1882 and then included among the "Discourses in America" delivered a year later. Like Gadamer, Arnold dwells on the importance of science (the work of science is *part* of "the best which has been thought and uttered" [*CPW*, 10:58]), but he notes that as a discipline, science is value-free: having no connection with human practice, it does nothing to satisfy our need for "conduct" or "beauty" or solidarity (61–62). (For Gadamer, one recalls, the scientific method works against solidarity.) Written partly in response to Thomas Huxley's lecture "Science and Culture," with its dismissal of "mere literary education" as a component of the practical student's curriculum, Arnold is alarmed by the lack of interest among scientists like Darwin in poetry or religion.[49] For the naturalist, he speculates, devotion to the facts of nature do not allow "time or inclination" for such matters as beauty or conduct (65). Once again, it is a case of Hellenism, the preoccupation with knowledge, detached from Hebraism, the concern with conduct—but lacking Hellenism's sense of (in Gadamer's phrase) "the Relevance [*Die Aktualitat*] of the Beautiful." Arnold's defense of letters is based on his sense of culture as a grand dialogue in which science has its due voice, but is not the dominating voice, and in which the work of "art and poetry and eloquence" from all ages and cultures provides a life-sustaining "criticism of life." (Arnold's argument is clearly inspired by Wordsworth's famous description of the poet, binding "together by passion and knowledge the vast empire of human society, as it is spread over the whole earth, and over all time." Poetry, as Wordsworth argues, *connects*; science individuates.)[50] And Greek culture, for Arnold and Gadamer, has shown itself historically to be that which best satisfies our need for beauty and truth. "If," Arnold asserts, "the instinct for beauty is served by

Greek literature and art as it is served by no other literature and art, we may trust to the instinct of self-preservation in humanity for keeping Greek as part of our culture" (10:71).

That human beings crave beauty and truth, that we find happiness in ethical behavior and solidarity—these are positions Gadamer and Arnold uphold despite the voices of relativists who deny the first premise and anarchistic technologists who ignore the second. For both of them, art matters to the degree that it provides truth. "Poetry is nothing less than the most perfect speech of man," Arnold says in his essay on Wordsworth, "that in which he comes nearest to being able to utter the truth" (CPW, 9:39). "In the midst of a world in which everything familiar is dissolving," Gadamer declares, art provides us with a valuable "mimesis," recognition of what and whom and where we are, as well as a "presentation of order."[51] Hence, for Arnold, the "future of poetry is immense," because in a world where not a "creed . . . is not shaken, . . . an accredited dogma . . . not shown to be questionable, . . . a received tradition which does not threaten to dissolve," poetry offers an interpretation of life "to console us, to sustain us." It is the poetry of Plato and the Bible that has endured, and Arnold avows, "most of what now passes with us for religion and philosophy will be replaced by poetry" (161–62). Poetry brings us "home," Gadamer insists: it fulfills itself by giving us something fundamental to dwell in; its truth "consists in creating a 'hold upon nearness.' " For this reason, Arnold praises Goethe (*"Art still has truth, take refuge there!"*) and Wordsworth, the latter of whom, more than any other modern English poet, "prosecutes his journey home" (47). "The recognition that the work of art procures for us," says Gadamer, "is always an expansion of that infinite process of making ourselves at home in the world which is the human lot."[52]

For, both agree, our home is in *this* world, and if art allows us a sense of beauty and order—if the beautiful serves, in Platonic fashion, "to bridge the chasm between the ideal and the real" (RB, 15)—we remain finite beings in a historically contingent world. It is as "moderns," then, that Gadamer and Arnold look to Greece or to the Bible, and it is the "modern element" in those worlds that speaks, for them, directly to our time. The lesson from Greek religion, notes Gadamer, is the awareness of the fact that "we are always other and much more than we know ourselves to be, and what exceeds our knowledge is precisely our real being."[53] It is through hermeneutics—the understanding of the other—that we understand ourselves as part of the other, and as involved in a historical process that bears us forward too: in a retranslation of John 3:3, Arnold affirms, " 'Except a man be born *from above*, he cannot have part in the society of the future' " (*CPW*, 11:369). Among the best of the literary essays Arnold wrote after ceasing to write religious hermeneutics is a tribute to George Sand, who felt "the poetry of the past," but who also aspired "towards a purged and renewed society." Like Wordsworth, she celebrated "nature and beauty" as the common human legacy (not as "the selfish and solitary joy" of the aesthete); and she resisted the world of suspicious intellectuals, with "their interminable flow of [in her words] 'stimulating phrases, cold as death' " (8:234, 220, 226, 234).

It is a ghastly irony that Arnold has been so consistently misunderstood in our time, that he has been reduced to a handful of phrases by critics willfully unfamiliar with his work and with the context of his work. And Gadamer, too, has been misappropriated by American academics—some of the same critics who dismiss Arnoldian humanism as an elitist enterprise have credited Gadamer with opening the door to readings in which the reader brings all the essential information to bear upon the text. (For others, Gadamer, with his appeal to tradition, is yet another elitist.) And yet each author has a sense of ironical perspective that allows them to laugh at the mistaken image. Arnold was amused by the Victorian reviewers who concocted a derisive image of the "apostle of culture"; and Gadamer, in his eighties, promised an American critic, impatient with an old man's faith in the existence of practical reason in the modern world, that he would read Habermas and Richard Rorty again: "perhaps I can still get something new into this old head."[54] What Arnold and Gadamer do not offer is definitive pronouncements. "We are all seekers still!" says Arnold of the humanist position (*CPW*, 3:289). What else is philosophy, asks Gadamer, but "the incessant though constantly unfulfilled striving after truth?" (*RAS*, 141).

To the end of his life, Arnold would "say with Solon: ('I grow old learning ever more things.')" (*CPW*, 11:386). The Spanish painter Goya, in his eighties and living in political exile, drew a witty and sardonic caricature of himself as a decrepit old man, walking with the aid of sticks and yet continuing to move on. He titled the drawing "Au aprendo" (I'm still learning), and the combination of realism and idealism bespeaks the humanist position in what is always a time of crisis. We are always "wandering between two worlds"—"Living in the Interregnum," as Nadine Gordimer calls a recent essay—and therefore, in Gordimer's words, "We must continue to be tormented by the ideal." We cannot abandon Plato, as Iris Murdoch argues, because the Platonic emphasis on "vision" provides us with an ethical light that allows us "to see our way" on life's journey.[55] The sense that we are part of a community that embraces all times and cultures, past and present, guarantees that "the" truth will never be arrived at, that "perfection" will never be attained; but it suffices us to know that there is a something outside of ourselves that compels our attention and our need to keep learning *if* we are ever to move toward (in Arnold's words, written near the end of his life) "a renovated and perfected human society on earth" (11:369).

Chapter Five

Arnold and the Pragmatists: Culture as Democracy

I am more and more convinced that the world tends to become
more comfortable for the mass, and more uncomfortable for those
of any natural gift or distinction—and it is as well perhaps that it
should be so—for hitherto the gifted have astonished and
delighted the world, but not trained or inspired or in ány real
way changed it—and the world might do worse than to dismiss
too high pretentions, and settle down on what it can see and
handle and appreciate.

Arnold to Arthur Hugh Clough, January 7, 1852

I am finite once for all, and all the categories of my sympathy are
knit up with the finite world *as such*, and with things that have a
history.

William James, *A Pluralistic Universe*

Our neglect of the traditions of the past, with whatever this
negligence implies in the way of spiritual impoverishment of our
life, has its compensation in the idea that the world is
recommencing and being remade under our eyes.

John Dewey, "The Development of American Pragmatism"

Here or nowhere is America!

Goethe, *Wilhelm Meister's Apprenticeship*

While pleased that Clough liked "The Scholar-Gipsy," Arnold persisted in asking his friend, "but what does it *do* for you?" The greatest
poets—Homer, Shakespeare—*animate;* and " 'The complaining millions of men [who] /Darken in labour and pain' " (Arnold is quoting
from his "The Youth of Nature") desire "something to *animate* and
enoble them—not merely to add zest to their melancholy or grace to
their dreams." In 1853 Arnold called this feeling "the basis of [his]
nature—and of [his] poetics."[1] What does poetry—or, for that matter,
criticism or culture—*do* for you? The utilitarian-sounding question
may seem strange coming from an Oxford-trained idealist; but, as I
have argued in the preceding chapter, Arnold's idealism is inextricably

linked to his emphasis on practice. Like his hermeneuticist descendant Hans-Georg Gadamer, Arnold sees knowledge and action, Hellenism and Hebraism, as incomplete without the other. By now we have seen an Arnold who upholds principles of unity and authority coexisting with an Arnold who praises diversity and who questions dogmas and traditions. There is the Arnold who defers to Burke and Newman, and the Arnold who identifies with Byron and Heine. And yet all these seemingly contradictory selves are part of an individual totality—the personal equivalent of what William James called our "multiverse"— and this polyphonic self pursues a pragmatic goal. If a pragmatist may be defined as a pluralist with standards—someone who believes in subjecting the doctrines inherited from the past, and the unexamined presumptions of the present, to critical reflection; one whose aim is the improvement of the kingdom of this earth, bolstered by humanist ideals that promote social solidarity and individual transformation— then Arnold must be seen as an important precursor of pragmatism.

While acknowledging it to be a "vague, ambiguous, and over-worked word," Richard Rorty nevertheless names pragmatism as "the chief glory of [America's] intellectual tradition. No other American writers have offered so radical a suggestion for making our future different from our past, as have James and Dewey." In recent years, in large part owing to Rorty, pragmatism has enjoyed a resurgence of popularity,[2] having become a philosophical refuge and sounding board for a variety of fin de siècle intellectuals: frustrated liberals and enraged radicals, post-Marxists and anti-Marxists, individualists and communitarians, aesthetes and social activists. At a time when many intellectuals feel themselves at odds with the establishment, and at the same time oppose the nihilism and fatalism implicit in some recent academic trends, pragmatism has offered a belief both in the potential for change and in the power of ideas and ideals to effectuate change. And yet, despite Arnold's tendency to regard "America" as symbol of what should be avoided by lovers of culture, this most American of philosophies restates, in many ways, and builds upon some of the Arnoldian attitudes I have been examining for the past four chapters.

Arnold has had an extraordinary appeal for American intellectuals, from North American Review editor Charles Eliot Norton down to the editor of Arnold's Complete Prose Works, R. H. Super. He has been admired by, and inspired, some of America's best minds, beginning with Emerson and Henry James. In recent years, he has attracted such New York intellectuals as Lionel Trilling, Irving Howe, and Morris Dickstein.³ It should not be a surprise, then, that American pragmatists have seen in Arnold a useful ally or a valuable adversary. Rorty includes him among the literary critics whose example he thinks philosophers may profit from. William James drew on Arnold's religious writings and (surprisingly, given his patriotism) praised Arnold's final and harshest piece on "Civilisation in the United States" as "very sensible and good."⁴ And Dewey conducted a dialogue with Arnold that extended over six decades. In 1890, two years after Arnold's death, Dewey devoted the major portion of a lecture on "Poetry and Philosophy" to a sensitive and highly revealing analysis of Arnold— all the more surprising coming from a philosopher often accused of being indifferent to the arts, but who, early on, showed sympathetic awareness of Arnold's depiction of mankind's tragic plight.

Dewey's apostle Sidney Hook has characterized pragmatism in terms both of its "melioristic" thrust and its "tragic sense of life." The hopeful aspect of pragmatism is contained within three of its premises: first, that "the universe [is] open," with the result that human "possibilities [are] real"; second, that "the future [depends] in part upon what" we do or leave undone; and, third, that ideas are "potentially plans of action." Rather than supporting a materialistic status quo, as some have charged, pragmatism must be seen as "a method of clarifying ideas" and thus as "a method of *criticism*." But along with this sense of the "efficacy of human ideals and actions" comes an awareness of "their inescapable limitations." For it is a finite world that we inhabit—one cut off from divine support or guidance—and living with finitude means accepting a world of "inescapable tragedy."⁵ Hook's emphasis on the tragic side of pragmatism is supported by a look at Dewey's 1890 lecture. Dewey begins by quoting the opening of Arnold's "The Study of Poetry," with its account of how, in a time of dying creeds and dissolving traditions, people are increasingly "turning to poetry for consolation, for stay, for interpretation." Speaking as one for whom philosophy and science should provide the "method and standard" for truth, Dewey nonetheless notes that Arnold's poetry—with its awareness of man's "isolation from nature, his isolation from fellow-man"—sounds a chord of authenticity that cannot be denied. Comparing Arnold's "Stoic" stance with Browning's more optimistic verses (Browning's sense that "the world was

made for man, and that man was made for man," which Dewey
would obviously prefer to be closer to the truth than Arnold's view),
Dewey contends that "Arnold's message has weight and penetration
with us, . . . because that message conveys something of the reality
of things." What the philosophy of 1890, by contrast, lacks is just such
an awareness of the *Zeitgeist* held by such poets as Arnold and Browning. What is needed, then, is a bridging of "this gap of poetry from
science," of a uniting of the poet's sense of reality with the philosopher's and scientist's method for transforming that reality.[6]

Even with his hopeful conclusion—and from the latter part of the
nineteenth until the middle of the twentieth century, Dewey was remarkable for his hopefulness—Dewey's recital of all those Arnold passages that undermine optimism ("Wandering between two worlds,
one dead / The other powerless to be born"; "The sea of faith / Was
once, too, at the full"; "Thou hast been, shalt be, art alone"; and so
on) indicate how closely he had studied the poet. But he had also
absorbed the hopeful side of Arnold the critic, the Arnold who looked
to education and the forces of culture to release humankind from its
tendency to anarchy, intolerance, and provinciality. In a fragment of
autobiography dating from 1930, Dewey, judging the present from
the point of view of the future, dismissed "the whole of western
European history [as] a provincial episode," and he called on philosophers "to help get rid of the useless lumber that blocks our highways
of thought, and strive to make straight and open the paths that lead to
the future." Not for the first time in his work, Dewey is echoing the
theme of "The Function of Criticism at the Present Time"; and to
underscore the resemblance, he concludes with Arnold's image of the
forward-looking critic as he wanders through the wilderness: "Forty
years spent in wandering in a wilderness like that of the present is not
a sad fate—unless one attempts to make oneself believe that the wilderness is after all itself the promised land."[7] It was Dewey's goal no
less than it had been Arnold's to counter the individual sense of
isolation with a social vision of solidarity.

In this chapter I will be exploring Arnold's affinities with the pragmatists: with William James, himself eminently Victorian in many of
his conflicting attitudes, and not least in his desire to reconcile individual and religious needs with societal and scientific claims; with Rorty,
whose mixture of private aestheticism and public liberalism, as well as
whose ironic stance, bears some resemblance to that of the Arnoldian

artist-critic; and finally with Dewey, whose faith in education as the instrument best capable of nourishing a cultivated and creative democracy resembles Arnold's own abiding faith. Arnold's description of himself, in the Introduction to *Culture and Anarchy*, as "a Liberal tempered by experience [and] reflection," as, "above all, a believer in culture" (*CPW*, 5:88) is not a bad description of Dewey too. For if Arnold's keyword *culture* gives way to Dewey's keyword *democracy*, the two terms were intertwined from the beginning in Arnold's mind. Arnold's culture was never meant to be a defense against democracy but was meant rather to be a preparation for, and safeguard of, democracy.[8] Apostles of culture, he repeatedly argued, are necessarily proponents of equality; and no culture is worth its name, he felt, that did not contain all its citizens ("all our fellow-men, in the East of London and elsewhere" [5:216]) in the goal of individual and societal transformation ("progress towards perfection"). As prelude to my last set of Arnoldian dialogues, therefore, I will be looking at perhaps the most pragmatic in tone of all his volumes, the fine and often overlooked collection of *Mixed Essays* (1879), which brings together his important essays on "Democracy" and "Equality," as well as his eloquent tributes to Falkland and George Sand.

The author of the *Mixed Essays* is a more earnest and appealing Arnold than the combative author of the more quotable *Culture and Anarchy*. The years spent inspecting schools, reevaluating literary and religious texts, and reflecting on the spirit of the age had all intensified Arnold's belief in the need for ideals and in the value of conduct. Without ceasing to be a Hellenist, an advocate of beauty and intelligence ("sweetness and light"), he is more passionate now in his defense of "civilization"—a term that has displaced "culture" in the Preface to the new volume. Arnold has, in part, returned to literary subjects—to George Sand, to the French critic Edmond Scherer (and, through him, to Milton and Goethe)—but in order to examine what part literature plays in the "whole" of civilization, whose aim is the "humanisation of man," all men, "in society." To signal the continuity of his interests, Arnold includes in his new book the essay on "Democracy" that had served, two decades earlier, as Introduction to *The Popular Education of France* (1861). To it he added essays on Clarendon's (and Thomas Arnold's) beloved "Falkland," on "Equality," on "Irish Catholicism and British Liberalism," and on the woeful state of British education

("Porro Unum Est Necessarium"). A "mixed" collection, indeed, and yet each essay illustrates Arnold's principle: "Whoever seriously occupies himself with literature will soon perceive its vital connection with other agencies" (*CPW*, 8:370).

The radical nature of Arnold's "Democracy" is evidenced if we put it in the context of the authors on the subject who preceded him, Tocqueville and Mill, and the pragmatists who succeeded him. *On Liberty* (1859) had appeared just two years before Arnold's *Popular Education;* but whereas Mill's argument is made in behalf of the "highly gifted" individual's right to develop himself, free from the dictates of the unreflecting "mass," Arnold's plea is in behalf of that mass's right: "no longer individuals and limited classes only, but the mass of a community—to develop itself with the utmost possible fulness and freedom" (*CPW*, 2:8). Mill shares Tocqueville's fear of the "tyranny of the majority," and he celebrates, in romantic fashion, the right of genius to resist and reshape public opinion. (Mill bristles, however, at the thought that he is "countenancing . . . 'hero worship' " of a Carlylean nature; the Millite genius must not force the public into doing his bidding, but he does claim "freedom to point out the way.")[9] But Tocqueville had warned not only of the conformist power of public opinion but also of the excesses of individualism in America, where "Everyone shuts himself up tightly within himself and insists upon judging the world from there." To the French observer, "individualism is of democratic origin": it encourages a self-reliance that prides itself on "contempt for tradition" and disregard for the past, but that also occasions an alienation between man and man, throwing "him back forever upon himself alone and [threatening] in the end to confine him entirely within the solitude of his own heart."[10] From Emerson to William James to Rorty, the individual has remained the romantic intellectual's focus of attention; and this romantic impulse has often pulled against pragmatism's activist streak. Thus, as a liberal of the laissez-faire school, Mill opposes state intervention in public education. He does not oppose the state's requiring that its children be educated, but he demands that parents be free "to obtain the education where and how they pleased." To his mind, a state-run education will only mould "people to be exactly like one another," and is thus to be resisted.[11] Mill's text has become a secular bible for conservatives and radicals alike, all those for whom freedom to go one's own way takes precedence over what Arnold, in *Popular*

Education, called "the strong bond of a common culture" (2:89). In "My Countrymen," Arnold assailed his fellow Liberals for failing to see that "Freedom . . . is a very good horse to ride;—but to ride somewhere" (5:22). And, like Dewey, he suggests that the worship of individual freedom is often done at the expense of the other two principles of the French Revolution, equality and fraternity.

Arnold begins "Democracy" with a glance at Mill's position that no amount of state action is permissible; but, unlike Mill, he accepts the fact that a new force is coming to power—that "democracy" is now in the process of "trying *to affirm its own essence; to live, to enjoy, to possess the world, as aristocracy has tried, and successfully tried, before it*" (*CPW*, 2:7). Supporting the legacy of the French Revolution, Arnold notes how in France democracy has flourished with the aid of a massive state-run educational system, and how the French support the state because they see it working in their name. (As Dewey will say of democracy, it is the one political system in which the dualism between governor and governed disappears.)[12] In England, however, with its traditions supporting self-reliance, there is no rallying point to provide the uneducated masses with a sense of ideals existing beyond the self. "Nations are not truly great solely because the individuals composing them are numerous, free, and active," Arnold maintains; "but they are great when these numbers, this freedom, and this activity are employed in the service of an ideal higher than that of an ordinary man, taken by himself" (2:18). Arnold is not setting up the state as an authoritarian ideal. Rather, he is positing an ideal of the solidarity of men, "a true bond of union," in which the "best self" of each citizen finds a "rallying-point for the intelligence and for the worthiest instincts of the community" (2:19). To those who demand, *"Leave us to ourselves!"* Arnold suggests that they look at the present state of England, to the widespread indifference to beauty, the paucity of intelligence, the scarcity of essential services that such an attitude has prompted: "The State can bestow certain broad collective benefits, which are indeed not much if compared with the advantages already possessed by individual grandeur, but which are rich and valuable if compared with the make-shifts of mediocrity and poverty. A good thing meant for the many cannot well be so exquisite as the good things of the few; but it can easily, if it comes from a donor of great resources and wide power, be incomparably better than what the many could, unaided, provide for themselves" (2:21). To charge Arnold with elitism (as so many do) is to ignore where he stands when it comes to the sharing of education, culture, even health care.

It is in Arnold, not Mill, that Dewey's faith in democracy finds its true forebear. Dewey's early "The Ethics of Democracy" (1888) builds upon Arnold's position that each individual in a democracy is not to be seen as a "disorganized fragment" (as Sir Henry Maine claimed in his attack on *Popular Government*) but rather as a member of an "organism." There is no such thing in reality as a "non-social individual," Dewey maintains, and the Platonic (and liberal) notion that "democratic freedom" means "doing what one likes," without respect for ideals, is wrongheaded. ("For men are solidary, or co-partners; and not isolated," Arnold says in a late religious essay [*CPW*, 8:43].) For Dewey, democracy is itself an ideal, an ideal allowing for each person's right to fulfill himself; and the "democratic ideal includes liberty, because democracy without initiation from within [without that is, in Arnoldian terms, regard for one's "best self"], without an ideal chosen from within and freely followed from within, is nothing." Dewey's democracy is thus "a social, that is to say, an ethical conception"; "it is a form of government only because it is a form of moral and spiritual association." Dewey's vision of democracy is more idealized than Arnold's; but for both educators, the goal of their vocation is the guidance of the masses toward ideals of self-fulfillment (affirming "one's *own essence*") and solidarity. Only a democracy enables every individual to follow the Nietzschean injunction to become what one is; only with "equality," Dewey and Arnold agree, do we have an "ideal of humanity." Dewey ends his essay on the same note with which Arnold ends his essay on George Sand: his may be an ideal, but (to cite James Russell Lowell) " 'I am one of those who believe that the real will never find an irremovable basis till it rests upon the ideal.' "[13]

The pragmatist thrust of Arnold's and Dewey's essays rests upon their belief in the efficacy of the ideal to move us forward. ("Perfection will never be reached," Arnold says in the conclusion to "Democracy"; "but to recognize a period of transformation when it comes, and to adapt ourselves honestly and rationally to its laws, is perhaps the nearest approach to perfection of which men and nations are capable" [*CPW*, 2:29].) And they share an awareness that "civilisation" or "culture" is connected to "character," to conduct. The Arnoldian sense of culture as *Bildung* (which I discussed in the last two chapters) is also Dewey's; and Dewey's democratic ideal (what he later calls "Creative Democracy") is precisely that which Arnold advocated in "A French Eton," wherein the transformation, the "growth in perfection," of the individual is paralleled by the transformation of society as well (2:312–13). To turn from Arnold to a contemporary pragmatist like Rorty is to see how tenaciously this faith in democracy as *Bildung* has persisted, even in one for whom *ideals* and *values* are merely localized and transitory terms.

Rorty's career as philosopher has been the attempt, by turns ironical and serious, to justify both the aesthetic doctrine of self-fulfillment and the liberal appeal to solidarity—despite his sense that there is no foundation to support either belief. In "The Priority of Democracy to Philosophy" (in the Cambridge University Press reprint, capital letters are coyly dispensed with), Rorty's position is that the democratic society we live in is a worthy one even if he cannot offer philosophical reasons to support the claim. (Elsewhere, he celebrates "bourgeois capitalist society as the best polity actualized so far, while regretting that it is irrelevant to most of the problems of most of the population of the planet.") Rorty supports a Rawlsian view of democratic society, in which the "Socratic commitment to free exchange of views [exists] without the Platonic commitment to the possibility of universal agreement"; and he is willing to accept an image of the self as a "centerless web of historically conditioned beliefs and desires." Any attempt to speak of enduring values existing outside or within the self is clearly a waste of time. Claiming Dewey as his source, Rorty argues that "communal and public disenchantment is the price we pay for individual and private spiritual liberation," and that this "liberation" is worth any regressive return to the realm of "philosophical reflection" or "religion." And yet, one can only marvel at the tenacity whereby this disbeliever in all absolutes (Rorty describes his procedure as a kind of Socratic slapstick, a "joshing" of his fellow citizens out of their earnestness) clings, with the sincerity of a romantic pragmatist, to the belief in "individual liberation" and to a faith in democracy as affording "experiments in cooperation."[14] Even without the capital letters, democracy retains a metaphysical sense of priority.

In the *Mixed Essays* Arnold readily admits the lack of absolute standards, and he denies the value of all systematic judgments ("altogether unprofitable"). Still, he points to the examples of Falkland and

Goethe and George Sand for having reflected lucidly and acted generously. Together, they embody an ideal of civilization whose components (in Arnold's view) are the liberty that allows for human "expansion" and a sense of "equality" that encourages human *civility* (*CPW,*
8:371–72). Falkland's personal civility during the time of the English
civil wars makes him "a martyr of sweetness and light" (8:206) to
Arnold. Choosing to fight on the Royalist side, despite his awareness
of its aristocratic "vices" and "delusions," Falkland realized that the
alternative was an unsound Puritan cause that promoted religious
"narrowness" and "intellectual poverty" (201). In giving "himself to
the cause which seemed to him least unsound" (204) because its opponent was opposed to the progressive spirit of the age, but which
contained no more "truth" than its antagonist, Falkland found himself in a "tragic"—and, for Arnold, *modern*—dilemma. A pragmatist's
"tragic sense," Hook argues, derives precisely from this sense that
one is often forced in practice to choose between what is "good" and
what is "right."[15] For Arnold, looking at the unsoundness of the Liberal and Conservative positions of his own time, the individual can
only act in behalf of what is right for the *future*. Falkland's "lucidity of
mind and largeness of temper," Arnold declares " . . . link him with
the nineteenth century. He and his friends, by their heroic and hope-
less stand against the inadequate ideas dominant in their time, kept
open their communications with the future, lived with the future . . .

> To our English race, with its insularity, its profound faith in
> action, its contempt for dreamers and failers, inadequate ideals in
> life, manners, government, thought, religion, will always be a
> source of danger. Energetic action makes up, we think, for imper-
> fect knowledge. We think that all is well, that a man is following
> "a moral impulse," if he pursues an end which he "deems of
> supreme importance." We impose neither on him nor on our-
> selves the duty of discerning whether he is *right* in deeming it so.
> Hence our causes are often as small as our noise about them is
> great. (8:204–5)

If the "impassioned seekers of a new and better world" such as
Falkland fail, Arnold notes, paraphrasing George Sand, that "proves
nothing . . . for the world as it is. Ineffectual they may be, but the
world is still more ineffectual, and it is the world's course which is

doomed to ruin, not theirs" (*CPW*, 8:223). Calling himself a liberal not of the present but "of the future," Arnold identified with the French novelist. In the eloquent essay devoted to her, he speaks of the power of ideals to form "a purged and renewed human society" (220). Sand's idealism is based on intense love—for nature, for the past, for all mankind, beginning with the French peasantry. He sees her as a Wordsworth devoid of any post-Wordsworthian Romantic egoism: "She regarded nature and beauty, not with the selfish and solitary joy of the artist who but seeks to appropriate them for his own purposes [but] . . . as a vast power of healing and delight for all" (226). But she is also a daughter of the Revolution, dismayed by the ideological hatreds of French intellectuals. Rorty has written, without irony, of the ethical power of "edifying" novelists. For Arnold, no novelist was more edifying than Sand, none more committed to what she called "the sentiment of the ideal life, which is none other than man's normal life as we shall one day know it" (219).[16]

Having invoked a pre-Deweyan faith in idealism in the pieces on Falkland and Sand, Arnold argues elsewhere in the *Mixed Essays* the pragmatic view that human development requires a critical examination of the defects of the present. (Pragmatism means "death on bunkum and pretentious abstractions," Hook says, "especially when they are capitalized as Success or Historical Destiny or Reality.")[17] In "Irish Catholicism and British Liberalism," Arnold blames the English, including his fellow Liberals, for failing to see the justice of Irish grievances; and he lambasts the middle class, which prides itself on "knowing how to make money, but not knowing how to live when they have made it" (*CPW*, 8:338). In "Porro Unum Est Necessarium," he points up once again (as Dewey will devote his life to arguing) the value of public education in creating a sense of "social solidity" (8:361), a solidarity that in France translates into an agreeable social life. "If there is one need more crying than another," he says, "it is the need of the English middle class to be rescued from a defective type of religion, a narrow range of intellect and knowledge, a stunted sense of beauty, a low standard of manners. And what could do so much to deliver them and to render them happier, as to give them proper education, public education, to bring them up on the first plane; to make them a class homogeneous, intelligent, civilised?" (369).

In the great essay "Equality" (a remarkable act of confrontation on Arnold's part, since his first audience was the Royal Institute,

" 'the most aristocratic and exclusive place out' " [*CPW*, 8:283]), Arnold attributes the lack of civilization in England to its "religion of inequality" (8:303). Civilization, "the humanisation of man in society," requires that we "make progress towards this, our true and full humanity" (286); but England, with its materialized upper class, its vulgarized middle class, and its brutalized working class, perpetuates a condition in which incivility rules. It is not by the widespread possession of material goods but "by the humanity of their manners that men are equal," Arnold contends. " 'A man thinks to show himself my equal,' " says Goethe, " 'by being *grob*,—that is to say, coarse and rude; he does not show himself my equal, he shows himself *grob*.' But a community having humane manners is a community of equals, and in such a community great social inequalities have really no meaning" (289). However, to attain a community of civility, there must be political equality. No one, Arnold daringly (and pragmatically) argues, has "natural rights"—neither peasant nor nobleman (285). Democratic France, thanks to its "spirit of society" (286), has produced an atmosphere in which people of all conditions feel a sense of companionship with, not alienation from, each other. And thus, Arnold notes (looking to the Liberals as they grapple with the Irish Question), the Alsatians *want* to be part of the affable French "social system," whereas "we offer to the Irish no such attraction" (291).

Acknowledging democracy to be the political power of the future, Arnold deplores the examples of the two classes who have hitherto held power: the aristocracy, incapable of ideas or an aesthetic sense ("They may imagine themselves to be in pursuit of beauty," he scoffs; "but how often, alas, does the pursuit come to little more than dabbling a little in what they are pleased to call art, and making a great deal of what they are pleased to call love!" (*CPW*, 8:301); the middle-class heirs to Puritanism, drugged with religion and business, not knowing, "good and earnest people as they were, that to the building up of human life there belong all those other powers also,—the power of intellect and knowledge, the power of beauty, the power of social life and manners" (294). In what is perhaps the most passionately argued of all his essays, Arnold charges "that we are trying to live on with a social organisation of which the day is over. Certainly equality will never of itself alone give us a perfect civilisation. But, with such inequality as ours, a perfect civilisation is impossible" (304). More than fifty years later, across the ocean, Dewey would make a case similar to Arnold's about the inefficacy of present-day (1935) liberalism, and would argue that it "must now become radical, meaning by 'radical' perception of the necessity of thoroughgoing changes in the set-up of institutions and corresponding activity to bring the changes to pass." And, for both writers, education is the "first object" of a "renascent liberalism," education's task being the encouragement of "the habits of mind and character, the intellectual and moral patterns, that are somewhere near even with the actual movements of events."[18] For the genuine "well-being of the many," as Arnold argues in "Equality," "comes out more and more distinctly . . . as the object we must pursue"(289).

Arnold's pragmatism is, in some respects, more progressive-minded than William James's. On the subject of democracy, for example, James resembles Carlyle more than he does Arnold or Dewey. "If democracy is to be saved," James avowed in 1907, "it must catch the higher, healthier tone" that intellectuals trained in the humanities possess. The aim of the humanities, he says, is to teach stimulating "biographies"—to show what great men have achieved so that we may be provided with diverse "standards of the excellent and durable." History, for Carlyle (for whom democracy meant "despair of finding any Heroes to govern you"), was synonymous with biography, the biographies of heroes. James's Carlylean hero worship is evident in the essays "Great Men and Their Environment" and "The Importance of Individuals" (1880) and in his celebration of those who act, who practice the "strenuous mood," who break the rules, and who exert their free will in defiance of deterministic philosophies. Philosophy itself, James states in *A Pluralistic Universe* (1909), is not the expression of a man's "reasons" but of his "vision": "all definitions of the universe are but the deliberately adopted reactions of human characters upon it."[19]

James's strong individualistic streak—a compound of Emerson's self-reliance, Carlyle's hero worship, and Mill's libertarianism—is accompanied by an unidealized view of the masses. Arnold's disgusted reaction to the Hyde Park rioters of 1866 (a prime example of "doing as one likes," in *Culture and Anarchy*) pales in comparison to James's reaction to demos in action, whether illustrated in the imperialist war fever occasioned by the Spanish-American War or in the "lynching epidemic" that occurred in Massachusetts in 1903. James's tribute to

the college-bred ("the only permanent presence that corresponds to
the aristocracy in older countries") as a bulwark "in our democracy,
where everything else is so shifting," is in keeping with his fear of
that human "carnivore," the uncivilized multitude. In 1892 James
urged teachers to "wean" students "from their native cruelty"; and in
his outcry against the lynchings, he gives way to a Darwinian pessimism absent (perhaps to their loss) in Arnold or Dewey: "The average
church-going Civilizee realizes, one may say, absolutely nothing of
the deeper currents of human nature, or of the aboriginal capacity for
murderous excitement which lies sleeping even in his own bosom.
Religion, custom, law and education have been piling their pressure
upon him for centuries mainly with the one intent that his homicidal
potentialities should be kept under."[20]

Nearly two decades prior to these remarks, James took issue with
Ernest Renan's virulently antidemocratic sentiments. While admitting
his own "dislike" for the Commune (Arnold, in contrast, had sympa-
thized with "that fixed resolve of the [French] working class to count
for something and *live*"), James maintained that the new "Democratic
religion which is invading the Western world" would probably provide for a "political or spiritual hero" to stand "firm till a new order
built itself around him." In the *Talks to Teachers,* he described his
"pluralistic or individualistic philosophy" as one whose "practical consequence . . . is the well-known democratic respect for the sacredness
of individuality," that is to say (with a nod to Mill), "the outward
tolerance of whatever is not itself intolerant." James renamed his
philosophy on several occasions—calling it, variously, "pragmatism"
(in lectures dedicated to Mill, "our leader were he alive today"),
"meliorism," "pluralism," and "radical empiricism"; but in all its incar-
nations, he sought to balance a "personal and romantic view of life"
with a scientific regard for the *"facts of experience."* Dewey perhaps
intended to minimize the confusions occasioned by such a balancing
act when he described James as being "possessed of the spirit of the
artist." One need not be too critical of a thinker who "sees the functions of the mind in terms of drama, and records his insights as
though he were writing for the theatre." But Dewey recognized that
if James veered toward singularity at times—a kind of romantic-
aesthetic waywardness—he also aimed at making artists of his auditors and readers. Paradoxically, the Carlylean individualist promoted

a "radical liberalism," a "philosophy which invites each man to create his own future world."[21]

In the lectures on *Pragmatism* James elaborates on the "creative" aspect of "cognitive" life. "The world stands really malleable," he declares, "waiting to receive its final touches at our hands" (*P,* 167). Truth, hence, is not something we find, but something we make and test: "Truth *happens* to an idea. It *becomes* true, is *made* true by events" (133). It is for remarks of this sort that Rorty has celebrated Jamesian pragmatism for having rejected all truths or values existing prior to the self (truths of science, religion, or "Philosophy") or pertaining to the self—for having promulgated the modernist "sense that there is nothing deep down inside us except what we have put there ourselves, no criterion that we have not created in the course of creating a practice, no standard of rationality that is not an appeal to such a criterion, no rigorous argumentation that is not obedience to our own conventions." What we are left with, thus, is a "post-Philosophical culture—in which men and women [feel] themselves alone, merely finite, with no links to something Beyond."[22] But Rorty's reading ignores the way in which James's pragmatism, like Arnold's, contains a wistful dialogue between the finite and the "Beyond"; it ignores the ways in which James is very much a man of his time, the late Victorian period, and in some respects even behind his time.

Born only twenty years after Arnold (in 1842), James found himself caught in the same dilemma as other Victorians, having seen the grounds for belief eroded by scientific discoveries and yet clinging to a "will to believe." James's pragmatism puts itself forward as a "solution" to those who want *both* "the scientific loyalty to facts . . . , but also the old confidence in human values and the resultant spontaneity, whether of the religious or of the romantic type" (*P,* 33, 26). Hence, F. C. S. Schiller, James's English disciple (who preferred the name "humanism" to "pragmatism"), speaks of the "middle path" this philosophy offers between naturalism and idealism: "it will neither reject ideals because they are not realised, nor yet despise the actual because it can conceive ideals."[23] To a considerable degree, James is updating Carlyle's own "solution," his "Natural Supernaturalism," which redirects human attention to this world and this time sphere. James's focus on the finite and the temporal restates Carlyle's view (expressed as early as 1831, in "Characteristics") that we are "beings that exist in Time, by

virtue of Time, and are made of Time." One might call James's philosophy a version of the Goethean idea, translated and preached by Carlyle
in *Sartor Resartus,* "that your 'America is here or nowhere.' . . . Yes
here, in this poor, miserable, hampered, despicable Actual, wherein
thou even now standest, here or nowhere is thy Ideal."[24] James cor-
rectly labels pragmatism "a new name for some old ways of thinking"
(empiricist methods, in his case, that extend back to Socrates and Aristotle), but he also sees his efforts as part of a "new dawn" in which the
acceptance of our finitude allows us to decide what we are going to
make of ourselves and our world (*P,* 45, 18, 86). "I am finite once for
all," he affirms in *A Pluralistic Universe,* "and all the categories of my
sympathy are knit up with the finite world *as such,* and with things that
have a history" (*APU,* 48). Yet it is a characteristic of our historical
natures to reach beyond ourselves, James avows—not to a Deweyan
sense of community but toward God. Using his pragmatic argument
that whatever "works satisfactorily in the widest sense of the word" is
"true," James is able to accept the divine hypothesis as one that "certainly does work" (192).

Gerald Myers has compellingly argued that James's "pragmatism
was developed to make room for faith."[25] Indeed, if "democracy" is
the thread in Dewey's writings and "culture" in Arnold's, then, "religion" is the omnipresent theme in James. "The most interesting and
valuable things about a man," James proclaims, "are his ideals and
over-beliefs" (*WB,* xiii). In this respect, James is echoing Arnold's
view, in his religious writings, that "the chief exercise of [mankind's]
higher thought and emotion which they have, is their religion" (*CPW,*
7:117); and James would scarcely dispute Arnold's sense that "the
chief guide and stay of conduct, so far as it has any at all, is their
religion" (117). Given his sense of humanity as "carnivores," James
might appear to be adopting a utilitarian defense of religion as an
instrument of control. But that is by no means the intention of the
essays that make up *The Will to Believe* (1897) or of the lectures that pay
tribute to *The Varieties of Religious Experience* (1902). His idol Mill had
modified his position on the "utility of religion": having argued in the
1850s that "those great effects on human conduct, which are com-
monly ascribed to motives derived directly from religion, have mostly
for their proximate cause the influence of human opinion," Mill suggested, two decades later in "Theism," that the "hope" born of religion might well promote a sense of fellow-feeling and duty in believ-

ers.[26] Mill's view (startling to his fellow Liberals, for whom, as Arnold complained, "religion is a noxious thing . . . that . . . must die out" [*CPW*, 7:117]), which denies certainty to both believer and atheist, is James's starting point in *The Will to Believe* volume. But James quickly makes it clear that what Mill condoned, and Arnold praised, as an aid to mankind's social well-being, was for himself the most *personal* of concerns.

In the Preface to *The Will to Believe*, James agrees, with Arnold, that most men lack a sense of Hellenism ("criticism") rather than a sense of Hebraism ("faith"), but the "academic audiences" he is addressing (and of which he is a member), "fed already on science, have a very different need" (*WB*, x). For such people, "criticism" is not what is wanted; and, for James in particular, the Hellenizing that Arnold brought to bear on the Bible is inadequate in certain respects. Where Arnold, for example, treats *Aberglaube* (the belief in miracles or immortality) as "a kind of fairy-tale," part of the Bible's "poetry" but not something subject to scientific verification (*CPW*, 6:212), James accepts this "extra-belief." He calls it "over-belief" in *The Varieties of Religious Experience*, and affirms that this "over-belief on which [he is] ready to make his personal venture" persuades him that "divine facts . . . exist."[27] Preeminent among these divine facts is God Himself; and here James rejects Arnold's abstract definition in *God and the Bible*. James wants "A power not ourselves, . . . which not only makes for righteousness, but means it, and which recognizes us" (*WB*, 122), a personal God, in short. In *A Pluralistic Universe*, James concedes "that the only God worthy of the name *must* be finite" (125) if human beings are to exert their freedom of will (an article of faith to Jamesian pragmatism). Elsewhere, James maintains, "The gods we stand by are the gods we need and can use, the gods whose demands on us are reinforcements of our demands on ourselves and on one another" (*VRE*, 264). Yet James wants to be true to the "unseen world" no less than to the "seen world" (295).

A guiding principle of the French critics admired by Arnold was "ne pas être dupe." James, by advocating the "right to believe" (the title he claims he should have given his famous essay), contends "that worse things than being duped may happen to a man in this world" (*WB*, 19). In an early essay on Renan (1876), James criticized the "dandified despair" flaunted by this favorite of his brother Henry and of Arnold; and his subsequent references to Renan are startling in their ferocity.[28] In *Varieties,* he assaults Renan's "Who cares?" attitude, the French critic's willingness to treat life as an ironic spectacle rather than a strenuous activity (46–47). "The name of Renan," he later notes, "would doubtless occur to many persons as an example of the way in which breadth of knowledge may make one only a dilettante in possibilities, and blunt the acuteness of one's living faith" (380). In "The Dilemma of Determinism," James assails this Renanian attitude as "subjectivism," a spectator's view of life that inevitably degenerates into "the corruptest curiosity," and whose worst sin is "ethical indifference" (*WB,* 170–71). Condemning the "romanticism" of Renan and his aesthetic kind, James invokes Carlyle to say for him, "Hang your sensibilities!" But if the Carlylean message is one Arnold would support ("It says conduct, and not sensibility, is the ultimate fact for our recognition" [174]), James implicates Arnoldian culture, in debased form, among his villains: "if the stupid virtues of the philistine herd do not then come in and save society from the influence of the children of the light," he snarls, "a sort of inward putrefaction becomes its inevitable doom" (172).

The James who pits Carlyle against Renan is not an author one might expect to appeal to another connoisseur of "irony," Richard Rorty. And Rorty is indeed uncomfortable with the James who writes (defying Rorty's antifoundationalism), "If this life be not a real fight in which something is eternally gained for the universe by success, it is no better than a game of private theatricals, from which we may withdraw at will." Rorty has written movingly of the pragmatist enterprise as a matter of "our loyalty to other human beings clinging together against the dark, not our hope of getting things right,"[29] yet he has also praised the Renanian aesthetic antihumanists, Nietzsche and Foucault, who mock such presumptions of solidarity. For James, our ethics and our sanity depend upon our having a something Out-there "which recognizes us." Never mind, he argues, the possibility that we may be duped: "The universe is no longer a mere *It* to us, but a *Thou,* if we are religious" (*WB,* 27). Despite Nietzsche's scorn for saintliness (an attitude James finds "itself sickly enough" [*VRE,* 295]), James compares the visions of saints to "Utopian dreams of social justice" (dreams like those Arnold found in George Sand) that "help to break the edge of the general reign of hardness and are slow leavens of a better order" (*VRE,* 285). In the conclusion to *Varieties,* James asserts that "we belong to" a region beyond self (call it "the mystical region, or the supernatural region") "in a more intimate sense than that in which we belong to the visible world, for we belong in the most intimate sense wherever our ideals belong" (399). In the last resort, he avows, we belong to the supreme "other," to whom James gives the name of God: "We and God have business with each other; and in opening ourselves to his influence our deepest destiny is fulfilled" (399).

James's pragmatist ethics requires a religious sphere, as well as a Carlylean work ethic, to draw mankind out of its isolation and potential murderousness. The melancholy tone of much of Arnold's poetry—the sense, that so haunted Dewey, that "We mortal millions live *alone*"—finds expression in the famous description, in James's *Principles of Psychology,* of the "stream of consciousness": "Absolute insulation, irreducible pluralism, is the law." What the scientist in James and the poet in Arnold had deduced required a counterweight: religion for James, culture for Arnold. For both, what the facts of "experience" reveal, the values emanating from something that transcends the self must counteract. In James's case, science may speak in support of determinism, but "ethics makes a counter-claim" to the effect that "our wills are 'free.' "[30] Comparing Arnold and James, one notes this paradox: while the stoical Englishman trusts to the future (what else is culture but an ideal guiding us forward?), the optimistic American instinctively retreats to the emotional position of a Carlyle or to the Tennyson of *In Memoriam,* who answers the voice of scientific determinism with a confident "I have felt." Whereas the melancholy poet in Arnold gave way to the critic speaking of social solidarity, the scientist in James inevitably bowed to the "personal and romantic" voice. Perhaps even more so than his brother or Arnold, William James was indeed "possessed by the spirit of the artist."

Of Rorty, too, it has been said that he writes with "A Touch of the Poet." One might describe Rorty's career to date as an attempt to redefine philosophy along the lines of romantic poetics, which Rorty sees as the progenitor of pragmatism. In an era when many English professors routinely profess their distaste for "literature"—seeing it as an agent of hegemonic forces, or else essaying to deconstruct its authorial pretensions—it is touching to find a philosopher who praises the power of literature so unstintingly and who draws on credos of literary modernism (such as "Make it new") that have become virtually threadbare through overuse. Lacking James's Victorian confidence in the seriousness of "this life," Rorty has occasionally taken refuge in an ironic posture (he calls it "light-minded aestheticism") that resembles Arnold's notorious "vivacity." Both have been criticized accordingly.[31] One thinks of the famous Max Beerbohm cartoon of Arnold being addressed by his earnest niece (the future novelist Mary Augusta Ward), "Why, Uncle Matthew, Oh why, will not you be always serious?" Arnold's reply ("My vivacity is but the last sparkle of flame before we are all in the dark, the last glimpse of colour before we all go into drab,—the drab of the earnest, prosaic, practical, austerely literal future" [CPW, 3:287]) is prelude to Rorty's apologia in "The Priority of Democracy." Here he claims that his aim of "joshing" his "fellow citizens . . . out of the habit of taking these [traditional philosophical] topics so seriously" is not without a "moral purpose."[32]

Arnold's targets were the enemies of enlightenment, the latter-day Philistines; and his goal, as he told his mother, was to do "what will sap them intellectually." But where Arnold saw Protestant Dissent, with its opposition to culture and state-run education, as the leading obstacle standing in the way of England's necessary transformation, Rorty initially saw "Philosophy," with its pretensions of having discovered universal truth, as the first obstacle to be cleared away. At most, according to Rorty, philosophers can provide an edifying conversation for the benefit of the Zeitgeist. Rorty's recent criticism of neo-Marxist ideologues resembles Arnold's criticism of the Dissenters— both groups sharing a naive faith in the truth of dogma; both incapable of appreciating beauty or art, but seeing them only as forms of "ideology." (Interestingly, Rorty, like Arnold, wrote poetry in his youth.) Attracted initially to the fashionably antifoundationalist views of Wittgenstein and Heidegger, Rorty soon realized that his closest affinity was to the unfashionable Dewey, whose hope had been "that philosophy will join with poetry as Arnold's 'criticism of life.' "[33]

As Rorty's enthusiasm for Heidegger has ebbed, his enthusiasm for Dewey has intensified. "What seems to me most worth preserving in Dewey's work," Rorty has recently affirmed, "is his sense of the gradual change in human beings' self-image which has taken place in recorded history—the change from a sense of their dependence upon something antecedently present to a sense of the utopian possibilities of the future, the growth of their ability to mitigate their finitude by a talent for self-creation." Beginning with Philosophy and the Mirror of Nature (1979), Rorty has praised Dewey's democratic vision: "in his ideal society, culture is no longer dominated by the ideal of objective cognition but by that of aesthetic enhancement."[34] Rorty's first book also draws on Gadamer's preference for "edifying" philosophy over "systematic" philosophy (a preference shared by Arnold), and he invokes Gadamer's substitution of "the notion of *Bildung* (education, self-formation) for that of 'knowledge' as the goal of thinking." However, this crucial German term, so important to Arnold's sense of culture and Gadamer's sense of the humanities (a term, for both of them, *linked* to knowledge), is translated by Rorty to mean "edification," a term that departs from Gadamerian hermeneutics to include personal projects that may be poetically "edifying" without being socially "constructive." And here one can see a source of tension between Rorty's Deweyan allegiance and his romantic-aesthetic predilections. Dewey, after all, sought to break down dualisms—as Arnold implicitly did when he defined knowledge in terms of practice, Hebraism in terms of Hellenism—particularly the dichotomy between self and society. For Rorty, aesthetic delight in the workings of the self (a mixture of Hellenism, Emersonian self-reliance, Germanic *Bildung*, and Bloomian genius-worship) coexists with, but does not necessarily interpenetrate his liberal Deweyan faith in the advancement of the community. For art, as Rorty realizes (to the dismay of the ideologues), does not necessarily serve the people. Like the poetic (but not the critical) Arnold, Rorty sees finite man as inescapably isolated— detached from anything "out there." Perhaps with Arnold's reversal of attitude in mind, Rorty contends, in *Consequences of Pragmatism* (1982) that there is *no* "something, not ourselves, which makes for rigor." "Both the Age of Faith and the Enlightenment seem beyond recovery." The modern self must give up any pretense of seeing "things steadily and [seeing] them whole," he says, and instead must "take a nominalistic, ironic view of oneself."[35]

Rorty's rejection of a humanistic hermeneutics in favor of aesthetic pragmatism has social and ethical "consequences," as he makes clear in his second book. Discussing the transformation of "Nineteenth-Century Idealism" into "Twentieth-Century Textualism," he traces the establishment of a romantically imbued cultural criticism (a critical dynasty extending from Coleridge to Arnold to Trilling) that uses literature to fill up the space left by the disappearance of metaphysical certainties. But humanistic "culture," for all its benign intent, lacks a unifying center; and the inevitable result of literature's displacement of

religious or Enlightenment certainties has been the emergence of the
private vocabularies of a Nietzsche or Foucault. The "strong" modernist textualist (admired by Harold Bloom) becomes, thus, for Rorty a
heroic pragmatist whose goal is to cultivate novelty, privacy, and sometimes (in the case of Nietzsche and Foucault) contempt for humanity—
all contrary to the ideal of the Arnoldian culture-critic. (In *Twilight of the
Idols,* Nietzsche expressed contempt for the spread of higher education, what he called the "democratism of *Bildung.*") "The stimulus to
the intellectual's private moral imagination provided by his strong mis-
readings [the inevitable consequence of making things new], by his
search for sacred wisdom," Rorty observes, "is purchased at the price
of his separation from his fellow-humans." It is to Rorty's credit that he
does not minimize the "moral cost" of the Nietzschean-Foucauldian
enterprise; yet, as a believer in democracy, Rorty champions a democratic society "in which there is room for subjectivity and self-
involvement, room for the kind of private spiritual development that
politically irrelevant philosophers and novelists help us to achieve."
Rorty's reverence for creative genius resembles James's infatuation
with heroism; but Rorty's democratic principles temper his wilder romantic flights. For just as Rorty is almost unique among academics in
his faith in literature, he is also unique in his refusal to hate the democratic society that allows such creativity and self-creation to flourish.[36]
    Dewey figures in Rorty's pantheon as a liberal who championed
solidarity and aesthetic self-creation, but who was perhaps too idealistic to see a potential conflict between the two aims, who saw them
rather as interdependent. In the nineteenth century, Mill had similarly
proposed a marriage of Coleridgean and Benthamite "half-truths," an
alliance of romantic ethics (true for all time) with a liberal faith in
progress (the *Zeitgeist* at work). For Rorty, liberalism and romanticism
make for necessary, if sometimes unwilling, bedfellows; and in place
of Coleridge and Bentham, he offers us Foucault and Habermas, the
former "an ironist who is unwilling to be a liberal," the latter "a liberal
who is unwilling to be an ironist." By embracing both figures, Rorty
concedes that Foucault may provide "a very bad model for a society,"
yet he deserves a "poet's privileges." For it is incumbent upon liberal
democrats that they support a society in which all voices are heard:
"The point of a liberal society is not to invent or create anything, but
simply to make it as easy as possible for people to achieve their wildly
different private ends without hurting each other." (Elsewhere, he

notes the usefulness of Foucault's work.)[37] Rorty's most unsatisfactory book, *Contingency, Irony, and Solidarity* (1989), speaks in behalf of private and public vocabularies, the Foucauldian language of ironic detachment and the Habermasian language of communitarian goals. But having jettisoned, in his early writings, any reason why we should sustain *either* vocabulary, let alone both, he can offer little more here than his personal vision of a "liberal utopia" in which "we ironists" cultivate private gardens while, at the same time, the social-minded dream of a "solidarity" that remains little more than a dream. Rorty's utopia contains an ivory tower for the ironists, plus a stable of writers below who produce edifying novels to sensitize the "nonintellectual" masses. Having reduced all intellectual positions to fictions alone, Rorty has no way to justify the value of his own distinctive fiction, his utopian vision.[38]

In recent years, perhaps in response to the charge of aesthetic detachment, Rorty has strenuously demonstrated his liberal allegiances, often in defiance of the pervasive antiliberalism coming from left and right. He has also spoken in favor of the cultural canon, again in defiance of academic trendiness. "One good reason for having a high culture," he maintains, in support of E. D. Hirsch, Jr.'s defense of a communal heritage, "is to provide an alternative set of fantasies to those current in mass culture"—fantasies that serve as "stimuli to social change." Like Arnold assailing his fellow-liberals for their lack of vision, Rorty has criticized the new left for clinging to an outmoded set of dogmas and for regarding itself as "a saving remnant which despises its opponents too much to argue with them." In *Objectivity, Relativism, and Truth* (1991), he attacks the ideologues within the American academy who preach hatred against the democratic society that supports them, and he criticizes the "Foucauldian left" for "its failure to offer such visions and such suggestions" for change as the Deweyan liberals once did. Only a democratically based culture, he argues (as did Dewey and Arnold), offers room for hope, room for change: "if there is social hope," he affirms, "it lies in the imagination—in people [like Dewey and Roberto Unger] describing a future in terms which the past did not use."[39]

"The School of Resentment," Rorty wittily observes, "made up of people who can single-handedly deconstruct a large social theory faster than a Third World village can construct a small elementary school, does not take kindly to romance." It prefers a "fruitless exercise in nostalgia" (Marxism) to the Deweyan faith in liberal democracy with its hope for the future. And yet, Rorty notes elsewhere, Dewey's philosophy of education does provide a vision and a method that have enabled society to move forward. At times Rorty's disdain for the past exceeds Dewey's own disdain. ("We think that Dewey and Weber absorbed everything useful Plato and Aristotle had to teach, and got rid of the residue.")[40] But because Dewey felt that certain "traditions of the past" stood in the way of progress, he was willing to accept a certain "spiritual impoverishment" in exchange for his pragmatist faith "that the world is recommencing and being remade under our eyes." "For the past as past is gone," Dewey declares in *Liberalism and Social Action* (1935), "save for aesthetic enjoyment and refreshment, while the present is with us. Knowledge of the past is significant only as it deepens and extends our understanding of the present." Such Deweyan disregard for the past might seem to mark a considerable gap between Dewey and Arnold, the former fixated (as Santayana complained) on the "foreground,"[41] the latter supposedly enmeshed (in the eyes of detractors) in a flimsy web called "culture." But many of Dewey's views are extensions or restatements of Arnoldian ideas, especially Arnold's views on education, culture, and democracy. The two men shared a common task as liberals and educators, and they shared a common faith in the efficacy of a democratic culture that included (or came to include, in Dewey's case) the fruits of science, religion, and art. For the remainder of the chapter, hence, I will be focusing on the Arnoldian side of Dewey, while underscoring, at the same time, Arnold's pragmatic side.

With regard to the past, Arnold is by no means animated by the nostalgia of Newman or Carlyle. "The past in itself has no attraction for him." Peter Keating observes; "it is only in so far as the past illuminates, guides, or acts in any way as a model for the present, that he speaks with approval of its study." Hence, Arnold looks for the "modern element" in past history (and literature), and he accuses liberals and Dissenters of failing to follow the spirit of the time. Dewey, too, takes a pragmatic view of the past. "We live," he writes, " . . . in a haphazard mixture of a museum and a laboratory. Now it is certain that we cannot get rid of the laboratory and its consequences, and we cannot by a gesture of dismissal relegate the museum and its specimens to the void. There is the problem of selection, of choice, of discrimination. What are the things of the past that are relevant to our own lives and how shall they be reshaped to be of use?"[42] What, in other words (to rephrase Arnold's question to Clough), can the past *do* for us, and what can we, thus edified, do for the future?

Dewey was born in the year of Mill's *On Liberty* and Darwin's *The Origin of Species* (1859)—the year also of Arnold's first inspection of the superior state-run schools on the Continent—and he quickly found himself in the position of Arnold's pilgrim, "wandering between two worlds." Although Dewey claimed that the loss of his religious beliefs did not affect his philosophic views, he nevertheless admitted to having undergone a "trying personal crisis." From his college days, he retained a strong residue of Hegelian idealism, allied with what he later called the Hegelian "glorification of the here and now."[43] Very early on, Dewey found in science one of the "articles" that constituted his "creed of life." Like Arnold (as well as like William and Henry James), the young Dewey was fascinated by the example of Renan, the seminarian turned science-lover turned ironic aesthete. For Dewey, Renan was fully justified in having put his faith in science: the youthful French author of *The Future of Science* (*L'Avenir de la science*) had seen that, thanks to the French Revolution, ideals were set forth in "practice [in Dewey's words]; knowledge into action." The "development of science" had allowed for that legacy of the Revolution that Arnold praised in "The Function of Criticism at the Present Time": it put "intelligence," for the first time, in the controls.[44]

Despite Dewey's disagreement with Arnold over the superiority of a scientific to a literary education, it should be noted here that in Dewey's earliest descriptions of the scientific method, science plays a role analogous to Arnold's "criticism" (a term Arnold himself partly owed to Renan). Indeed, for Dewey the terms *science, intelligence,* and *criticism* are often interchangeable. As Robert B. Westbrook notes, Dewey regarded science as "a strictly *methodological* conception. . . . The scientific attitude of mind, he said, was apparent whenever beliefs were not simply taken for granted but established as the conclusions of critical inquiry and testing." Arnold's description of criticism as "a free play of the mind on all subjects" (*CPW*, 3:270) suits the experimental role of the Deweyan scientist no less than the (Henry) Jamesian literary critic. In the late essay "Construction and Criticism"

(1930), Dewey restates Arnold's thesis of the necessary connection between criticism and creation ("Critical judgment is . . . not the enemy of creative production but its friend and ally"), and he defines criticism as a universal task whereby we discover how much our beliefs are still "validated and verified in present need, opportunity, and application."[45]

In "Science as Subject-Matter and as Method" (1909), Dewey does take issue with what he interprets to be Arnold's underestimation of a scientific education. (Although Dewey often defers to Arnold, here he sides with Arnold's friendly opponent, T. H. Huxley.) "Without ignoring in the least the consolation that has come to men from their literary education," Dewey argues, "I would even go so far as to say that only the gradual replacing of a literary by a scientific education can assure to man the progressive amelioration of our lot. Unless we master things, we shall continue to be mastered by them; the magic that words cast upon things may indeed disguise our subjection or render us less distinguished with it, but after all science, not words, casts the only compelling spell upon things." That philosophy or criticism should be (in Wittgenstein's memorable phrase) "a battle against the bewitchment of our intelligence by means of language"[46] was an idea shared by Arnold and Dewey. But the notion that science provided the only key to a more humane future was doubted by Arnold. In *Friendship's Garland,* Arnold humorously notes how the well-intending utilitarian "educational creed" of "Archimedes Silverpump, Ph.D" ("We must be men of our age. . . . Useful knowledge, living languages, and the forming of the mind through observation and experiment"), becomes perverted into the illiberal views of Silverpump's pupil, the businessman Bottles: "Original man, Silverpump! fine mind! fine system! None of your antiquated rubbish—all practical work—latest discoveries in science—mind constantly kept excited—lots of interesting experiments—lights of all colours—fizz! fizz! bang! bang! That's what I call forming a man" (*CPW,* 5:70–71). Without disputing the importance of science (he invokes science in his religious writings), Arnold foresaw the possibility that the language of science might become yet another bewitching jargon. At its best, however, science, by liberating mankind from past errors, cleared the way so that "the value of humane letters, and of art also," might "be felt and acknowledged, and their place in education be secured" (10:68–69).

As Dewey gradually came to see the importance of art and religion—and as the twentieth century gave increasing evidence of the potential misuse of science—he qualified some of his earlier scientific optimism. But just as Arnold saw in culture the means of prodding his countrymen toward the future, Dewey saw in the scientific method the means of encouraging us to deal with a universe not "closed" but rather "infinite in space and time, having no limits here or there," a world capable of being transformed by our own efforts and intelligence. Science, he argues in *The Quest for Certainty* (1929), allows us to become artists, working on the inexhaustible "material" afforded by nature (*QC*, 100). Here too, Renan may have affected the young Dewey by having developed a principle of "evolution" (a decade before Darwin's *Origins*) as the law for individuals and society alike. " 'Each individual travels in his turn,' " Dewey in 1890 quotes from Renan's early work, " 'along the line which the whole of mankind has followed, and the series of the development of human reason is parallel to the progress of individual reason.' " To a professional educator, this was a pregnant idea indeed; and by 1893 Dewey was praising "Self-Realization as the Moral Ideal," arguing that the unending activity of education is not a means but "an end in itself."[47] ("There is nothing which a scientific mind would more regret," Dewey says in *The Quest for Certainty*, "than reaching a condition in which there were no more problems" [101].) In practice, Dewey is drawing upon Arnold's activist sense of culture as continuous *Bildung*. For if the author of *Culture and Anarchy* described the sense of "a growing and a becoming [as] the characteristic of perfection as culture conceives it," he also noted that the aim of culture is to beget "a dissatisfaction" with the status quo "which is of the highest value in stemming the common tide of men's thoughts in a wealthy and industrial society" (*CPW*, 5:94, 98).

Only in a democracy, Dewey felt, could the principles of *Bildung* be applied to everyone. But while he defined "Culture and Culture Values" in the Germanic-Arnoldian sense of their aiding the individual expansion of one's talents, Dewey also adopted Arnold's sense of culture as something that prepares the individual for society. (He questions Arnold's "humanistic notion, . . . not in its end, but in its exclusive reliance upon literature and history as means of reaching this end"—missing Arnold's repeated inclusion of science among the ingredient of culture.) "From the broader point of view," Dewey states, "culture may be defined as the habit of mind which perceives and estimates all matters with reference to their bearing on social values and aims." In one of his most suggestive phrases, Arnold calls "education . . . the road to culture";[48] and in one of his last works, a "Special Report" on Continental "Elementary Education" (1886), based on a recent inspection tour, he praises the humanities-centered schools abroad for *humanizing* their students. The fault of English elementary education, he complains, is "that it is so little formative; it gives the children the power to read the newspapers, to write a letter, to cast accounts, and gives them a certain number of pieces of knowledge, but it does little to touch their nature for good and to mould them." Why shouldn't *all* English children, Arnold asks, have the right (hitherto reserved for the privileged classes) to a "fuller cultivation of taste and feeling?" (*CPW*, 11:28).

Dewey's philosophy of education expands upon three basic Arnoldian premises: that in a democracy all students should have access to the best, that critical thinking should be encouraged, and that education should instill a sense of social solidarity. "Education must have a tendency, if it is education, to form attitudes," he asserted in 1936. But "The tendency to form attitudes which will express themselves in intelligent social action is something very different from indoctrination"; education consists, for Dewey, in learning not what to think, but rather in learning to think critically and to think as part of a social dialogue. In response to Walter Lipmann and others who felt (in the 1920s) that democracy had failed to create an enlightened, responsible public, Dewey argued that it was education's task to do just this. "We are born organic beings associated with others," he contends in *The Public and Its Problems* (1927), "but we are not born members of a community. The young have to be brought within the traditions, outlook and interests which characterize a community by means of education; by unremitting instruction and by learning in connection with the phenomena of overt association."[49] The fullest expression of Dewey's pedagogic views is found in *Democracy and Education* (1916); here, he combines Mill's sense of a progressive society as one that allows for "the play of diverse gifts and interests" with an Arnoldian sense of culture as something that encourages solidarity as well as free play of mind ("the capacity for constantly expanding the range and accuracy of one's perception of meanings") for everyone. In a brief account of "The Aims and Ideals of Education," Dewey in 1921 condensed the Arnoldian program into two goals: to transmit "the 'best of what has been thought and said' " and to work for the reformation of society.[50]

Arnold's views on education came out of his experience as inspector of schools and his fight with the Liberal Party's tendency to favor individual rights at the expense of communal responsibilities. He took issue, moreover, with the insensitivity of Liberal leaders like Robert Lowe, for whom public education was treated as little more than a means of training students to pass examinations (Lowe's policy of "payment by results") rather than a means of instructing them in the "power of reading." As a future-oriented liberal, Arnold deplored the negative strain of his party, which permitted, under the slogan of "doing as one likes," a widespread national neglect of minds and bodies. In his reports on English schools, Arnold called attention to the lack of "humanizing" instruction. Unlike "rich" children, who had opportunities to read good books outside of class, the working-class children Arnold inspected were at the mercy of "second or third-rate literature," which would remain henceforth their "principal literary standard"; they (and their middle-class counterparts) received an education that reflected the national obsession with "mechanical processes" at the expense of "intelligence." (Arnold cites, approvingly, Bishop Butler's comment, "Of education, . . . *information itself is really the least part*.") To those skeptical of his "high estimate of the value of poetry in education," Arnold retorts, pragmatically, "Good poetry does undoubtedly tend to form the soul and character; it tends to beget a love of beauty and of truth in alliance together, it suggests, however indirectly, high and noble principles of action, and it inspires the emotion so helpful in making principles operative."[51] In *Culture and Anarchy*, Arnold called for a rethinking of Liberal premises ("turning a stream of fresh and free thought upon our stock notions and habits" [*CPW*, 5:233]) in order to promote an inward and social change. Instead of praising the fruits of industrialism (as Liberals tended to do), we should, he argues, be tending to the increase of education, thereby advancing common goals of "increased sweetness, increased light, increased life, increased sympathy" (5:109).

Arnold's political essays of the 1880s harp on the theme of Liberal irresponsibility. In "The Future of Liberalism" (1882), he derides the Liberal celebration of "heroes of industrial enterprise," who, in their hurry to make a fortune, "have not made the fortunes of the clusters of men and women whom they have called into being to produce for them" (*CPW,* 9:146), and who have left behind a legacy of slums ("hell-holes") and widespread illiteracy. And he mourns the Liberal coddling of the badly educated middle class, with its "effusion and confusion," its lack of ideas and its addiction to empty phrases. (The natural human instinct for "beauty . . . , intellect and knowledge has been maltreated and starved; because the schools for this class, where it should have called forth and trained this instinct, are the worst of the kind anywhere" [9:147–48].) Elsewhere, Arnold laments the English mistreatment of Ireland and the specious (as he sees it) Liberal support for Home Rule as a way of ensuring continued Irish misery. If in the early lectures on Celtic literature Arnold had highlighted the indispensible Celtic components of the English imagination, in his later writings he was incapable of imagining a political disjunction of the two countries that would not be harmful to both sides. Supporting political separatism, he felt, was equivalent to supporting the negative Liberal sense of human beings as detached atoms.

However questionable Arnold's views on Ireland may seem in hindsight, they are consistent with his sense of himself as a "Liberal of the future," one believing in solidarity within nations and co-dependency between nations. (He believed that Ireland and England were as codependent, and mutually supportive, as Alsace and France or Alabama and the Northern States.) Arnold held an organic view of society in which classes and individuals could rise above partisan interests "to the idea of the whole community" (Arnold's idealized "state" [*CPW,* 5:134]). And so did Dewey, whose faith in democracy was sustained from the beginning by his sense "that men are not isolated non-social atoms, but are men only when in intrinsic relations to men."[52] Dewey's faith in democracy is Arnold's belief in culture writ large. If Dewey inherits Arnold's future-oriented liberalism, he does so, like Arnold, in revolt against the outmoded view of liberalism as the party of laissez-faire individualism. Democracy, like culture, provides for the liberation of creative energies; but, Dewey cautions, "Doing as one pleases signifies a release from truly *intellectual* initiative and independence, unless taste has been well developed as to *what* one pleases." And just as the school provides, in Dewey, the educational means for the development of taste (with the help of teachers who "guide the child," as Westbrook notes, "in the subject matter of science and history and art"), so too does the democratic community provide lessons in cooperation and interdependence. The future-oriented liberal, hence, is not one who is "jealous of every extension of governmental activity," but rather one "committed to the principle that organized society must use its powers to establish the conditions under which the mass of individuals can possess actual as distinct from merely legal liberty." But liberalism, according to Arnold and Dewey, must also wean the public and itself from the addiction to "clap-trap" (Arnold's term), from the force of "party politics" wherein (in Dewey's phrase) "words not only take the place of realities but are themselves debauched." It is because of such debasement that Dewey looked to scientific "intelligence"—just as Arnold had appealed to "criticism"—to create a climate of "greater honesty and impartiality [Arnold's "disinterestedness"], even though these qualities be now corrupted by discussion carried on mainly for purposes of party supremacy and for imposition of some special but concealed interest."53

Rorty has characterized Dewey's educational philosophy as one "calculated to change the character of American institutions—to move society to the political left by moving successive generations of students to the left of their parents." But this is another way of saying that Dewey was a lifelong liberal, believing (with Arnold) in the promise of the future despite all the blunders of the present. Dewey himself maintained, in 1936, that the "new social ideals" implicit in his educational views were only "a new version of the very same ideals that inspired the Declaration of Independence," the ideals of democracy forever renewing themselves, and those of liberty and equality finally being applied to all people. As liberals of the future, Dewey and Arnold saw that the real strength of liberal ideals remained to be tested. Both trusted to the idea of liberalism, despite the inevitable debasement of the term, and despite jeers from left and right alike at liberal pretensions.54 They never lost sight of a liberal vision of society and its inhabitants in constant development, always moving toward the unreachable goal Arnold called "perfection." But liberalism also meant, for both, a communal ideal, a dream of associations of men and women (what John Rawls, the most recent defender of the liberal ideal, calls "the idea of overlapping consensus") forming common bonds, as Dewey says, "for the better realization of any form of experience which is augmented and confirmed by being shared." In the end, they invoke a sense of liberalism implicit in the word's original meaning: this is what Arnold's heir Lionel Trilling means when he calls the "job of criticism" a recalling of "liberalism to its first essential imagination of variousness and possibility"; and it is what Rawls means when he describes the ideal social union in terms of an orchestra whose various musicians need one another's complementary gifts in order to flourish individually. Like the Arnold of *Essays in Criticism,* with its appeal "To try and approach truth on one side after another" (*CPW,* 3:286), Dewey in his eighties defined the liberal mission as the "quiet and patient pursuit of truth, marked by the will to learn from every quarter."[55]

What is obvious in even a brief examination of Dewey's and Arnold's views on education and liberalism is the fact that these terms run into each other, and that they keep ending up in Arnold's "culture" and in Dewey's "democracy." Their common mentor, here, is Emerson, whose concept of culture as something that combines the principles of *Bildung* (cultivation of the "best") with a corrective to human isolation anticipates both Arnold's culture and Dewey's democracy. "Culture," says Emerson, "is the suggestion, from certain best thoughts, that a man has a range of affinities through which he can modulate the violence of any master-tones that have a droning preponderance in his scale, and succor him against himself. Culture redresses his balance, puts him among his equals and superiors, revives the delicious sense of sympathy and warns him of the dangers of solitude and repulsion."[56] Arnold's culture and Dewey's democracy resemble each other because they are both processes and ideals, something to steer by and something to steer toward. As Dewey moved toward his own journey's end, he never lost his democratic faith, but, increasingly, he saw democracy as a cultural ideal that needed more than the stimulus supplied by science. By the 1920s, even as he rebutted Lipmann's critique of democracy, Dewey was replacing the pragmatic trust in "experience" with the larger term of *culture.* He realized, soon after its publication, that *Experience and Nature* (1925) should have been titled *Culture and Nature*—the term referring, he explained, to more than what Arnold and his followers meant by *culture:* "the whole body of beliefs, attitudes, dispositions which are scientific and 'moral' "; a world in which facts and values are no longer at odds and in which the "scientific" coexists with the " 'ideal' (even the name 'spiritual,' if intelligibly used)."[57]

The later Dewey, hence, turns increasingly to the world of art and religion to extend the range of experience available in a democratic culture. And here his Arnoldian affinities cause him to adopt a rather different position from the one Rorty claims for Dewey—"following [in the unlikely company of Foucault and Derrida] through on Enlightenment secularization by, roughly, pragmatizing and demetaphysicizing culture." On the contrary, Dewey, as early as 1920, in *Reconstruction in Philosophy*, imagined a revival of "the religious spirit," set within the kingdom of the earth (this resembles Arnold's position in his religious writings) and inspiring a poetry and religion that arise out of hope, not fear. That the "old beliefs have dissolved" (*QC*, 71) Dewey knew no less than did the Arnold of "The Study of Poetry" ("not a creed which is not shaken, not an accredited dogma which is not shown to be questionable" [*CPW*, 9:161]), but that does not prevent the desire for "standards, principles, rules." Like Arnold, he redefines these standards as "hypotheses" that are endlessly "tested and confirmed—and altered," losing "all pretence of finality—the ultimate source of dogmatism" (*QC*, 277). In *Reconstruction* Dewey updates Arnold's appeal to "criticism," calling for a new "poetry and religious feeling," born of the union between "science and emotion" that has been facilitated by a new, clearsighted "philosophy."[58]

Arnold's massive attempt at Hellenizing the Bible led him to the conclusion that, in spite of the efforts of "modern liberalism," people "cannot do without" religion, even as "they cannot do with it as it is." In wanting the joy provided by religious faith, they "are on firm ground of experience" (*CPW*, 7:378–81). Mill came round to this position (which William James never lacked), and eventually, in his own way, so did Dewey. In *Human Nature and Conduct* (1922) Dewey questions Arnold's habit of treating cognition and righteous action, Hellenism and Hebraism, as separate faculties. (In the conclusion to *Literature and Dogma*, Arnold, somewhat disingenuously, claimed that "In praising culture, we have never denied that conduct, not culture, is three-fourths of human life" [*CPW*, 6:407].) "Potentially," Dewey retorts, "conduct is one hundred per cent of our acts." In *A Common Faith* (1934), his Jamesian defense of the religious impulse (as opposed to organized religion), Dewey again challenges the Arnoldian "opposition between Hellenism and Hebraism," not realizing that Arnold himself had implicitly been arguing all along that knowledge and action, the love of truth and beauty and right conduct, are interlinked. Arnold was pleased by the popular success of these rhetorical terms, and while he spoke of their being a "distinction on which more and more will turn,"[59] he nevertheless did not doubt "the old and true Socratic thesis of the interdependence of virtue and knowledge" (8:162). For, as Dewey argues, "Intelligence becomes ours in the degree in which we use it and accept responsibility for consequences" (*HNC*, 314). But humanity requires "symbols" to draw forth their "reverences, affections, and loyalties," and perhaps the most potent symbol of the "communal sense" (330) is that which finds expression in the religious impulse.[60]

As much as Dewey would have liked for the democratic community to constitute the only needful source of faith, and as much as he might have wished for science to provide the only earthbound hypotheses, he was obliged to recognize, in *A Common Faith*, the psychological need for a belief that links the real world and the ideal. "I should describe this faith," he offers, "as the unification of the self through allegiance to inclusive ideal ends, which imagination presents to us and to which the human will responds as worthy of controlling our desires and choices" (*ACF*, 33). "In a distracted age," there is a particular need for an "*active* relation between ideal and actual to which [Dewey gives] the name 'God' " (51), and such a name "may protect man from a sense of isolation and from consequent despair or defiance" (53). In the end, however, Dewey's own faith is in the union of knowledge and conduct that (like Arnold in the *Mixed Essays*) he calls "civilization." "The things in civilization we most prize," he says, "are not of ourselves. They exist by grace of the doings and sufferings of the continuous human community in which we are a link. Ours is the responsibility of conserving, transmitting, rectifying and expanding the heritage of values we have received that those who come after us may receive it more solid and secure, more widely accessible and more generously shared than we have received it" (87).

In *Art as Experience* (1934) the Arnoldian faith in the humanizing power of civilization reaches its Deweyan climax. Here, the man accused by Lewis Mumford of having no aesthetic sense, no appreciation of the imagination, writes knowingly, and sometimes eloquently of art as the consummate human "experience." Dewey describes art's capacity to imagine a better world as the consummate "criticism of life." (The book's wealth of citations reveals that Dewey, in 1934, was as familiar with Cezanne, van Gogh, and Matisse as he was with Goethe, Johnson, Keats, Shelley, George Eliot, Tolstoy, Pater—and, of course, Arnold.) Arnold's "dictum that poetry is criticism of life" is true, Dewey contends, because art imagines "possibilities that contrast with actual conditions. A sense of possibilities that are unrealized and that might be realized are when they are put in contrast with actual conditions, the most penetrating 'criticism' of the latter that can be made." Moreover, in a world in which "mortal millions live *alone*," "works of art are the only media of complete and unhindered communication between man and man that can occur in a world full of gulfs and walls that limit community and experience."[61] There are other (and nonpragmatic) ways to describe and defend artistic experience, but Dewey here provides perhaps the fullest answer to the Arnoldian query, "What does it *do* for you?"

In stressing areas where Arnold and Dewey have shared interests, I have underplayed their differences in taste and sensibility. Arnold makes more of the internal dimension of culture and education than does Dewey, although both ultimately agree on the social ends of these two forces. And even though his aesthetic sensibility is less refined and more utilitarian than, say, Pater's or Henry James's, Arnold had a far deeper awareness than Dewey of the qualitative nature of beauty and art (of poetry's "natural magic," for example [*CPW*, 3:33]). In the essay on Wordsworth, Arnold faults those who prize the "philosophy" over the "poetry" (9:48). Still, Arnold and Dewey were critics active in the public arena, fighting in behalf of a liberal society that they saw beckoning in the future. "That promised land it will not be ours to enter," Arnold realized; ". . . but to have desired to enter it, to have saluted it from afar, is already, perhaps, the best distinction among contemporaries" (3:285). Opposing (like Falkland) "the inadequate ideals dominant in their time," Arnold and Dewey "kept open their communications with the future, lived with the future."

All his life, Dewey sought a way for philosophy to bridge the gap between the old order and the new, between a feudal and a democratic world. In 1946 (Dewey's eighty-seventh year), with yet another terrible reminder of man's cruelty to man recently experienced, he once more cited Arnold in connection with the fate of humanity, "Wandering between two worlds, one dead, / The other powerless to be born." But he remained confident in the possibility of philosophy—a philosophy that transmuted Arnold's belief in civilization into his own faith in "creative democracy"—to project pragmatic ideals sufficient to "give intelligent direction to men in search for ways to make the world more one of worth and significance, more homelike, in fact. There is no phase of life, educational, economic, political, religious, in which inquiry may not aid in bringing to birth that world which Matthew Arnold rightly said was as yet unborn."[62]

Notes

All Arnold prose quotations cited in the text (as *CPW*) are from *The Complete Prose Works of Matthew Arnold*, ed. R. H. Super, 11 vols. (Ann Arbor: University of Michigan Press, 1960–77).

INTRODUCTION

1. A. C. Benson describes the occasion of Arnold's Eton lecture in *Memories and Friends* (New York: G. B. Putnam's Sons, 1924), 20–21.
2. Gadamer, *Dialogue and Dialectic: Eight Hermeneutical Studies on Plato*, trans. P. Christopher Smith (New Haven: Yale University Press, 1980), 126, 154, 152; Pater, *Plato and Platonism* (London: Macmillan, 1901), 188; Michael Holquist, *Dialogism: Bakhtin and his World* (London: Routledge, 1990), 25; Gadamer, *Truth and Method*, trans. Joel Weinsheimer and Donald G. Marshall (New York: Crossroad, 1991), 14.
3. Pater similarly discusses the tension between Greece's "centrifugal tendency" ("that passion for novelty noted in them by Saint Paul," that "Ionian ideal" that reflected Athens's "roaming," seafaring spirit) and the centripetal Dorian pull toward order (*Plato and Platonism*, 23–24).
4. Collini, *Public Moralists: Political Thought and Intellectual Life in Britain, 1850–1930* (Oxford: Clarendon Press, 1991). Arnold mentions his fondness for disparate kinds of writers and cultures in a letter to Lady Louisa de Rothschild, and he describes Goethe and Wordsworth as "the two moderns (very different) I most care for" (Arnold, *Letters*, ed. George W. E. Russell, 2 vols. [New York: Macmillan, 1895], 1:280). When, shortly after finishing the Wordsworth anthology for Macmillan, Arnold set to work on a collection of Byron's poetry, his publisher expressed astonishment: "But what a strange pair to have to hand to the British Public, with your blessing on each!" (See William E. Buckler, *Matthew Arnold's Books: Toward a Publishing Diary* [Geneva: Librairie Droz, 1958], 148). Among the many studies devoted to Arnold and his sources, three that I have found particularly useful are Warren D. Anderson, *Matthew Arnold and the Classical Tradition* (Ann Arbor: University of Michigan Press, 1965); Ruth apRoberts, *Arnold and God* (Berkeley: University of California Press, 1983); and Joseph Carroll, *The Cultural Theory of Matthew Arnold* (Berkeley: University of California Press, 1982).
5. Gadamer, *Philosophical Hermeneutics*, trans. and ed. David E. Linge (Berkeley: University of California Press, 1976), 66; Samuel Taylor Coleridge, *Writings on Shakespeare*, ed. Terence Hawkes (New York: Capricorn Books, n.d.), 167; Carlyle, "Characteristics," in *The Works of Thomas Carlyle*, ed. H. D. Traill, 30 vols., Centenary

Edition (London: Chapman and Hall, 1898–1901), 28:7. "Intentionally or not,"
Tzvetan Todorov argues in *Mikhail Bakhtin: The Dialogical Principle* (trans.
Wlad Gozich [Minneapolis: University of Minnesota Press, 1984], x), "all discourse is in
dialogue with prior discourses on the same subject, as well as with discourses yet
to come, whose reactions it foresees and anticipates. A single voice can make itself
heard only by blending into the complex choir of other voices already in place." A
number of the contributors to *Matthew Arnold 1988: A Centennial Review*, ed. Miriam
Allott, *Essays and Studies* 41 (John Murray, 1988), stress Arnold's dialogical nature
(e.g., John P. Farrell's " 'What You Feel, I Share': Breaking the Dialogue of the
Mind with Itself," 45–61). Donoghue, *Walter Pater: Lover of Strange Souls* (New
York: Knopf, 1995).

6. Honan, *Matthew Arnold: A Life* (New York: McGraw Hill, 1981), chap. 17 (e.g., pp.
398–99, 407–9).

7. In *Friendship's Garland* Arnold plays with the image reviewers have constructed of
him, that of an "elegant Jeremiah," a "transcendentalist" who writes in a "half-
foreign style" and who prattles on about the values of "culture." See *Matthew
Arnold, Prose Writings: The Critical Heritage*, ed. Carl Dawson and John Pfordresher
(London: Routledge & Kegan Paul, 1979), 209–24 (Henry Sidgwick), 198–201
(Fitzjames Stephen), 225–37 (Frederic Harrison's "Culture: A Dialogue," which
Arnold said caused him to laugh till he cried).

8. In the introduction to his edition of *Culture and Anarchy and Other Writings* (Cambridge: Cambridge University Press, 1993), Stefan Collini discusses Arnold's "heterodox and remarkably radical" theme in "Equality," all "the more so for the fact
that it was first given as an address to the gathering of scientists, literati, and members of society who made up the audience of the Royal Institution" for the Promo-
tion, Diffusion, and Extension of Science and of Useful Knowledge (xxiii). With
similar audacity, Arnold, in his essay "The Future of Liberalism" (1880), invited
Lord Derby, a eulogist of England's industrial progress, to take a look at the
industrial slums located within close reach of his estate at St. Helens. (Lord Derby
subsequently introduced Arnold when he delivered his "Liverpool Address.")

9. Bakhtin, *Problems of Dostoevsky's Poetics*, trans. Caryl Emerson (Minneapolis: Uni-
versity of Minnesota Press, 1984), 6, 166. And see Todorov, *Mikhail Bakhtin*, 87; and
Morson and Emerson, *Mikhail Bakhtin: Creation of a Prosaics* (Stanford: Stanford
University Press, 1990), 61. Morson and Emerson, fittingly, cite George Eliot and
Gerard Manley Hopkins ("Glory be to God for dappled things") to illustrate Bakh-
tin's position. I discuss the German influence on the Victorians in "Meredith and
Bakhtin: Polyphony and Bildung," *Studies in English Literature* 28 (Autumn 1988),
693–712; and "Goethe and the Victorians," *Carlyle Annual* 13 (1992/93): 17–34.

10. Dickstein, *Double Agent: The Critic and Society* (New York: Oxford University Press,
1992), 28. Miriam Allott, in " 'Both/and' or 'either/or'?: Arnold's Mind in Dialogue
with Itself" (*The Arnoldian*, Centenary issue, 15 [Winter 1987–88]: 1–13), writes, "If
it is Arnold's inveterate mental habit to move between alternatives, it is also his
habit to exploit the movement for whatever it will contribute towards the making
of a firm 'assiette.' . . . His own 'movement of mind' is less a fluctuation than a
perpetuum mobile between certain fixed polarities whose values are determined
by the needs of successive 'epochs' of cultural history" (12).

11. Those who currently call for ending the "culture wars" by institutionalizing the teaching of the conflicts would attract Arnold's scorn, I think, because of their underlying assumption that individual instructors are capable of only a single point of view: "Older Male Professor" versus "Young Feminist Professor," for example. Exposing students to a variety of attitudes is not the same thing as exposing them to a variety of ideas. (See Gerald Graff, "How to Save 'Dover Beach,' " in *Beyond the Culture Wars* [New York: Norton, 1992], 37–63.) Arnold's response to those who prefer teaching attitudes to teaching literature might resemble his response to the Nonconformist minister who boasted of the squabbles between religious factions in his parish: " 'Only think of all the zeal and activity which the collision calls forth!' 'Ah, but, my dear friend,' I answered, 'only think of all the nonsense which you now hold quite firmly, which you would never have held if you had not been contradicting your adversary in it all these years!' " (*CPW,* 5:244).

12. Charles Augustin Sainte-Beuve, "Lettres d'Eugénie de Guérin," *Nouveaux lundis* 9 (Jan. 2, 1865): 250; Sainte-Beuve, "What Is a Classic?" in *Selected Essays,* trans. and ed. Francis Steegmuller and Norbert Guterman (Garden City: Doubleday Anchor Books, 1964), 11.

CHAPTER ONE

1. James, *Literary Criticism* (henceforth *LC*), ed. Leon Edel and Mark Wilson, 2 vols. (New York: Library of America, 1984), 1:723, 720, 730. James's virtually complete library of Arnold's books is catalogued (with one or two omissions) by Edel and Adeline R. Tintner, in *The Library of Henry James* (Ann Arbor: UMI Press, 1987), 19.

2. James, *William Wentworth Story and His Friends,* 2 vols. in one (New York: Grove Press, 1957), 2:208; James, *Autobiography,* ed. F. W. Dupee (New York: Criterion, 1956), 507.

3. James, Sr., quoted in F. O. Matthiessen, *The James Family* (New York: Knopf, 1961), 219 (Arnold is referring to Jesus [see, e.g., *CPW,* 6:115]; James, *A Little Tour in France* (Boston: Houghton, Mifflin, 1884), 160, 225, 242–43 (James is quoting from memory Arnold's "A Southern Night," "Morality," and "The Church at Brou"); *The Awkward Age* (London: Penguin, 1987), 58 (reference to Arnold's "To a Friend," l. 10, which James cites again in 1899 in "The Present Literary Situation in France" apropos of Zola; *LC,* 1:122); "The Pupil," in *Complete Tales of Henry James* (henceforth *CT*), ed. Leon Edel, 12 vols. (Philadelphia: Lippincott, 1961–64), 7:417; *The Tragic Muse* (London: Penguin, 1978), 125; "Lady Barberina," *CT,* 5:223, 255, 287; *The Portrait of a Lady* (London: Penguin, 1986), 107 (I have restored the three "own"s from the 1881 text.) In *The Sacred Fount,* James transforms Arnold's famous description of God, "the eternal power, not ourselves, which makes for righteousness" (*God and the Bible, CPW,* 7: 201), into a description of love as "the power not one's self . . . that made for passion" (*The Sacred Fount* [New York: Grove Press, 1953], p. 17).

4. James, *Portrait,* 79; *The Wings of the Dove* (London: Penguin, 1986), 107; *The Golden Bowl* (London: Penguin, 1987), 172; *The Ambassadors* (London: Penguin, 1986), 112.

5. See, for example, Chris Baldick, *The Social Mission of English Criticism: 1848–1932* (New York: Oxford University Press, 1987); or Cornel West, "Decentering Europe: A Memorial Lecture for James Snead," *Critical Quarterly* 33 (Spring 1991): 6–9. Mary W. Schneider, in *Poetry in the Age of Democracy: The Literary Criticism of Matthew Arnold* (Lawrence: University Press of Kansas, 1989), argues in Arnold's defense that he "was offering a new declaration of the rights of humankind—the right to know the best" (104).

6. James, *Autobiography*, 95, 94.

7. *LC*, 1:172. Before writing the essay "Mr. and Mrs. Fields" (1915), from which these words come, James emphasized, in a memo to himself, "don't drop above all the Matthew Arnold reference" concerning the *Essays* "and with what intense emotion I read 'em." James, *The American Essays*, ed. Leon Edel (New York: Vintage, 1956), 282.

8. *LC*, 1:714, 711–12 (*North American Review*, July 1865).

9. For Arnold's favorable reception in America (by James and Emerson, among others), see John Henry Raleigh, *Matthew Arnold and American Culture* (Berkeley: University of California Press, 1957), and Leon Edel, *Henry James: The Untried Years* (Philadelphia: Lippincott, 1953), 205–8, 223–27. James, "An American Art Scholar: Charles Eliot Norton" (1909), *American Essays*, 120–21, 127. For Arnold's influence on James's criticism, see Susan B. Daugherty, *The Literary Criticism of Henry James* (Athens: Ohio University Press, 1981); Vivien Jones, *James the Critic* (New York: St. Martin's Press, 1985); Morris Roberts, *Henry James's Criticism* (Cambridge: Harvard University Press, 1929).

10. See Alwyn Berland, "Henry James and the Aesthetic Tradition," *Journal of the History of Ideas* 23 (July–Sept. 1962): 407–19; Edward Engelberg, "James and Arnold: Conscience and Consciousness in a Victorian 'Kunstlerroman,' " *Criticism* 10 (Spring 1968): 93–115.

11. Both Arnold and James believed that a nation's "civilization" could be gauged by the quality of its stage. (See James, *The Scenic Art*, ed. Allan Wade [New York: Hill and Wang, 1957], 22.) Arnold, "The French Play in London," *CPW*, 9:64–85. When writing *Guy Domville*, James was perhaps consciously trying to be part of this civilizing mission. (It was at the theater, after all, that his "free play of mind" was first activated.) See James's preface to the New York edition of *The Tragic Muse* (*LC*, 2:1116), where he recalls Arnold's plea for an "organized theater."

12. *LC*, 1:718; 2:434. James's review of Scherer (*Nation*, April 6, 1876) preceded Arnold's "A French Critic on Goethe" by nearly a year. His success with the 1865 Arnold review and the first (*Nation*, Oct. 12, 1865) of his pieces on Scherer prompted James to ask Norton if he could write on "Recent French Criticism"—an offer he retracted a few months later, feeling "incompetent to the enterprise." See James, *Letters*, ed. Leon Edel, 4 vols. (Cambridge: Harvard University Press, 1974–84), 1:62, 64.

13. *LC*, 1:857 (*Nation*, Dec. 21, 1865: Dickens), 1317 (*Nation*, July 13, 1865: Trollope), 958 (*Galaxy*, March 1873: Eliot), 629, 631–33 (*Nation*, Nov. 16, 1865: Whitman).

14. Lionel Trilling, *Matthew Arnold* (1939; reprint, New York: Meridian Books, 1955), 361.

15. *LC*, 2:803.

16. *LC*, 1:7 (*North American Review*, April 1866); Arnold, "To a Friend," 1. 1.

17. *LC*, 2:669 (*Nation*, Feb. 18, 1875), 684, 681, 679 (revising this Jan. 1880 *North American Review* piece on Sainte-Beuve in 1904, James changed "unliterary function" to "unliterary condition").

18. James, *Letters*, 1:77.

19. Quoted in Edel, *The Untried Years*, 322; James, *Letters*, 1:77. Arnold's tribute to America, in "My Countrymen," is ascribed to a fictive "friend," who also notes the American worship of "Buncombe" (hence, James's insistence that he is speaking "without cant"?).

20. *LC*, 1:714; James, *The Art of Travel*, ed. Morton Dauwen Zabel (Garden City: Doubleday Anchor Books, 1962), 145; "A Passionate Pilgrim," *CT*, 2:289–94; "The Madonna of the Future," *CT*, 3:15, 18 (by "critical" James here means "realistic"); Arnold, *Letters*, ed. George W. E. Russell, 2 vols. (New York: Macmillan, 1895), 2:55.

21. "The Author of 'Beltraffio,' " *CT*, 5:331, 334.

22. James, *French Poets and Novelists* (1878; reprint, New York: Grosset & Dunlap, 1964), 89, 65, 243, 185.

23. *Roderick Hudson* (London: Penguin, 1968), 123; *The American* (London: Penguin, 1986), 105–6; *The Ambassadors*, 512. Gay Wilson Allen, in *William James: A Biography* (New York: Viking Press, 1967), suggests that Babcock is a satiric portrait of William (207).

24. *LC*, 2:1208.

25. "A Bundle of Letters," *CT*, 4:448, 455, 463–64, 439–40. The derogatory phrase was applied to James by Robert Buchanan (*Universal Review* 3 [March 1889]: 355–59; reprinted in *Henry James: The Critical Heritage*, ed. Roger Gard [London: Routledge & Kegan Paul, 1968], 187). In the year of "A Bundle of Letters," Richard Grant White, reviewing *The Europeans*, bracketed James with Arnold as French-schooled writers of "fastidious taste" (*North American Review* 128 [Jan. 1879]: 101–6; reprinted in *Critical Heritage*, 56).

26. "The Point of View," *CT*, 4:504–8; *Hawthorne*, in *LC*, 1:351; "The Point of View," *CT* 4:506, 508.

27. *CT* 4:486–88, 503, 495, 497–98; James, *Letters*, 2:162; "The Point of View," *CT* 4:512–13.

28. James, *Notebooks*, ed. F. O. Matthiessen and Kenneth B. Murdock (New York: Oxford University Press, 1961), 23–24; James, *Letters*, 1:209; 2:20 (Flaubert and his circle "are extremely narrow," he wrote his mother in 1876, "and it makes me rather scorn them that not a mother's son of them can read English"), 2:135, 120.

29. James, *Wentworth Story*, 1:208; *Letters*, 2:371 (to Alice); *Autobiography*, 593. Edel suggests, in *Henry James: The Conquest of London* (Philadelphia: Lippincott, 1962), that James was particularly put off by Arnold's monocle (122–25).

30. James, *Letters*, 2:342; Park Honan, *Matthew Arnold: A Life* (New York: McGraw-Hill, 1981), 400; Edel, *Conquest of London*, 394.

31. Higginson, *North American Review* 272 (July 18, 1879): 99; Arnold, *Letters*, ed. Russell, 2:232–33. See Super on the Arnold-James interchange in *CPW*, 10:449–51.

32. Arnold, *The Letters of Matthew Arnold*, ed. Cecil Y. Lang (Charlottesville: University Press of Virginia, 1996–), 1:95 (Professor Lang very kindly provided me with the

galleys for volume one of this edition-in-progress). As Super notes (*CPW*, 5:450), Bright had probably spoken of American "inventions," not "information," as the *Times* (Arnold's source) quoted it. See *CPW*, 7:49, where Arnold cites Renan to disprove Higginson's claims for America.

33. "The Point of View," *CT* 4:508; Higginson, 99.

34. Arnold, *Letters*, ed. Russell, 1:326; James, *Letters*, 1:152; Arnold, *Letters*, ed. Russell, 1:213, 359–60.

35. Arnold, *Letters*, ed. Russell, 1:326; Arnold on *Roderick Hudson*, quoted by Super, *CPW*, 10:452. Arnold's phrase about Americans who hop "backwards and forwards over the Atlantic" comes from a columnist in the *Boston Daily Advertiser* (Nov. 18, 1879) who reproached him for basing his poor opinion of America on the abominable tourists he saw and on those expatriates who complain of their small remittances. If Arnold wishes to see America at its best ("a manner of life belonging to the highest civilization"), he should leave the big cities (with their "Keltic" immigrants) and wander into the interior, to towns and states unknown to him or to those Americans ashamed of their country (2). It was this last suggestion that perhaps led to Arnold's extensive citing of a British traveler's account of a Denver family whose narrowness mirrored the Philistine prototype in England.

36. In *The Princess* James uses the terms *socialism* and *democracy* interchangeably (see chaps. 17–18, for example).

37. "If Matthew Arnold lectures in Boston," James wrote Grace Norton in October 1883, "*do* go and hear him—not because he will lecture well; but because I want him to succeed!" (*Letters*, 3:12). To Perry, a month later, James regretted his friend's disappointment at "poor dear old Mat. I like him—love him rather—as I do my old portfolio, my old shoe-horn: with an affection that is proof against anything he may say or do today, and proof also against taking him too seriously." At age forty, ten years after the meeting in Rome, James felt the need to demonstrate to Perry that he was standing on his own feet now, which perhaps accounts for the tone of these comments and the description of his recent essay on Arnold as having been written "in a manner absolutely fulsome" (*Letters*, 3:14). Shortly before his return trip to England, Arnold wrote James to thank him for his "more than kind article. . . . I remember hearing with pleasure, when first you came over to Europe, of your telling some one that you felt to owe me a debt for gratification received from my writings; if you so felt, you have now paid your debt indeed." (I am grateful to Cecil Y. Lang for providing me with a copy of this letter, which will appear in his ongoing edition of Arnold's letters.)

38. *LC*, 1:726–27; Griffin, *Fortnightly Review* 41 (Jan. 1884): 61, 63. (In "Civilisation in the United States," Arnold cites Griffin's harsh view of America.)

39. Arnold makes the same point about Goethe in the essay on Heine.

40. Arnold to James (March 7, 1884), quoted by Super, *CPW*, 10:518–19. See Arnold, *Unpublished Letters*, ed. Arnold Whitridge (New Haven: Yale University Press, 1923), 54–55.

41. James, *LC*, 2:351–52. James and Arnold were at one, in the 1880s, in seeing the modern newspapers as symptoms of the "sinking of *manners*, in so many ways, which the democratization of the world brings with it" (James, *Notebooks* for Nov. 17, 1887, 82).

42. W. C. Brownell astutely describes Arnold's unhappiness "in dealing with America. He could not let us alone. He seemed to be haunted by the desire to subject us, also, to his discrimination. But he could not, I fancy, quite characterize us to his satisfaction" (*Victorian Prose Masters* [New York: Scribner, 1901], 173). And see Trilling, *Matthew Arnold*, 357–67.

43. James, *Partial Portraits* (1888; reprint, Ann Arbor: University of Michigan Press, 1970), 92. Arnold admitted to liking Turgenev's novels (see Super, *CPW*, 11:467), but he rarely chose to write about a contemporary; in this, he differed from James, who generally wrote only about his contemporaries.

44. James, *Partial Portraits*, 124, 2, 29–30; Brownell, *Victorian Prose Masters*, 155.

45. James, *Partial Portraits*, 292, 322, 370. Jones, in *James the Critic*, sees Arnold as James's target, but Ruskin is clearly intended: see James's essay on Venice (written in 1882, a year before the "Du Maurier"), where he speaks of Ruskin's "narrow theological spirit, the moralism à tout propos, the queer provincialities and pruderies" (reprinted in *The Art of Travel*, 335–36). Arnold, by contrast, was Du Maurier's and James's ally in the fight against Philistinism.

46. James, *Partial Portraits*, 296–97, 406, 381, 406.

47. James, *Letters*, 3:244; "An Animated Conversation," *LC*, 1:72–73. James had also left far behind the rather superficially "cosmopolitan" stance he had claimed for himself in 1877, as one "seeing many lands and feeling at home in none," as one so detached from any one country as to see "the merits of all peoples" (*Portraits of Places* [Boston: J. R. Osgood and Company, 1884], 75–78). Adeline R. Tintner, in *The Cosmopolitan World of Henry James* (Baton Rouge: Louisiana State University Press, 1991), examines the evolution of James's cosmopolitanism, and notes that the ideal itself changed during James's lifetime.

48. James, *LC*, 1:651–52, 665, 695.

49. *LC*, 1:652; James, *The Question of Our Speech; The Lesson of Balzac: Two Lectures* (Boston: Houghton Mifflin, 1905), 10; *The American Scene*, New York: Horizon Press, 1967), 54, 64.

50. James, *The American Scene*, 85, 124 (*LC*, 1:664), 133, 374. Arnold, with his romantic feeling for "lost causes," was less negatively disposed to the South than James. See Sidney Coulling, "Matthew Arnold and the American South," in *Matthew Arnold in His Time and Ours: Centenary Essays*, ed. Clinton Machann and Forrest D. Burt (Charlottesville: University Press of Virginia, 1988), 40–56. A touch of Southern blood in a Jamesian protagonist (Roderick Hudson, Basil Ransom) is generally enough to doom him to ineffectuality.

51. Kaplan, *Henry James: The Imagination of Genius* (New York: Morrow, 1992), 291–96. Sidney Coulling describes the press's reaction to Arnold on Wales in *Matthew Arnold and His Critics* (Athens: Ohio University Press, 1974), 174.

52. From Renan's "La poésie des races celtiques" (first published in the *Revue des Deux Mondes* in 1854), Arnold got his four Celtic groupings, his sense of the defiant and melancholy mood pervasive in the Celtic race (and of its feeling for nature), and the recommendation of chairs in Celtic studies. Renan later qualified his romanticized view of racial characteristics: in "What Is a Nation?" (1882), he pointed to other qualities that unite a nation.

53. See Frederic E. Faverty, *Matthew Arnold the Ethnologist* (Evanston: Northwestern

University Press, 1951) for Arnold's treatment of race in light of the views (especially the French views) of his time. "One of his chief aims," which distinguishes him from others writing on this subject, notes Faverty, "is conciliation. Even when his facts are wrong, or his premises unsound, or his conclusions questionable, his animating purpose is usually right. He desires not to divide races or nations, but to bring them together. Ignorance and insularity, he believes, accompany each other" (11). For Honan, Arnold is "occasionally" mocking the racial views described (*Matthew Arnold*, 333). But Super says, apropos of Arnold's research for the lectures, he "looked in the right places" (*CPW*, 3:495). Besides Renan, he drew on Henri Martin, Michelet, Taine, and Amédée Thierry, and on Taine for the distinction between Celt and Teuton. Among the many studies of the lectures are William E. Buckler, "On the Study of Celtic Literature: A Critical Reconsideration," *Victorian Poetry* 27 (Spring 1989): 61–76; John Kelleher, "Matthew Arnold and the Celtic Revival," *Perspectives of Criticism*, ed. Harry Levin (Cambridge: Harvard University Press, 1950), 197–221; Leonard Orr, "The Mid-Nineteenth Century Irish Context of Arnold's Essay on Celtic Literature," and Saundra Segan Wheeler, "*On the Study of Celtic Literature* and the Young Writer: A Place in Arnold's Poetics," the latter two in *Matthew Arnold in His Time and Ours*, 135–56, 157–70.

54. James, *LC*, 1:716. See Ruth apRoberts's stimulating discussion of Arnold's interest in world religions in *Arnold and God* (Berkeley: University of California Press, 1983), esp. pp. 157–75. Arnold's essay on Islam, "A Persian Passion Play" (1871), was added to the third edition of *Essays in Criticism* (1875). (Super notes that on this occasion, Renan followed in Arnold's footsteps, rather than the reverse, by also writing on the annual Shiite ritual-drama depicting the death of Hussein: *CPW*, 7:405.) We have the testimony of the distinguished Jewish scholar Emanuel Deutsch (George Eliot's model for Mordecai in *Daniel Deronda*) that he would not have found an audience for his work on the Talmud if Arnold's interest in Hebraism had not prepared the ground (Arnold, *Letters*, ed. Russell, 1:458–59). And see James Whitlark, "Matthew Arnold and Buddhism," *Arnoldian* 9 (Winter 1981): 5–16.

55. Kelleher, "Arnold and the Celtic Revival," 197, 218. "How well one knows these sentences of Arnold," Yeats declares in "The Celtic Element in Literature," *Essays and Introductions* (New York: Macmillan, 1968), 174.

56. See Super *CPW*, 10:479–80 for an account of Arnold's influence on playwright Henry Arthur Jones.

57. James, "Collaboration," *CT*, 9:425. Following Arnold in this as in other respects (see chapter 5), John Dewey declares, in *Art as Experience* (1934; reprint, New York: Perigree Books, 1980), "The differences between English, French and German speech creates barriers that are submerged when art speaks" (335).

58. Wilde, "The Critic as Artist," in *The Works of Oscar Wilde*, ed. G. F. Maine (London: Collins, 1948), 995–96.

CHAPTER TWO

1. Richard M. Chadbourne, *Ernest Renan as an Essayist* (Ithaca: Cornell University Press, 1957), 185.

2. See Joseph Carroll, *The Cultural Theory of Matthew Arnold* (Berkeley: University of California Press, 1982), 62–63.

3. Arnold to his mother, cited in Park Honan, *Matthew Arnold: A Life* (New York: McGraw-Hill, 1981), 33; Arnold, *The Letters of Matthew Arnold*, ed. Cecil Y. Lang (Charlottesville: University Press of Virginia, 1996–), 1:89, 92; Louis Bonnerot, *Matthew Arnold, poète* (Paris: Didier, 1947), 535; Carlyle, *Sartor Resartus*, in *The Works of Thomas Carlyle*, ed. H. D. Traill, 30 vols., Centenary Edition (London: Chapman and Hall, 1898–1901), 1:63.

4. Sainte-Beuve, "Histoire de l'Académie française," *Causeries du lundi* 14 (July 19, 1856): 209; Bonnerot, *Matthew Arnold, poète*, 518–19; the first part of the translation is by R. H. Super; "Documents in the Matthew Arnold-Sainte-Beuve Relationship," *Modern Philology* 60 (Feb. 1963): 206 (see *Letters*, ed. Lang, 1:284).

5. Bonnerot, *Matthew Arnold, poète*, 535, 531; Arnold, *Letters*, ed. Lang, 1:495; Sainte-Beuve, "Lettres d'Eugénie de Guérin," *Nouveaux lundis* 9 (Jan. 2, 1865): 250. Arnold was especially pleased when Sainte-Beuve quoted from his poem "Obermann" in his book on Chateaubriand. "I value his praise both in itself," Arnold wrote his mother, "and because it carries one's name through the literary circles of Europe in a way that no English praise can carry it" (Arnold, *Letters*, ed. George W. E. Russell, 2 vols. [New York: Macmillan, 1895], 1:154–55).

6. Arnold, *Letters*, ed. Russell, 1:155; Stephen, "Matthew Arnold and His Countrymen," *Saturday Review* (Dec. 3, 1864): 683–85; reprinted in *Matthew Arnold, Prose Writings: The Critical Heritage*, ed. Carl Dawson and John Pfordresher (London: Routledge & Kegan Paul, 1979), 118; Marzials, "M. Sainte-Beuve," *Quarterly Review* 119 (Jan. 1866): 55; Gross, *The Rise and Fall of the Man of Letters* (New York: Macmillan, 1969), 60. "Whatever his limitations," F. R. Leavis declares in "Arnold as Critic," "Arnold seems to be decidedly more of a critic than the Sainte-Beuve to whom he so deferred" (*A Selection from Scrutiny*, 2 vols. [Cambridge: Cambridge University Press, 1968], 1:268). Swinburne, in 1867, felt that Arnold was praising the wrong French writers and that his "faith in the French Academy and in the *Revue des deux mondes* . . . is nothing short of pathetic" ("Mr. Arnold's New Poems," *Fortnightly Review* 8 [Oct. 1867]: 441). But Swinburne was writing in the journal that Anthony Trollope and associates, fired by Arnold's enthusiasm, had just founded as an English version of the *Revue*. (See N. John Hall, *Trollope: A Biography* [Oxford: Clarendon Press, 1990], 270.)

7. Sainte-Beuve, *Selected Essays*, ed. and trans. Francis Steegmuller and Norbert Guterman (Garden City: Doubleday Anchor Books, 1964), 309; Arnold, *Unpublished Letters*, ed. Arnold Whitridge (New Haven: Yale University Press, 1923), 65–66.

8. Arnold on Sainte-Beuve (a canceled passage from "Culture and Its Enemies"), *CPW*, 11:542. For Arnold and Taine, see F. J. W. Harding, *Matthew Arnold, the Critic and France* (Geneva: Librairie Droz, 1964), 126.

9. Edward Said, "Foucault and the Imagination of Power," in *Foucault: A Critical Reader*, ed. David Couzens Hoy (Oxford: Basil Blackwell, 1986), 151. (Said is an admiring critic of Foucault.)

10. See, for example, Paul Bové, *Intellectuals in Power: A Genealogy of Critical Humanism* (New York: Columbia University Press, 1986), in which Foucault and Said (the proper sort of "oppositional critics") are pitted against Arnold.

11. Wellek, *A History of Modern Criticism: 1750–1950*, 7 vols. so far (New Haven: Yale University Press, 1955–), 3:34; James, *Literary Criticism* (henceforth *LC*), ed. Leon Edel and Mark Wilson, 2 vols. (New York: Library of America, 1984), 1:668. See Arnold Whitridge, "Matthew Arnold and Sainte-Beuve," *PMLA* 53 (March 1938): 303–13; and Harding, *Arnold and France*, chap. 4.

12. Sainte-Beuve, *Selected Essays*, 8–12. See Irving Babbitt on Sainte-Beuve in *The Masters of Modern French Criticism* (1912; reprint, New York: Farrar, Strauss and Company, 1963), 79–188. Richard M. Chadbourne's *Charles-Augustin Sainte-Beuve* (Boston: Twayne, 1977) is a useful introduction to Sainte-Beuve, a companion to his 1968 Twayne volume on Renan.

13. Sainte-Beuve, *Selected Essays*, 299–310.

14. See *CPW*, 11:282, for Arnold's citation of Sainte-Beuve ("The ideal has ceased, the lyric vein is dried up; the new men are cured of lyricism and the ideal"). Sainte-Beuve's review of *Madame Bovary* is in *Selected Writings*, 275–90.

15. Sainte-Beuve, "Maurice de Guérin," *Causeries du lundi* 15 (Sept. 24 and Oct. 1, 1860): 1–34; "Lettres d'Eugénie du Guérin," *Nouveaux lundis* 9 (Jan. 2,, 1865): 240–57; "Eugénie de Guérin," *Causeries du lundi* 12 (Feb. 9, 1856): 231–47. To the modern reader wondering at Arnold's lavish praise for Guérin's literary achievement (which Swinburne found much inferior to Keats's), one might cite the Goncourts, in 1861, on the "only . . . modern writer who was able to discover a tongue with which to make the ancients speak: . . . Maurice de Guérin in *Le Centaure*" (*Journals*, ed. and trans. Lewis Galantiere [Garden City: Doubleday Anchor Books, 1958], 101).

16. Sainte-Beuve treats Joubert extensively in *Chateaubriand et son groupe littéraire sous l'Empire* (1860; reprint, 2 vols., Paris: Calmann Levy, 1878), as well as in an 1838 portrait collected in *Portraits littéraires* (1844; reprint, 3 vols., Paris: Garnier, 1864) 2: 306–26, and an early *Causerie* for December 1849. Lionel Trilling shrewdly compares Arnold and Joubert in *Matthew Arnold* (1939; reprint, New York: Meridian Books, 1955), 197–201. And see Robert A. Donovan, "The Method of Arnold's *Essays in Criticism*," *PMLA* 71 (Dec. 1956): 922–31.

17. Sainte-Beuve, "Histoire de l'Académie française," *Causeries du lundi* 14 (July 19, 1856): 208.

18. Sainte-Beuve, *Selected Essays*, 8. See R. H. Super's notes, *CPW*, 3:400.

19. Arnold, *Letters*, ed. Lang, 1:282; Arnold, *Letters*, ed. Russell, 1:234.

20. Goncourt, *Journals*, 155, 178; Sainte-Beuve, *Selected Essays*, 24–125; Goncourt, *Journals*, 257.

21. Chadbourne, *Ernest Renan* (Boston: Twayne, 1968), 148.

22. Arnold, *Letters*, ed. Lang, 1:515–16. See *The Note-Books of Matthew Arnold*, ed. Howard Foster Lowry, Karl Young, and Waldo Hilary Dunn (London: Oxford University Press, 1952), e.g., pp. 194, 503 (altogether, there are scores of Renan quotations, many of them repeated).

23. Renan, *Life of Jesus* (London: Dent, 1927), 24; *Recollections of My Youth* (*Souvenirs d'enfance et de jeunesse*, henceforth *SEJ*), trans. C. B. Pitman (Boston: Houghton, Mifflin, 1929), 115.

24. James, *LC*, 1:633–34; Arnold, "Numbers," *CPW*, 10:155 (Arnold is conflating three separate passages from the *Souvenirs*: see 114, 137, 315).

25. Arnold, "George Sand," *CPW*, 8:234–35; *Letters*, ed. Russell, 2:184 (and see 414); preface to *Irish Essays*, *CPW*, 9:316 (this phrase recurs throughout the *Note-Books*, e.g., p. 318).

26. Arnold, *Letters*, ed. Russell, 1:234; Chadbourne, *Renan as Essayist*, xxi; and see Chadbourne, "Renan and Sainte-Beuve," *Romanic Review* 44 (April 1953): 127–35; Renan, *Studies of Religious History and Criticism* (*Etudes d'histoire religieuse*, henceforth *EHR*), trans. O. B. Frothingham (New York: Carleton, 1864), 37.

27. Renan, *EHR*, 219, 51, 55, 185.

28. See Arnold, "The Bishop and the Philosopher," *CPW*, 3:40–55; Renan, *EHR*, 55 ("Humanity is not made up of scholars and philologists. It is frequently deceived, or rather it is necessarily deceived").

29. Arnold, *CPW*, 6:5, 275. Renan, while seeing Paul's "reign drawing to a close," felt that "Jesus, on the contrary, lives more than ever": *Saint Paul*, third volume of the *Origines*, trans. Ingersoll Lockwood (New York: Carleton, 1869), 330. Although Renan's name, in recent years, has become little more than a target for Edward Said and his followers in the crusade against Eurocentrism, the author of the *Origines du christianisme* had, for Edmund Wilson, written "a masterpiece— perhaps the greatest of all histories of ideas" (*To the Finland Station* [1940; reprint, Garden City: Doubleday Anchor Books, 1953], 43).

30. See, for example, Joseph W. Angell, "Matthew Arnold's Indebtedness to Renan's *Essais de morale et de critique*," *Revue de Littérature Comparée* 14 (1934): 714–33; Sidney M. B. Coulling, "Renan's Influence on Arnold's Literary and Social Criticism," *Florida State University Studies*, no. 5 (1952): 95–112; Harding, *Arnold and France*, chap. 5; Lewis F. Mott, "Renan and Matthew Arnold," *Modern Language Notes* 33 (Feb. 1918): 65–73. Among recent Arnoldians, R. H. Super (in his superb notes to the *Complete Prose Works*), Douglas Bush, in *Matthew Arnold* (New York: Macmillan, 1971: 176), and Ruth apRoberts, in *Arnold and God* (Berkeley: University of California Press, 1983; e.g., pp. 32, 135–36, 147), have stressed Renan's importance to Arnold.

31. Renan, Preface, *Essais de morale et de critique* (henceforth *EMC*), in *Oeuvres Complètes*, ed. Henriette Psichari, 10 vols. (Paris: Calmann-Lévy, 1947–61), 1:17; "M. de Sacy et l'école libérale," *EMC*, 50.

32. Renan, "La Poésie de l'Exposition," *EMC*, 242; "L'Académie française," *EMC*, 236–37.

33. Chadbourne, in *Renan as Essayist*, notes that "*résistance*" and "*idéalisme*" are "key words" in the *Essais* (96); Renan, *SEJ*, xxxviii.

34. Renan, "Marcus Aurelius" and "Henri-Fréderic Amiel," in *The Poetry of the Celtic Races, and Other Studies*, trans. William G. Hutchison (Port Washington: Kennikat Press, 1970), 161, 189, 212.

35. Goncourt, *Journals*, p. 155. See "M. Sainte-Beuve," *Quarterly Review* 119 (Jan. 1866):54.

36. James, *LC*, 1:802–7.

37. Scherer, "Taine's History of English Literature," *Essays on English Literature* (henceforth *EEL*), trans. George Saintsbury (London: Sampson Low, 1891), 78; Babbitt, *Masters of French Criticism*, 208 ("Scherer did instinctively what Arnold regretted Amiel does not do," Babbitt observes: "he escaped the vertigo of the abyss by

turning literary critic"; 197); Renan, "La Poésie de l'Exposition," *EMC*, 251; Scherer, preface to Henri-Fréderic Amiel, *Fragments d'un journal intime*, 2 vols. (Geneva: Georg, 1892), lxviii–lxix.

38. Arnold, *Letters*, ed. Russell, 1:303.

39. Scherer, "Milton and 'Paradise Lost,' " *EEL*, 98–131 (of *Paradise Lost*, "an unreal poem, a grotesque poem, a tiresome poem," Scherer asks, "By what effort of imagination or of faith can we read the history of Adam as part of our own history . . . ?"; 129, 122); Scherer, "Goethe," *Etudes sur la littérature contemporaine* 6 (Paris, 1886): 295–351. See Wellek, *History of Modern Criticism*, 4:83.

40. Scherer, "*Daniel Deronda*," *EEL*, 45–46; "Wordsworth and Modern Poetry in England," *EEL*, 154–58.

41. Habermas, "Taking Aim at the Heart of the Present," in *Foucault: A Critical Reader*, 107; and see Habermas's lectures on Foucault in *The Philosophical Discourse of Humanity*, trans. Frederick Lawrence (Cambridge: MIT Press, 1987), 238–93. Bonnerot's *Matthew Arnold, poète* is a reminder that Arnold once (1947) was not absolutely unknown in France.

42. For Foucault on humanism, see "Revolutionary Action: 'Until Now,' " in *Language, Counter-Memory, Practice: Selected Essays and Interviews* (henceforth *LCP*), ed. Donald Bouchard and Sherry Simon (Ithaca: Cornell University Press, 1977), 221–22; Foucault, introduction to *The Archaeology of Knowledge* (published with "The Discourse on Language"), trans. A. M. Sheridan Smith (New York: Pantheon, 1972), 17; Megill, *Prophets of Extremity: Nietzsche, Heidegger, Foucault, Derrida* (Berkeley: University of California Press, 1985), 184.

43. See David Macey, *The Lives of Michael Foucault* (henceforth *LMF*) (London: Hutchinson, 1993), 210–13, 385; H. D. Harootunian, "Foucault, Genealogy, History: The Pursuit of Otherness," in *After Foucault: Humanistic Knowledge, Postmodern Challenges*, ed. Jonathan Arac (New Brunswick: Rutgers University Press, 1988), 110–37; Renan, *SEJ*, 15–16.

44. Eribon, *Michel Foucault* (henceforth *MF*), trans. Betsy Wing (Cambridge: Harvard University Press, 1991), 256 (he is citing Foucault's colleague at the Collège, Emmanuel Le Roy Ladurie); Miller, *The Passion of Michel Foucault* (henceforth *PMF*), (New York: Simon & Schuster, 1993).

45. Nicholas Murray, *A Life of Matthew Arnold* (London: Hodder & Stoughton, 1996); Miller, *PMF* (on Foucault's lecture, "radically subversive in its declared intentions, yet reassuringly classical in its display of eloquence and learning"), 184; Edward Said (on his tone of voice), "Michel Foucault, 1926–1984," in *After Foucault*, 7; *I, Pierre Rivière, having slaughtered my mother, my sister, and my brother . . .* , ed. Foucault, trans. Frank Jellinek (Lincoln: University of Nebraska Press, 1982), x, 206; Eribon, *MF*, 276.

46. Arnold, *Letters*, ed. Russell, 1:269–70; During, *Foucault and Literature: Toward a Genealogy of Writing* (London: Routledge, 1992), 13.

47. Foucault, *Maurice Blanchot: The Thought from Outside* (published with Blanchot, "Michel Foucault as I Imagine Him"), trans. Brian Massumi (New York: Zone Books, 1990), 55; Foucault, "Nietzsche, Genealogy, History," *LCP*, 162. In *The Archaeology of Knowledge*, Foucault, drawing on Nietzsche, argues that humanity has no refuge or "abode" either in history or in language (11–14).

48. Foucault, "The Functions of Literature," in *Politics, Philosophy, Culture: Interviews and Other Writings, 1977–1984* (henceforth *PPC*), ed. Lawrence D. Kritzman, trans. Alan Sheridan (New York: Routledge, 1988), 312; Foucault, *Raymond Roussel*, translated as *Death and the Labyrinth: The World of Raymond Roussel* by Charles Ruas (New York: Doubleday, 1986), 174, 16, 175, 156. David Carroll considers Foucault's use of literary texts in *Paraesthetics: Foucault, Lyotard, Derrida* (New York: Methuen, 1987), 53–79, 107–29.

49. Foucault, "A Preface to Transgression," *LCP,* 33, 30–31; Foucault, *Blanchot,* 17.

50. Foucault, *Blanchot,* 12, 15, 22–26.

51. Foucault, "What Is an Author?," *LCP,* 121. "It certainly takes an author," Zhang Longxi observes in *The Tao and the Logos: Literary Hermeneutics, East and West* (Durham: Duke University Press, 1992), "to make the authoritative announcement of the death of the author" (195).

52. Foucault, "Practicing Criticism," *PPC,* 156; Foucault, "The History of Sexuality," in *Power/Knowledge: Selected Interviews and Other Writings, 1972–77,* ed. Colin Gordon (New York: Pantheon, 1980), 193; Macey, *LMF,* 432. See also Foucault, *Remarks on Marx: Conversations with Duccio Trombadori,* trans. R. James Goldstein and James Cascaito (New York: Semiotext[e], 1991), on the autobiographical and fictional nature of his writings (e.g., pp. 27, 37).

53. Megill, *Prophets of Extremity,* 183; Foucault, *LCP,* 230; Eagleton, *The Ideology of the Aesthetic* (Oxford: Basil Blackwell, 1990), 388. See also Michel de Certeau on Foucault's aesthetic seductiveness in "The Black Sun of Language: Foucault," in *Heterologies: Discourse on the Other,* trans. Brian Massumi (Minneapolis: University of Minnesota Press, 1986), 171; or Frank Lentricchia on the "aesthetic anarchy" of Foucault and his New Historicist followers in *Ariel and the Police* (Madison: University of Wisconsin Press, 1988), 101; or Charles Taylor on the aesthetic tidiness of Foucault's historical scenario in *Philosophy and the Human Sciences* (Cambridge: Cambridge University Press, 1985), 182. Miller links Foucault with Nietzsche in preferring "externalized" to "internalizing cruelty. . . . Better internalized cruelty than no cruelty at all" (*PMF,* 238).

54. Foucault, *Madness and Civilization: A History of Insanity in the Age of Reason,* trans. Richard Howard (from the revised 1964 edition of *Histoire de la folie,* originally published 1961 as *Folie et deraison*) (New York: Vintage Books, 1973), 288–89, x; Derrida, "Cogito and the History of Madness," in *Writing and Difference,* trans. Alan Bass (Chicago: University of Chicago Press, 1978), 31–63; Deleuze, *Foucault,* trans. and ed. Séan Hand (Minneapolis: University of Minnesota Press, 1986), 13; Foucault, *The Order of Things: An Archaeology of the Human Sciences* (*Les Mots et les choses*), trans. unidentified (New York: Vintage Books, 1973), 55. In the Preface to *Lyrical Ballads,* Wordsworth compares the poet, who binds people together, with the scientist, who seeks a truth that distances individuals from nature and from each other.

55. Macey, *LMF,* 353.

56. Foucault, *Discipline and Punish: The Birth of the Prison* (*Surveiller et punir*), trans. Alan Sheridan (New York: Vintage Books, 1979), 304.

57. Ibid., 205; Stephen, in *Arnold: The Critical Heritage,* 118, 121, 122.

58. Foucault, "Qu'est-ce que la critique?," *Bulletin de la Société française de Philosophie,*

84th year (April–June 1990): 38, 39 (I am using Miller's translation, *PMF*, 302), 41, 40. "What Is Enlightenment?" is included in *The Philosophy of Kant*, ed. Carl J. Friedrich (New York: Modern Library, 1949), 132–39. Besides Miller's helpful discussion of Foucault on Kant (see, e.g., pp. 301–4), see also John Rajchman, *Michel Foucault: The Freedom of Philosophy* (New York: Columbia University Press, 1985), chap. 3 ("The Transformation of Critique").

59. Foucault, "What Is Enlightenment?," trans. Catherine Porter, in *The Foucault Reader*, ed. Paul Rabinow (New York: Pantheon, 1984), 42–43, 41–42, 44–45; Hubert L. Dreyfus and Paul Rabinow, *Michel Foucault: Beyond Structuralism and Hermeneutics*, 2d ed. (Chicago: University of Chicago Press, 1982), 236. The Dreyfus-Rabinow book chronicles Foucault's evolution toward an ethics; and see their essay, "What Is Maturity?: Habermas and Foucault on 'What Is Enlightenment?' " in *Foucault: A Critical Reader*, 109–21.

60. Foucault, *The Use of Pleasure* (New York: Vintage Books, 1986), 10–11; and see *The Care of the Self* (New York: Vintage Books, 1988), 43, 50; Dreyfus and Rabinow, *Beyond Structuralism and Hermeneutics*, 231; Pater, *The Renaissance* (New York: Oxford University Press, 1986), 141. In *The Use of Pleasure*, Foucault cites Jacob Burckhardt on the theme of the Renaissance "aesthetics of existence" (11). (In *The Archaeology of Knowledge*, by contrast, Foucault had mocked the idea of "development," whether historical or individual; [14].) In the next two chapters, I consider the importance of the idea of *Bildung* for Arnold, Nietzsche, and Gadamer.

61. Foucault, *The Use of Pleasure*, 72–73; and see Foucault, "The Minimalist Self," in *PPC*, 14.

62. See "The Ethic of Care for the Self as a Practice of Freedom," in *The Final Foucault*, ed. James Bernauer and David Rasmussen (Cambridge: MIT Press, 1988), 1–20 (on the theme of one's responsibility to others, see pp. 7–9); Thomas Flynn describes Foucault's lectures on truth-telling in the same volume (102–18). In *The Care of the Self*, Foucault draws on Galen and Seneca to consider "the interplay of the care of the self and the help of others" (53); Eribon, *MF*, 279.

63. Foucault, *The Care of the Self*, 46–47; Eribon, *MF*, 294; Foucault, "The Masked Philosopher," *PPC*, 326; Renan, *SEJ* (I have used James's translation in *LC*, 1:643), 76.

64. Foucault, *The Use of Pleasure*, 8–9.

CHAPTER THREE

1. Although Nietzsche's poor work in mathematics nearly caused him to fail, his exceptional showing in classics prompted one examiner to ask whether the school planned to flunk "the best pupil Pforta ever had?" (cited in R. J. Hollingdale, *Nietzsche: The Man and His Philosophy* [Baton Rouge: Louisiana State University Press, 1965], 23). For Arnold on Schulpforta, see *Schools and Universities on the Continent* (1868) in *CPW*, 4:187.

2. Brooks is cited in John Henry Raleigh, *Matthew Arnold and American Culture* (Berkeley: University of California Press, 1957), 151; David S. Thatcher, *Nietzsche in England: 1890–1914* (Toronto: University of Toronto Press, 1970), 273, 12. George

Steiner compared Arnold to Nietzsche (to the latter's advantage) at the 1988 Liverpool Arnold Conference. Geoffrey H. Hartman pits Nietzsche against Arnold in *Criticism in the Wilderness* (New Haven: Yale University Press, 1980), e.g., p. 5; and see his "The Culture of Criticism," *PMLA* 90 (Jan. 1984): 381, 384.

3. Arnold, "The Study of Poetry" (1880), *CPW*, 9:161; Nietzsche, *Human. All Too Human* (1878; henceforth *HH*), trans. R. J. Hollingdale (Cambridge: Cambridge University Press, 1986), 25 (and see pp. 117–18).

4. Nietzsche, *Selected Letters*, ed. and trans. Christopher Middleton (Chicago: University of Chicago Press, 1969), 284; Arnold, "Stanzas from the Grande Chartreuse," ll. 85–86, in *The Poems of Matthew Arnold*, ed. Kenneth Allott and Miriam Allott, 2d ed. (London: Longman, 1979), 305 (further quotations of the poems are from this edition and are cited in the text); James, "Matthew Arnold," in *Literary Criticism*, ed. Leon Edel and Mark Wilson, 2 vols. (New York: Library of America), 1:727.

5. Arnold, *Letters*, ed. George W. E. Russell, 2 vols. (New York: Macmillan, 1895), 1:287; Nietzsche, *Selected Letters*, 62; *The Will to Power* (1883–88; henceforth *WP*), ed. and trans. Walter Kaufmann with R. J. Hollingdale (New York: Vintage Books, 1968), 225. For the development of the idea of *Bildung* to its "final development in Nietzsche," see W. H. Bruford's hostile study, *The German Tradition of Self-Cultivation: "Bildung" from Humboldt to Thomas Mann* (Cambridge: Cambridge University Press, 1975), esp. pp. 164–89.

6. Nietzsche on Thucydides, *Twilight of the Idols* (1888), in *The Portable Nietzsche* (henceforth *PN*), ed. and trans. Walter Kaufmann (New York: Viking Press, 1954), 558; Goethe (on Spinoza), *Autobiography*, 2 vols., trans. John Oxenford (Chicago: University of Chicago Press, 1974), 1:261; for Arnold on Schopenhauer, see *CPW*, 8:159–60; Nietzsche, *Untimely Meditations* (henceforth *UM*), trans. R. J. Hollingdale (Cambridge: Cambridge University Press, 1983), 10.

7. Nietzsche, *HH*, 332; Coulling, *Matthew Arnold and His Critics* (Athens: Ohio University Press, 1974), 22; Nietzsche, *Selected Letters*, 90; for Nietzsche on Socrates, see Walter Kaufmann, *Nietzsche: Philosopher, Psychologist, Antichrist*, 3d ed. (New York: Vintage Books, 1968), 391–411; and Alexander Nehamas, *Nietzsche: Life as Literature* (Cambridge: Harvard University Press, 1985), 24–32.

8. Kaufmann, *Nietzsche*, 376; Stephen, in *Matthew Arnold, Prose Writings: The Critical Heritage*, ed. Carl Dawson and John Pfordresher (London: Routledge & Kegan Paul, 1979), 96; Arnold, *Letters*, ed. Russell, 1:233.

9. Arnold, *St. Paul and Protestantism* (1870), *CPW*, 6:73; "The Bishop and the Philosopher" (1862), *CPW*, 3:52; "A Word More about America" (1885), *CPW*, 10:213. Leslie Stephen recalls wishing, as he read Arnold, "that I too had a little sweetness and light that I might be able to say such nasty things of my enemies" (*Critical Heritage*, 421).

10. P. J. Keating says of Arnold, "elusiveness is his most characteristic quality," "Arnold's Social and Political Thought," in *Writers and Their Background: Matthew Arnold*, ed. Kenneth Allott (Athens: Ohio University Press, 1976), 208.

11. Nietzsche, *Selected Letters*, 47; Arnold, *The Letters of Matthew Arnold*, ed. Cecil Y. Lang (Charlottesville: The University Press of Virginia, 1996–), 1:128.

12. Arnold, *Letters*, ed. Russell, 1:360; Nietzsche, *Ecce Homo* (henceforth *EH*), ed. and trans. R. J. Hollingdale (Harmondsworth: Penguin, 1979), 65, 88.

13. Nietzsche, *Selected Letters*, 44; Arnold, *Letters*, ed. Russell, 2:50.

14. Arnold, *Letters*, ed. Lang, 1:233. As a teenager, Nietzsche claimed that Humboldt had inspired in him "an unusual urge towards knowledge, towards general culture [*Bildung*]"; cited in Hollingdale, *Nietzsche*, 27.

15. Arnold, "Common Schools Abroad" (1886), *CPW*, 11:89, 102, 105; Nietzsche, *The Future of Our Educational Institutions* (1871), trans. J. M. Kennedy, in *Complete Works*, ed. Oscar Levy, 18 vols. (1909; reprint, New York: Russell & Russell, 1964), 3:74. (In the 1909 preface, Kennedy suggests that the reader compare Nietzsche on education with Arnold.) In *Human, All Too Human*, Nietzsche advises the elite to "live as higher men and perform perpetually the deeds of higher culture" (177).

16. By 1879, in his address to the Ipswich Working Men's College, Arnold urged his audience to demand better schooling for the middle classes so that workers would have "a more civilised middle class to rise into" (*Letters*, ed. Russell, 2:175).

17. Nietzsche, *PN*, 510; *The Future of Our Educational Institutions*, 75, 62. Nietzsche's educational views are considered by Eliyahu Rosenow, "Nietzsche's Concept of Education," in *Nietzsche as Affirmative Thinker*, ed. Yirmiyahu Yovel (Dordrecht: Martinus Nijhoff, 1986), 119–31; and Daniel O'Hara, "The Prophet of Our Laughter: Or Nietzsche As—Educator?" in *Why Nietzsche Now?*, ed. O'Hara (Bloomington: Indiana University Press, 1985), 1–19. (O'Hara links Nietzsche with Arnold's "aesthetic humanism," 10.) A key study of the origins of *Bildung* and its elitist implications is W. H. Bruford's *Culture and Society in Classical Weimar: 1775–1806* (Cambridge: Cambridge University Press, 1962). In chapter 4 of *The German Tradition of Self-Cultivation*, Bruford acknowledges a movement in Goethe from self-cultivation to work on behalf of others (88–112).

18. Nietzsche, *Selected Letters*, 28, 183, 191; *The Future of Our Educational Institutions*, 131.

19. Arnold, *Letters*, ed. Lang, 1:143; Nietzsche, *Selected Letters*, 207. Whether citing Pindar or the Stoics, Arnold and Nietzsche ultimately look back to Socrates and the Delphic Oracle's "Know thyself."

20. Arnold, *Letters*, ed. Russell, 1:289; "A New History of Greece," *CPW*, 5:270; Nietzsche, *The Birth of Tragedy* (henceforth *BT*), trans. Walter Kaufmann (New York: Vintage Books, 1967), 137. On Arnold's misconception of Greece, see Richard Jenkyns, *The Victorians and Ancient Greece* (Cambridge: Harvard University Press, 1980), e.g., p. 273; Warren D. Anderson, *Matthew Arnold and the Classical Tradition* (Ann Arbor: University of Michigan Press, 1965); and Anderson, "Arnold and the Classics," in *Writers and Their Background*, 259–85. Nietzsche's indebtedness to the Greeks is discussed in *Studies in Nietzsche and the Classical Tradition*, ed. James C. O'Flaherty, Timothy F. Sellner, and Robert M. Helm (Chapel Hill: University of North Carolina Press, 1976); and E. M. Butler, *The Tyranny of Greece Over Germany* (Cambridge: Cambridge University Press, 1935), 307–15.

21. Winckelmann, cited in Butler, *Tyranny of Greece*, 46. What Nietzsche calls "Dionysian" in his late works is actually, Kaufmann claims, "a union of Dionysus and Apollo" (*Nietzsche*, 281–82). For Arnold's sense of myth, see Ruth apRoberts, *Arnold and God* (Berkeley: University of California Press, 1983), esp. chap. 4; and see Allan Megill on "Nietzsche and Myth," in *Prophets of Extremity: Nietzsche, Heidegger, Foucault, Derrida* (Berkeley: University of California Press, 1985), 65–102.

22. Arnold, *Letters*, ed. Lang, 1:382; Nietzsche, *The Gay Science* (henceforth *GS*), trans. Walter Kaufmann (New York: Vintage Books, 1974), 272. Paul de Man's influential reading of Nietzsche is based on the supposition that the philosopher never outgrew his Schopenhauerian phase (*Allegories of Reading: Figural Language in Rousseau, Nietzsche, Rilke, and Proust* [New Haven: Yale University Press, 1979], 79–102).

23. Nietzsche, *PN*, 475–76. Nietzsche directly links dialectic with science ("*Wissenschafft*") in *The Birth of Tragedy*, section 14. However, as Arthur Danto points out, Nietzsche uses the term *Wissenschafft* to refer to more than "scholarly investigation"; elsewhere, it refers to the natural sciences (*Nietzsche as Philosopher* [New York: Macmillan, 1965], 67). While Nietzsche, in *The Birth of Tragedy*, follows Arnold in viewing science as inferior to the humanities, he subsequently thought of turning to the "natural sciences, in order to give his philosophy a firm foundation" (*Selected Letters*, 193n.).

24. M. M. Bakhtin, "Epic and Novel," *The Dialogic Imagination*, trans. Caryl Emerson and Michael Holquist (Austin: University of Texas Press, 1981); Arnold, *Letters*, ed. Russell, 2:37. Nietzsche's dialectical approach is considered by Kaufmann, *Nietzsche*, 132–33; and Nehamas, *Life as Literature*, 18. Arnold's "lively dialectical interplay of elements" is discussed briefly by David J. DeLaura (*Review* 7 [1985]: 128), and in detail by Walter J. Hipple, Jr. in "Matthew Arnold, Dialectician" (*University of Toronto Quarterly* 32 [Oct. 1962]: 1–26). Hipple refers to Arnold's "dialectic of becoming, rather than of being"—in contrast to Platonic dialectic. But for Hans-Georg Gadamer, in *Dialogue and Dialectic: Eight Hermeneutical Studies on Plato*, trans. P. Christopher Smith (New Haven: Yale University Press, 1980), Plato's dialectic is seen as a dialogical method of questioning that is "unending and infinite" (152), hence closer to Arnold's practice.

25. Nietzsche, *BT*, 52, 60; Arnold, *On Translating Homer* (1861), *CPW*, 1:102, 108; "Dover Beach," ll. 17–18; "On the Modern Element in Literature," *CPW*, 1:28.

26. Nietzsche, *PN*, 563. See Murray Krieger," 'Dover Beach' and the Tragic Sense of Eternal Recurrence," *University of Kansas Review* 23 (Oct. 1956): 73–78.

27. Nietzsche, *Beyond Good and Evil* (1886), trans. Walter Kaufmann (New York: Vintage Books, 1966), 123; *Selected Letters*, 5.

28. Anderson, *Arnold and the Classical Tradition*, 39.

29. See Kenneth Allott, "A Background for 'Empedocles on Etna,' " *Essays and Studies 1968*, ed. Simeon Potter (London: John Murray, 1968), 80–100; and Allott on Arnold and Byron in *Notes and Queries*, n.s., 9 (1962): 300–303. Nietzsche at seventeen wrote an essay on *Manfred* in which he used the word "*Übermensch*" for the first time to describe Byron's protagonist. He subsequently composed a musical "meditation" based on the poem; and in the late *Ecce Homo*, he claimed to be "profoundly related" (58) to Byron's outlaw-hero.

30. Nietzsche, *PN*, 515; Arnold, *Letters*, ed. Russell, 2:220–21; *Last Essays on Church and Religion* (1877), *CPW*, 8:72.

31. Nietzsche, *Selected Letters*, 7. Eugene Goodheart discusses Arnold's "problematic" relation to Protestantism in *The Failure of Criticism* (Cambridge: Harvard University Press, 1978), 33; and one may detect a current of Protestant individualism in Nietzsche's beliefs. Ray Monk, in *Ludwig Wittgenstein: The Duty of Genius* (New

York: Viking Press, 1990), notes that Wittgenstein accepted Nietzsche's (and William James's) view that Christianity "is not a *belief* but a practice" (122).

32. Arnold, *Literature and Dogma* (1873), *CPW*, 6:171; Vaihinger, *The Philosophy of "As If": A System of the Theoretical, Practical, and Religious Fictions of Mankind*, trans. C. K. Ogden (London: Kegan Paul, 1935), 361; Nietzsche, "On Truth and Lies in a Nonmoral Sense," in *Philosophy and Truth: Selections from Nietzsche's Notebooks of the Early 1870's*, ed. and trans. Daniel Breazeale (Atlantic Highlands, N.J.: Humanities Press, 1979), 96; *The Antichrist* (1988), in *PN*, 613–16; *Selected Letters*, 12–13.

33. Arnold, *Letters*, ed. Russell, 2:20; Nietzsche, *PN*, 652.

34. Arnold, *Critical Heritage*, 309, 319–23; apRoberts, *Arnold and God* (similarities between Nietzsche and Arnold are noted on pp. 51, 155, 231, 237); Willey, *Nineteenth-Century Studies* (1949; reprint, Harmondsworth: Penguin, 1964), 288. And see R. H. Super, *The Time-Spirit of Matthew Arnold* (Ann Arbor: University of Michigan Press, 1970), 61–91.

35. Arnold, *CPW*, 6:258, 218; and see *CPW*, 11:187 ("For undoubtedly what Jesus meant by the kingdom of God or of Heaven was the reign of saints, the ideal future society on earth"); Nietzsche, *PN*, 610, 607, 612.

36. Arnold, *God and the Bible* (1875), *CPW*, 7:234; Altizer, "Eternal Recurrence and the Kingdom of God," in *The New Nietzsche: Contemporary Styles of Interpretation*, ed. David B. Allison (Cambridge: MIT Press, 1985), 239; Nietzsche, *Thus Spoke Zarathustra* (1883–92), *PN*, 608–9, 610, 607, 612; Arnold, "The Better Part," l. 10.

37. Heidegger, "The Word of Nietzsche: 'God Is Dead,' " in *The Question Concerning Technology and Other Essays*, trans. William Lovitt (New York: Harper and Row, 1977), 100; Nietzsche, *PN*, 318. For Arnold and Nietzsche on Darwin, see *CPW*, 7:222–23; *GS*, 292.

38. Nietzsche, *PN*, 554; *WP*, 434. Arnold cites Goethe frequently, in many contexts, and at every point in his career. It is surprising, thus, to find scholars playing down the connection; see James Simpson, in "Arnold and Goethe" (*Writers and Their Background*, 286–318); and David J. DeLaura, in "Arnold and Goethe: The One on the Intellectual Throne," *Victorian Literature and Society: Essays Presented to Richard D. Altick*, ed. James R. Kincaid and Albert J. Kuhn (Columbus: Ohio State University Press, 1984); and in *Hebrew and Hellene in Victorian England: Newman, Arnold, and Pater* (Austin: University of Texas Press, 1969), e.g., p. 189. I (briefly) consider the matter in "Goethe and the Victorians," *Carlyle Annual* 13 (1992/93): 17–34.

39. Kaufmann, *Nietzsche*, 414; Megill, *Prophets of Extremity*, 99–102; Nehamas, *Life as Literature*, 8; Madden, *Matthew Arnold: A Study of the Aesthetic Temperament in Victorian England* (Bloomington: Indiana University Press, 1967); Levine, "Matthew Arnold: The Artist in the Wilderness," *Critical Inquiry* 9 (March 1983): 476.

40. Nietzsche, *PN*, 522; *Daybreak: Thoughts on the Prejudices of Morality*, trans. R. J. Hollingdale (Cambridge: Cambridge University Press, 1982), 228. See Park Honan on Emerson and Arnold in *Matthew Arnold: A Life* (New York: McGraw- Hill, 1981), 75–76. The Emerson quotations ("Experience" and *The Conduct of Life*) are taken from *Selected Writings*, ed. Donald McQuade (New York: Modern Library, 1981), 347, 723.

41. Nietzsche, *Beyond Good and Evil*, 117; Arnold, "Numbers" (1884), *CPW*, 10:143–64; "Joseph de Maistre on Russia" (1879), *CPW*, 9:86–87.
42. Cited in Honan, *Matthew Arnold*, 398.
43. Arnold, *Letters*, ed. Lang, 1:402.
44. Kaufmann, *Nietzsche*, 66.
45. Williams, *Culture and Society: 1780–1950* (Garden City: Doubleday Anchor Books, 1960), 128.

CHAPTER FOUR

1. Ricoeur, "Hermeneutics and the Critique of Ideology," in *Hermeneutics and the Human Sciences*, ed. and trans. John B. Thompson (Cambridge: Cambridge University Press, 1981), 64–78 (discussion of Gadamer); *Freud and Philosophy*, trans. Denis Savage (New Haven: Yale University Press, 1970), 27, 32–35 (on the "school of suspicion").
2. Schleiermacher, *General Hermeneutics*, trans. J. Duke and J. Forstman, excerpted in *The Hermeneutics Reader*, ed. Kurt Mueller-Vollmer (New York: Continuum, 1985), 76; Arnold, *Letters*, ed. George W. E. Russell, 2 vols. (New York: Macmillan, 1895), 1:442. See Ruth apRoberts, *Arnold and God* (Berkeley: University of California Press, 1983), 65–66.
3. Gadamer, *Truth and Method* (henceforth cited in the text as *TM*), trans. revised by Joel Weinsheimer and Donald G. Marshall (New York: Crossroad, 1991), 195–96; Gadamer (on tradition), "The Heritage of Hegel," in *Reason in the Age of Science* (henceforth *RAS*), trans. Frederick G. Lawrence (Cambridge: MIT Press, 1981), 60. Georgia Warnke discusses Gadamer's mixture of traditional and pluralistic values in *Gadamer: Hermeneutics, Tradition, and Reason* (Stanford: Stanford University Press, 1987); David Couzens Hoy, in *The Critical Circle: Literature, History, and Philosophical Hermeneutics* (Berkeley: University of California Press, 1978), emphasizes the dialogical nature of Gadamer's view of tradition (61–72). Among the many useful accounts of *Truth and Method* are Joel C. Weinsheimer, *Gadamer's Hermeneutics: A Reading of "Truth and Method"* (New Haven: Yale University Press, 1985) and Richard E. Palmer, *Hermeneutics: Interpretation Theory in Schleiermacher, Dilthey, Heidegger, and Gadamer* (Evanston: Northwestern University Press, 1969), 162–217. In *Hermeneutics Ancient and Modern* (New Haven: Yale University Press, 1992), Gerald Bruns says, "Gadamer is, in a way, a secular Luther who has substituted tradition for the Holy Scriptures" (158).
4. Arnold, "To Marguerite—Continued," ll. 4, 16.
5. Gadamer, "The Universality of the Hermeneutical Problem," in *Philosophical Hermeneutics* (henceforth *PH*), ed. and trans. David E. Linge (Berkeley: University of California Press, 1976), 16.
6. Bloom, "Literature as the Bible," *New York Review of Books* (March 31, 1988), 25; Benjamin, "Theses on the Philosophy of History," in *Illuminations*, ed. Hannah Arendt, trans. Harry Zohn (New York: Schocken, 1969), 256, 255; Murdoch, *Metaphysics as a Guide to Morals* (Harmondsworth: Penguin, 1993), 198.

7. Thus, Gerald Graff, in *Professing Literature* (Chicago: University of Chicago Press, 1987), hammers away at "The Humanist Myth," an elitist Arnoldian position that flourished in American English departments until the advent of a more correct approach. Jonathan Arac observes, in "Matthew Arnold and English Studies: The Power of Prophecies" (*Critical Genealogies: Historical Situations for Postmodern Literary Studies* [New York: Columbia University Press, 1987]), that even those who find Arnold irrelevant echo one aspect of his thought or another (117–38).

8. Gadamer, *Philosophical Apprenticeships* (henceforth *PA*), trans. Robert R. Sullivan (Cambridge: MIT Press, 1985), 3, 8, 9, 63–66 (the Krüger circle read everything from Homer to Meredith), 58 (on Bultmann), 193, 48 (on Heidegger). For the importance of Marburg, see Gadamer, *PA*, 7–19; "Martin Heidegger and Marburg Theology" and "On the Problem of Self-Understanding" (on Bultmann) in *PH*, 198–212, 44–58; Fritz K. Ringer, in *The Decline of the German Mandarins: The German Academic Community, 1890–1933* (Cambridge: Harvard University Press, 1969), e.g., pp. 305–6; and Robert R. Sullivan, *Political Hermeneutics: The Early Thinking of Hans-Georg Gadamer* (University Park: Penn State University Press, 1989).

9. Gadamer, "*Destruktion* and Deconstruction," in *Dialogue and Deconstruction: The Gadamer-Derrida Encounter* (henceforth *DD*), ed. Diane P. Michelfelder and Richard E. Palmer (Albany: State University of New York Press, 1989), 104, 24 ("Text and Interpretation"), 33. See Arnold on the modernity of Thucydides' "critical spirit" (*CPW*, 1:25). A selection of Heidegger's writings on the effects of modern technology (e.g., "The Age of the World Picture") is in *The Question Concerning Technology and Other Essays*, trans. William Lovitt (New York: Harper & Row, 1977). Karl Jaspers, in his influential *Man in the Modern Age*, published in 1931, warned of the resurgence of sophistry in modern Germany: whenever the classical world is forgotten, Jaspers contends, "barbarism has always revived" (trans. Eden and Cedar Paul [Garden City: Doubleday Anchor Books, 1957], 125).

10. See Sullivan, *Political Hermeneutics*; Gadamer (on the use of the Goethe quotation): it "was well camouflaged . . . and thus not quite a heroic act. But it was also not an accommodation" (*PA*, 78). See also Richard J. Bernstein, *Beyond Objectivism and Relativism: Science, Hermeneutics, and Praxis* (1983; reprint, Philadelphia: University of Pennsylvania Press, 1988), 253 n. 66. Gadamer, "Plato and the Poets," in *Dialogue and Dialectic: Eight Hermeneutical Studies of Plato*, trans. P. Christopher Smith (New Haven: Yale University Press, 1980), 64–65; "Plato's Educational State," 73.

11. Gadamer, *The Idea of the Good in Platonic-Aristotelian Philosophy*, trans. P. Christopher Smith (New Haven: Yale University Press, 1986). John P. Farrell draws upon Bakhtinian dialogism to argue that Arnold, even in his poetry, moves from self-preoccupation to engagement:" 'What You Feel I Share': Breaking the Dialogue of the Mind with Itself," in *Matthew Arnold 1988: A Centennial Review*, ed. Miriam Allott (London: John Murray, 1988, *Essays and Studies*), 45–61.

12. Bernstein, *Beyond Objectivism and Relativism*, 180. Like Bernstein (168), Weinsheimer, in *Gadamer's Hermeneutics*, notes that Gadamer's views of science and methodology are stereotyped and dated (2–3). But Gadamer's anxiety that a scientific worldview has supplanted a human-centered worldview is a romantic position that is by no means moribund.

13. Gadamer, "Rhetoric, Hermeneutics, and the Critique of Ideology: Metacritical

Comments on 'Truth and Method,' " in *The Hermeneutics* Reader, 289. While there is no evidence that Gadamer ever read Arnold, the fact that his position resembles Arnold's speaks favorably of the value of that position.

14. The Herderian *"concept of self-formation, education, or cultivation* (Bildung)," claims Gadamer, " . . . was perhaps the greatest idea of the eighteenth century" (*TM,* 9). Bruford, *The German Tradition of Self-Cultivation: "Bildung" from Humboldt to Thomas Mann* (Cambridge: Cambridge University Press, 1975), e.g., p. 164. There is no guarantee, of course, that the self-cultivated individual will turn his or her talents and sympathies outward, as Goethe, Arnold, and Gadamer believe. Weinsheimer, interestingly, compared the structure of *Bildung* ("alienation and return, excursion and reunion") to the story of the prodigal son (*Gadamer's Hermeneutics,* 70).

15. Arnold's targets here are the German Higher Critics of the Bible, who are "carried away by theorising; they affirm confidently where one cannot be sure; and, in short, prove by no means good and safe judges of the evidence before them" (*CPW,* 7:244). In his introduction to the English edition of Jauss's *Toward an Aesthetic of Reception* (trans. Timothy Bahti [Minneapolis: University of Minnesota Press, 1982], xi), Paul de Man notes that Gadamer's former pupil reproaches his teacher "for his commitment to a canonical idea of tradition," for privileging classical over modern authors. This "predilection for the classics" (Jauss, 54) is shared by Arnold; but their description of the hermeneutic effects of canonical texts (the Bible, the Greek tragedies) can also be applied to modern texts *provided* that one is willing to allow for a truth-claim in the text that transcends author and reader. What de Man refuses to allow for (in Gadamer or in Bakhtin) is a dialogical principle at work.

16. Heidegger, *Being and Time,* trans. John Macquarrie and Edward Robinson (New York: Harper & Row, 1962), 194. Heidegger's sense of the "forestructure" of understanding—that for the interpreter to understand, he "must already have understood what is to be interpreted"—leads into his discussion of the hermeneutic circle. For Gadamer, however, understanding moves one forward, not backward (see *DD,* 57).

17. "Unlike art, science destroys its past," notes Thomas Kuhn, in "Comments on the Relations of Science and Art," *The Essential Tension: Selected Studies in Scientific Tradition and Change* (Chicago: University of Chicago Press, 1977), 345.

18. Gadamer elaborates on the Protestant underpinnings of the idea of self-understanding (*Selbstverständnis*) in a letter to Fred Dallmayer, reprinted in *DD:* self-understanding does not lead to a sense of self-sufficiency; on the contrary, the reminder of one's human limitations leads Protestants to "the path of faith." Applying this principle to hermeneutics is to make us realize that "we are . . . something unfulfillable, an ever new undertaking and an ever new defeat" (97). Gadamer's privileging of the work of art is done in the traditionally romantic sense whereby the classic (a Grecian urn or Keats's "Ode on a Grecian Urn") survives as a something-out-there outlasting death. In "The Question of the Classic" (*Philosophical Hermeneutics and Literary Theory* [New Haven: Yale University Press, 1991], 125–26), Joel Weinsheimer disputes the view of Robert Scholes and other theorists that in a democracy "all texts are created equal" and that the idea of the "classic" implies an oppressive hierarchy. Weinsheimer contends that a classic exists not

only by virtue of its being constantly questioned, but also by its ability "to interrogate its inquisitors" (129). See Sainte-Beuve, "What Is a Classic?," in *Selected Essays*, trans. and ed. Francis Steegmuller and Norbert Gutterman (Garden City: Doubleday Anchor Books, 1964), 9, 11. And see Frank Kermode, *The Classic: Literary Images of Permanence and Change* (New York: Viking Press, 1975). Kermode, at this early point in his use of hermeneutics, presumes that the aim of the hermeneuticist is to recapture a text's original meaning. Four years later, in *The Genesis of Secrecy* (Cambridge: Harvard University Press, 1979), Kermode applies hermeneutics to the Bible and other texts to demonstrate their contemporaneity to the modern reader.

19. Gadamer, *Hegel's Dialectic: Five Hermeneutical Studies*, trans. P. Christopher Smith (New Haven: Yale University Press, 1976), 97. And see *TM*, 402. For Heidegger's view of how we come to "dwell" in language, see the essays collected in *Poetry, Language, Thought*, trans. Albert Hofstadter (New York: Harper & Row, 1971), esp. "Language" (189–210).

20. *DD*, 25; Derrida's response, 52–54; Gadamer's reply, 55–57. Derrida, "Violence and Metaphysics: An Essay on the Thought of Emmanuel Levinas," in *Writing and Difference*, trans. Alan Bass (Chicago: University of Chicago Press, 1978), 153. For the deconstructionist, meaningful dialogue is an impossibility: see, for example, Paul de Man on Bakhtin, in "Dialogue and Dialogism," *The Resistance to Theory* (Minneapolis: University of Minnesota Press, 1986); or J. Hillis Miller's dismissal of Paul Ricoeur ("the real action these days in narrative theory," Miller boasts, belongs to deconstructionists, not reactionary hermeneuticists) in *TLS* (Oct. 9, 1987), 1104–5; or John Caputo on "Gadamer's Closet Essentialism: A Derridean Critique," in *DD*, 258–64. (As the fortunes of deconstructionism have ebbed in the past decade, some former practitioners, like Geoffrey Hartmann, have claimed that what they are really doing is a form of Midrash, creative interpretation.)

21. Habermas, "On Hermeneutics' Claim to Universality," in *The Hermeneutics Reader*, 317, 316. Gadamer, "The Hermeneutics of Suspicion," in *Hermeneutics: Questions and Prospects*, ed. Gary Shapiro and Alan Sica (Amherst: University of Massachusetts Press, 1984), 54; "Rhetoric, Hermeneutics, and the Critique of Ideology," *Hermeneutics Reader*, 290–91. Two philosophers who see no need to oppose reason and tradition are Paul Ricoeur (who speaks of the Enlightenment's own "tradition" in "Hermeneutics and the Critique of Ideology," 99–100) and Karl R. Popper in "Towards a Rational Theory of Tradition," in *Conjectures and Refutations: The Growth of Scientific Knowledge* (New York: Basic Books, 1962), 120–35.

22. Gadamer, "Rhetoric, Hermeneutics, and the Critique of Ideology," 291; Habermas, *The Philosophical Discourse of Modernity*, trans. Frederick G. Lawrence (Cambridge: MIT Press, 1987), 183; Bernstein, *Beyond Objectivism and Relativism*, 263–64.

23. Bernstein, *Beyond Objectivism and Relativism*, 264–65. Allan Megill has an interesting comparison of Gadamer and Heidegger in *Prophets of Extremity: Nietzsche, Heidegger, Foucault, Derrida* (Berkeley: University of California Press, 1985), 20–25. Heidegger, "Letter on Humanism," in *Basic Writings*, ed. David F. Krell (New York: Harper & Row, 1977), 189–242. Heidegger opposes the "humanism" of Sartre and others "because it does not set the *humanitas* of man high enough" (210); this is

loftily stated, but the result is to place an abstract state of Being above the "merely human" (213, 221).

24. Newman, *Apologia Pro Vita Sua,* ed. David J. DeLaura (New York: Norton, 1968), 188. DeLaura overstates the nature of Newman's influence ("No other figure in Arnold's development—not Goethe, or Wordsworth—is so frequently found at the center of Arnold's total humanistic vision"), but he admits huge divergences of opinion too (*Hebrew and Hellene in Victorian England: Newman, Arnold, and Pater* [Austin: University of Texas Press, 1969]; compare pp. 152–61 with pp. 60–61, 89, 111–12). Joseph Carroll offers a corrective to DeLaura in "Arnold, Newman, and Cultural Salvation," *Victorian Poetry* 26 (Spring/Summer 1988): 163–78.

25. Arnold, *Unpublished Letters,* ed. Arnold Whitridge (New Haven: Yale University Press, 1923), 62–66; Newman, *Discussions and Arguments on Various Subjects* (1872; reprint, New York: Longmans, Green, and Co., 1924), 293. ("The Tamworth Reading Room" was first published in 1841.)

26. Quoted in Ian Ker, *John Henry Newman: A Biography* (Oxford: Oxford University Press, 1988), 93. Arnold cites Jesus' phrase as early as the Introduction to *The Popular Education in France* (reprinted later as "Democracy"), applying the injunction to the need of men and nations to transform themselves (*CPW,* 2:29).

27. Newman, *The Idea of a University,* ed. Martin J. Svaglic (New York: Holt, Rinehart, and Winston, 1960), 94, 91. Habermas, *Philosophical-Political Profiles* (Cambridge: MIT Press, 1983), 189–97.

28. See Isaiah Berlin's chilling account of de Maistre's conservatism in *The Crooked Timber of Humanity* (New York: Knopf, 1991), chap. 5.

29. Ker, *Newman,* 118; Newman, *An Essay on the Development of Christian Doctrine* (1845; reprint, Notre Dame: University of Notre Dame Press, 1989), 40. "Where by 'development' Newman meant (among other metaphors) something like the unfolding of the implications of an original germinative thought, Arnold . . . tends to mean something closer to the *alteration, deletion,* and eventual *extirpation* of Christian theology" (DeLaura, *Hebrew and Hellene,* 89). Ker, *Newman,* 171; Hirsch, *Validity in Interpretation* (New Haven: Yale University Press, 1967), 245–64.

30. See George Levine, "Matthew Arnold's Science of Religion: The Uses of Imprecision," *Victorian Poetry* 26 (Spring/Summer 1988): 143–62; David G. Riede, *Matthew Arnold and the Betrayal of Language* (Charlottesville: University Press of Virginia, 1988); J. Hillis Miller, *The Disappearance of God: Five Nineteenth-Century Writers* (Cambridge: Harvard University Press, 1963), chap. 5. For positive accounts of Arnold's religious hermeneutics, see apRoberts, *Arnold and God;* James C. Livingston, *Matthew Arnold and Christianity: His Religious Prose Writings* (Columbia: University of South Carolina Press, 1986); and Nathan A. Scott, Jr., *The Poetics of Belief* (Chapel Hill: The University of North Carolina Press, 1985).

31. Peter Allan Dale, in *The Victorian Critic and the Idea of History: Carlyle, Arnold, Pater* (Cambridge: Harvard University Press, 1977), discusses Arnold's Viconian pessimism, "inherited" from his father (97–104): according to Dale, Arnold uses the Viconian-derived phrase "the Modern Element" to show that England may well follow in the footsteps of Greece and Rome.

32. Quoted in *CPW,* 6:417.

33. See Kermode, *The Classic* ("the survival of the classic must . . . depend upon its possession of a surplus of signifier"; 140). "The true Past departs not," Carlyle declared in "Characteristics" (1831), "nothing that was worthy in the Past departs; no Truth or Goodness realised by man ever dies, or can die; but is all still here, and, recognised or not, lives and works through endless changes" (*The Works of Thomas Carlyle*, ed. H. D. Traill, 30 vols., Centenary Edition [London: Chapman and Hall, 1898–1901]), 28:38.

34. Arnold follows Newman in stressing the hold of the imagination rather than "logical reasonings" "over the affections" and in the formation of character ("Tamworth Reading Room," 297): Arnold cites this passage in his *Note-Books* (ed. H. F. Lowry, K. Young, and W. H. Dunn [London: Oxford University Press, 1952], 326).

35. Schleiermacher, *Hermeneutics Reader,* p. 83.

36. See Auerbach, *Mimesis: The Representation of Reality in Western Literature,* trans. Willard Trask (Garden City: Doubleday Anchor Books, 1957), p. 12.

37. Arnold, *Letters,* ed. Russell 2:99.

38. Alter, "Introduction to the Old Testament," in *The Literary Guide to the Bible* (Cambridge: Harvard University Press, 1987), 16–17; Kermode, "The Canon," 607. (Gadamer is invoked by several of the individual contributors—e.g., Gerald L. Bruns on "Midrash and Allegory," 636, or Kermode, 606.) Scott, *The Poetics of Belief,* 55, 59.

39. One notes the pervasive influence of Spinoza on Arnold's religious writings. In a number of early essays, including "The Bishop and the Philosopher," "Dr. Stanley's Lectures on the Jewish Church," "Tractatus Theologico-Politicus," and "Spinoza and the Bible" (1863), he repeats the idea that the "truth of religion" and the "truth of science" are not synonymous" (*CPW,* 3:74). See apRoberts, *Arnold and God,* on the Arnold-Spinoza connection (e.g., pp. 121–29).

40. Bultmann, "On the Problem of Demythologizing," in *"New Testament and Mythology" and Other Basic Writings,* trans. and ed. Schubert M. Ogden (Philadelphia: Fortress Press, 1984), 99, 122; and see Ricoeur, *The Symbolism of Evil,* trans. Emerson Buchanan (Boston: Beacon Press, 1967), 350. Howard W. Fulweiler, in "Literature or Dogma: Matthew Arnold as Demythologizer" (*The Arnoldian* 15 [Winter 1987/1988]: 37–47, notes considerable differences between Arnold and Bultmann (e.g., while Arnold relates Jesus and his teaching to this world, for Bultmann "the 'kingdom of God transcends the historical order' "; 45).

41. Bultmann, "Problem of Demythologizing," 118. Arnold is quoting Pope's "Essay on Man" " Oh Happiness! our being's end and aim!" (4.1).

42. Arnold, *Letters,* ed. Russell 2:55, 135.

43. Tulloch, "Amateur Theology," *Blackwood's Magazine* 113 (June 1873): 678–92, reprinted in *Matthew Arnold, Prose Writings: The Critical Heritage,* ed. Carl Dawson and John Pfordresher (London: Routledge & Kegan Paul, 1979), 287–96. Unsigned review, "The Bible as Interpreted by Mr. Arnold," *Westminster Review* 45 (April 1874): 309–23; reprinted in *Critical Heritage,* 307, 309.

44. Cited by Ker, *Newman,* 685. For Arnold's sympathy with the French Communards, see *Letters,* ed. Russell, 2:62, 65–66; for his non-sympathy with the Church of England's "Tory and squirearchical connexion," see 2:97.

45. Gadamer, "The Hermeneutics of Suspicion," 54; "The Philosophical Foundations of the Twentieth Century," in *PH*, 128.

46. Kuhn, "The Essential Tension: Tradition and Innovation in Scientific Research," *The Essential Tension*, 239; Gadamer, "What Is Practice?," in *RAS*, 87.

47. Gadamer, "Plato's Unwritten Dialectic," in *Dialogue and Dialectic*, 127–28, 125.

48. Gadamer, *"The Relevance of the Beautiful" and Other Essays* (henceforth *RB*), trans. Nicholas Walker, ed. Robert Bernasconi (Cambridge: Cambridge University Press, 1986), 48. (I have used Stephen Mitchell's translation of Rilke's "Archaic Torso of Apollo," l. 14, rather than David E. Linge's in the essay cited: "Aesthetics and Hermeneutics," *PH*.) One value of humanism, as Charles Altieri argues in *Canons and Consequences: Reflections on the Ethical Force of Imaginative Ideas* (Evanston, Ill.: Northwestern University Press, 1990), is that it looks "to idealized texts and to voices from the past [to provide] a history of efforts to escape" social iniquities (11–12).

49. Huxley (a friend of Arnold and friendly to Arnold's idea of culture) was speaking at the newly opened Science College of Birmingham, whose founder had decried the study of letters for science students; for them, Huxley contends, a "classical education is a mistake." (Sir Josiah Mason had decried "mere literary education.") To understand the Greeks, Huxley notes, we must appreciate how their "criticism of life . . . was affected by scientific conceptions. We falsely pretend to be the inheritors of their culture, unless we are penetrated, as the best minds among them were, with an unhesitating faith that the free employment of reason, in accordance with scientific method, is the sole method of reaching truth" ("Science and Culture," in *Science and Education* [New York: Appleton, 1896], 153, 152). See Arnold, *Letters*, ed. Russell, 2:143.

50. Wordsworth, Preface to *Lyrical Ballads*.

51. Gadamer, "Art and Imitation," in *RB*, 104, 103. In a letter to his mother, Arnold notes that while it is good to have "true feeling in poetry," it is better still for poetry to "give true *thoughts* as well" (*Letters*, ed. Russell, 1:241).

52. Gadamer, "On the Contribution of Poetry to the Search for Truth," in *RB*, 113; Arnold, "Memorial Verses," 28. (Wordsworth, the subject of "Memorial Verses," memorably articulated, in the preface to *Lyrical Ballads*, such ideas as the superiority of poetry to science, poetry's claim to truth, and its moral role on the reader— ideas pointing to Arnold's poetics and hermeneutics. Gadamer's ideas and phrasing, in the above paragraph, are similarly derived from his mentor, Heidegger.)

53. Gadamer, "Image and Gesture," in *RB*, 78.

54. Bernstein, *Beyond Objectivism and Relativism*, 265.

55. Gordimer, "Living in the Interregnum," in *The Essential Gesture*, ed. Stephen Clingman (London: Penguin, 1989), 284 (elsewhere, Gordimer cites Arnold as a fellow-liberal in "Speak Out: The Necessity for Protest," *Essential Gesture*, 101); Murdoch, *Metaphysics as a Guide to Morals*, 461–62.

CHAPTER FIVE

1. Arnold, *The Letters of Matthew Arnold*, ed. Cecil Y. Lang (Charlottesville: University Press of Virginia, 1996–), 1:233, 282.

2. Rorty, "Pragmatism, Relativism, and Irrationalism," *Consequences of Pragmatism* (henceforth *CP*) (Minneapolis: University of Minnesota Press, 1982), 160. See, for example, Richard J. Bernstein, "The Resurgence of Pragmatism," *Social Research* 59 (Winter 1992): 813–40, and *Philosophical Profiles: Essays in a Pragmatic Mode* (Philadelphia: University of Pennsylvania Press, 1986); John Patrick Diggins, *The Promise of Pragmatism* (Chicago: University of Chicago Press, 1994); Giles Gunn, *Thinking Across the American Grain: Ideology, Intellect, and the New Pragmatism* (Chicago: University of Chicago Press, 1992); John J. McDermott, *The Culture of Experience* (New York: New York University Press, 1976) and *Streams of Experience* (Amherst: University of Massachusetts Press, 1989); John Rajchman and Cornel West, eds., *Post-Analytic Philosophy* (New York: Columbia University Press, 1985); Cornel West, *The American Evasion of Philosophy: A Genealogy of Pragmatism* (Madison: University of Wisconsin Press, 1989).

3. See John Henry Raleigh, *Matthew Arnold and American Culture* (Berkeley: University of California Press, 1957). "Ever since Arnold found that reflecting upon the place of poetry in an industrial society led him to worry about 'a girl named Wragg,' " Irving Howe writes in *A Margin of Hope* (San Diego: Harcourt Brace Jovanovich, 1982), "the most valuable critics have often doubled as cultural spokesmen, moral prophets, political insurgents" (147). The finest recent contribution to Arnoldian criticism is Morris Dickstein's *Double Agent: The Critic and Society* (New York: Oxford University Press, 1992). Arnold "believed not simply in the spread of knowledge and the free play of mind," Dickstein observes, "but above all in usable knowledge, knowledge that could take on flesh and blood and make a difference, knowledge that was also poetry" (11). Cornel West, in *American Evasion*, dubs Trilling a "Pragmatist as Arnoldian Literary Critic" (164–81); but Diggins, in *Promise of Pragmatism*, finds divergencies as well as affinities between Trilling and Dewey (3–4, 382–84).

4. Rorty, "Private Irony and Liberal Hope," *Contingency, Irony, and Solidarity* (henceforth *CIS*) (Cambridge: Cambridge University Press, 1989), 81. James, quoted in Ralph Barton Perry, *The Thought and Character of William James*, 2 vols. (Boston: Little, Brown, 1935), 1:407.

5. Hook, *Pragmatism and the Tragic Sense of Life* (New York: Basic Books, 1974), 3–5, 22.

6. Dewey, "Poetry and Philosophy," in *John Dewey: The Early Works, 1882–1898*, ed. Jo Ann Boydston. 5 vols. (Carbondale: Southern Illinois University Press, 1969–72), 3:110, 123, 115, 120, 122, 123.

7. Ibid., 114–15; Dewey, "From Absolutism to Experimentalism," in *The Philosophy of John Dewey*, ed. John C. McDermott, 2 vols. (New York: Putnam's, 1973), 1:13.

8. "To read Arnold as the foe of democracy is false," observes Ruth apRoberts. "Democracy is the spring and the motive of *Culture and Anarchy* and of Arnold's whole career" ("Nineteenth-Century Culture Wars," *American Scholar* 64 [Winter 1995]): 147.

9. Mill, *On Liberty*, in *Autobiography and Other Writings*, ed. Jack Stillinger (Boston: Houghton Mifflin, 1969), 413–14. For Arnold on Mill, see Arnold, *Letters*, ed. Lang, 1:468. Edward Alexander compares the two in *Matthew Arnold and John Stuart Mill* (New York: Columbia University Press, 1965).

10. Alexis de Tocqueville, *Democracy in America*, ed. Philips Bradley, 2 vols. (New York: Vintage Books, 1960), 2:4, 104, 42, 106.

11. Mill, *On Liberty*, 452–53. Herbert Spencer, following Mill, attacked the "tyrannical system" of state-run education in "From Freedom to Bondage," 1891 (reprinted with *The Man versus the State*, ed. Donald MacRae [Harmondsworth: Penguin, 1969], 325). For a splendid recent account of Mill's position, see Stefan Collini, *Public Moralists: Political Thought and Intellectual Life in Britain, 1850–1930* (Oxford: Clarendon Press, 1991).

12. Dewey, "The Ethics of Democracy," *Early Works*, 1:237.

13. Ibid., 235, 232, 244, 245, 240, 246, 249.

14. Rorty, "The Priority of Democracy to Philosophy," *Objectivity, Relativism, and Truth* (henceforth *ORT*) (Cambridge: Cambridge University Press, 1991), 191, 188, 194, 193, 196.

15. Hook, *Pragmatism and the Tragic Sense of Life*, 13–14.

16. For Arnold's attachment to Sand, see Patricia Thomson, *George Sand and the Victorians* (New York: Columbia University Press, 1977), chap. 6.

17. Hook, *Pragmatism and the Tragic Sense of Life*, 4.

18. Dewey, *Liberalism and Social Action*, in *John Dewey: The Later Works, 1925–1953*, ed. Jo Ann Boydston, 17 vols. (Carbondale: Southern Illinois University Press, 1981–91), 11:45, 44.

19. James, "The Social Value of the College-Bred," in *Works of William James: Essays, Comments, and Reviews* (henceforth *ECR*) (Cambridge: Harvard University Press, 1987), 111, 118; Carlyle, *Past and Present*, in *The Works of Thomas Carlyle*, ed. H. D. Traill, 30 vols., Centenary Edition (London: Chapman and Hall, 1898–1901), 10:25; "Biography," *Works*, 28:46; James, *A Pluralistic Universe* (henceforth cited as *APU* in text) (1909; reprint, New York: Longman's, 1920), 20.

20. See James's letters to various newspapers on "The Philippine Tangle" (etc.), *ECR*, 154 ff.; "The Social Value of the College-Bred," *ECR*, 110; *Talks to Teachers* (New York: Norton, 1950), 131; "A Strong Note of Warning Regarding the Lynching Episode," *ECR*, 171.

21. For Arnold on the Paris Commune, see *Letters*, ed. George W. E. Russell, 2 vols. (New York: Macmillan, 1895), 2:65–66; James, "Renan's Dialogues," *ECR*, 330–31; *Talks to Teachers*, 19; *Pragmatism* (henceforth cited in text as *P*) (1907; reprint, New York: Meridian Books, 1955), 11; *The Will to Believe and Other Essays in Popular Philosophy* (henceforth cited in text as *WB*) (1897; reprint, New York: Dover, 1956), 325; Dewey, *Three Contemporary Philosophers*, in *John Dewey: The Middle Works, 1899–1924*, ed. Jo Ann Boydston, 15 vols. (Carbondale: Southern Illinois University Press, 1976–83), 12:206, 250.

22. Rorty, *CP*, xlii–xliii.

23. Schiller, *Humanism: Philosophical Essays* (1903; reprint, Freeport: Books for Library Press, 1969), xxiv.

24. Carlyle, "Characteristics," *Works*, 28:37; *Sartor Resartus*, *Works*, 1:156.

25. Myers, *William James: His Life and Thought* (New Haven: Yale University Press, 1986), 305. And see Hilary Putnam with Ruth Anna Putnam on Jamesian ethics in *Philosophy with a Human Face* (Cambridge: Harvard University Press, 1990), 217–31.

26. Mill, "The Utility of Religion," *Three Essays on Religion* (New York: Henry Holt and Co., 1874), 87; "Theism," Ibid., 249, 255–56. Noting the similarity between Arnold's and James's religious views, Lionel Trilling remarks, in *Matthew Arnold* (1939; reprint, New York: Meridian Books, 1955), "had James not read Arnold, we might have argued that Arnold had read James, for the earlier writer argued the pragmatic position with which the name of the latter is more intimately associated" (291).

27. James, *The Varieties of Religious Experience* (henceforth cited in text as *VRE*) (1902; reprint, New York: Collier Books, 1961), 401; and see *WB*, 89 (on "what Matthew Arnold likes to call *Aberglaube*").

28. James, "Renan's Dialogues," *ECR*, 331. R. W. B. Lewis suggests, in *The Jameses: A Family Narrative* (New York: Farrar, Straus and Giroux, 1991), that the real target of the Renan review is brother Henry ("William discerned in [Renan's *Dialogues*] an exaggerated version of everything that . . . he most feared about Henry: priggishness, fussy self-regard, and a disdainful—by implication, an anti-American—elitism"; 269–70). Henry James's response to William's Renan review was to agree with his brother about French "superficiality" (see Gay Wilson Allen, *William James: A Biography* [New York: Viking Press, 1967], 206). Perhaps William was taking the occasion, in the Renan review, to scourge his own aesthetic leanings.

29. Rorty, *CP*, 174, 166.

30. James, *Psychology, Briefer Course* (1892; reprint, New York: Fawcett, 1963), 148, 402. In the first passage James seems to echo the words of Arnold's follower, Walter Pater, in *The Renaissance:* "Every one of [our] impressions is the impression of the individual in his isolation, each mind keeping as a solitary prisoner its own dream of a world" (Oxford: Oxford University Press, 1986; 151).

31. Rorty, *ORT*, 193. Among those disturbed by Rorty's aesthetic turn are Richard J. Bernstein, in "One Step Forward, Two Steps Backward: Richard Rorty on Liberal Democracy and Philosophy," *Political Theory* 15 (Nov. 1987): 538–63; Nancy Fraser, "Solidarity or Singularity? Richard Rorty between Romanticism and Technology," *Unruly Practices: Power, Discourse, and Gender in Contemporary Social Theory* (Minneapolis: University of Minnesota Press, 1989); Jürgen Habermas, *The Philosophical Discourse of Modernity*, trans. Frederick Lawrence (Cambridge: MIT Press, 1990), 206–7; Frank Lentricchia, *Criticism and Social Change* (Chicago: University of Chicago Press, 1983), 15–19; the various contributors to the collection *Reading Rorty*, ed. Alan R. Malachowski (Oxford: Basil Blackwell, 1990); and Cornel West in *American Evasion* (194–210) and his afterward to *Post-Analytic Philosophy* (deploring Rorty's unashamed "ethnocentrism" and his non-Marxism: 259–72). For Alexander Nehamas, on the other hand, Rorty is insufficiently Nietzschean, insufficiently ironic ("A Touch of the Poet," *Raritan* 10 [Summer 1990]: 101–25).

32. See R. H. Super, "Sweetness and Light: Matthew Arnold's Comic Muse," in *Matthew Arnold in His Time and Ours*, ed. Clinton Machann and Forrest D. Burt (Charlottesville: University Press of Virginia, 1988), 183–96; Rorty, *ORT*, 193.

33. Arnold, *Letters*, ed. Russell, 2:20; Rorty, *CP*, 45.

34. Rorty, *ORT*, 17; *Philosophy and the Mirror of Nature* (Princeton: Princeton University Press), 13.

35. See Arnold, *CPW*, 3:53, 179 (on Spinoza's "edifying" versus Strauss's unedifying

views); 9:254; Rorty, *Philosophy and the Mirror of Nature*, 359–60; *CP*, 24, 175; *Essays in Heidegger and Others* (henceforth *EH*) (Cambridge: Cambridge University Press, 1991), 152.

36. Rorty, "Nineteenth-Century Idealism and Twentieth-Century Textualism," *CP*, 148–49, 158; Nietzsche, *Twilight of the Idols*, in *The Portable Nietzsche*, trans. and ed. Walter Kaufmann (New York: Viking Press, 1954), 510; Rorty, "Thugs and Theorists," *Political Theory* 15 (Nov. 1987): 573; (Rorty deploring the sense of "alienation" in Lentricchia and others) "Two Cheers for the Cultural Left," *South Atlantic Quarterly* 89 (Winter 1990): 228, 233 n; "The Unpatriotic Academy," *New York Times* (Feb. 13, 1994), 15.

37. Rorty, *CIS*, 61; *EH*, 196–98. Foucault's emergence as a human rights advocate in the late 1870s and early 1880s is touched on in chapter 2.

38. See "Private Irony and Liberal Hope," *CIS*, esp. pp. 87–95. "Why language that is not stable enough to support truth," Diggins wonders in *Promise of Pragmatism*, "can be clear enough to forge solidarity as a unifying principle held by different people remains unexplained" by Rorty (476).

39. Rorty, "Two Cheers," pp. 234 n, 229; *ORT*, 15–16; *EH*, 186.

40. Rorty, *EH*, 183; "Thugs and Theorists," 571. Rorty's fondness for Harold Bloom (who coined the phrase "School of Resentment") has led him to the dubious position that "strong modern" authors are always better than their predecessors. "Once we had Yeats's later poems in hand," Rorty says (*CIS*, 20), "we were less interested in reading Rossetti's." It is this kind of crassness that gives pragmatism a bad name in aesthetic matters.

41. Dewey, "The Development of American Pragmatism," in *Philosophy of John Dewey*, 1:56; *Liberalism and Social Action*, in *Later Works*, 11:52; George Santayana, "Dewey's Naturalistic Metaphysics," in *The Philosophy of John Dewey*, ed. Paul Arthur Schilpp (Evanston, Ill.: Northwestern University Press, 1939), 251.

42. Keating, "Arnold Social and Political Thought," in *Writers and Their Background: Matthew Arnold*, ed. Kenneth Allott (Athens: Ohio University Press, 1976), 222; Dewey, "Construction and Criticism," *Later Works*, 5:142.

43. Dewey, "From Absolutism to Experimentalism," 7, 8–9; *The Quest for Certainty* (henceforth cited in text as *QC*) (1929; reprint, New York: Perigree Books, 1980), 62. James, in 1903, noted in a letter to Dewey that while he had come "from empiricism," his fellow pragmatist had reached "much the same goal" even though proceeding "from Hegel" (Perry, *Thought and Character*, 2:521).

44. Dewey, "Science as Subject-Matter and as Method," *Middle Works*, 6:78; "Two Phases of Renan's Life," *Early Works*, 3:174–79; "Renan's Loss of Faith in Science," *Early Works*, 4:11–18. Dewey supports Renan's position (which Renan later abandoned) that science, in supplanting religion, presents "us with a deeper truth," and that the "practical outcome" of science should be "made the possession of all men" (4:14–15). See Arnold, *CPW*, 3:264–65.

45. Westbrook, *John Dewey and American Democracy* (Ithaca: Cornell University Press, 1991), 141. And see Richard J. Bernstein, *John Dewey* (New York: Washington Square Press, 1967), esp. chap. 9. In "Science as Solidarity," Rorty suggests that Dewey saw the community of "scientific inquirers" as a noteworthy example of democracy in action (*ORT*, 43). Dewey, "Construction and Criticism," 134, 142.

46. Dewey, "Science as Subject-Matter," 78; Ludwig Wittgenstein, *Philosophical Investigations*, trans. G. E. M. Anscombe (New York: Macmillan, 1968), 47e.

47. Dewey, *Reconstruction in Philosophy, Middle Works*, 12:114; "Two Phases of Renan's Life," 174–75; "Self-Realization as the Moral Ideal," *Early Works*, 4:50.

48. Dewey (defining "Culture" for *A Cyclopedia of Education*), *Middle Works*, 6:406; Arnold, canceled passage from *Culture and Anarchy, CPW*, 5:527.

49. Dewey, "The Challenge of Democracy to Education," *Later Works*, 11:189; *The Public and its Problems* (1927; reprint, Athens: Ohio University Press, 1991), 154. See Lipmann, *The Phantom Public* (New York: Harcourt, Brace, 1925).

50. Dewey, *Democracy and Education* (New York: Macmillan, 1916), 357, 145; "The Aims and Ideals of Education," *Middle Works*, 13:399–405.

51. See W. F. Connell, *The Educational Thought and Influence of Matthew Arnold* (London: Routledge & Kegan Paul, 1950); G. H. Bantock, "Matthew Arnold, H. M. I.," *Scrutiny* 18 (1951): 32–44; Vincent L. Tollers, "A Working Isaiah: Arnold in the Council Office," in *Matthew Arnold 1988: A Centennial Review*, ed. Miriam Allott, *Essays and Studies* 41 (John Murray, 1988): 108–24; Peter Smith and Geoffrey Summerfield, eds., *Matthew Arnold and the Education of the New Order* (Cambridge: Cambridge University Press, 1969), 239, 215–16, 223–24, 227 (selections from Arnold's inspector reports). Bantock notes Arnold's emphasis on "the value of the [student's] inner life" (which Dewey neglects), and he applauds "Arnold's insistence that the teachers should have a high standard of culture" (35, 39). Connell points to Arnold's and Dewey's joint stress on individual "growth" for the sake of social progress (279). In their good anthology (and introduction), Smith and Summerfield demonstrate Arnold's commitment to his task as school inspector, his anxiety over the deprivations endured by working-class children, and his sense that teachers were undervalued. The most stinging of Arnold's published rebukes of the Liberal mishandling of British education is his tract on "The Twice-Revised Code" (the policy dictating, for example, payment to schools on the basis of examination results): *CPW*, 2:212–43.

52. Dewey, "Ethics of Democracy," 231. Trilling pertinently notes that Arnold "demanded that men think not of themselves but of the whole of which they are a part" (52).

53. Dewey, "Construction and Criticism," 132; Westbrook, *Dewey And Democracy*, 100 (Westbrook also notes that "Dewey clearly differentiated his pedagogy" from that of "child-centered" educators who failed "to connect the interests and activities of the child to the subject matter of the curriculum"; 99); Dewey, *Liberalism and Social Action*, 21, 51–52.

54. Rorty, introduction to *Dewey: Later Works*, 8:xi–xii; Dewey, "Education and Social Ideals," *Later Works*, 11: 167. Two recent assaults on liberalism from within the academy emanate from Stanley Fish, who, in *There's No Such Thing as Free Speech and It's a Good Thing, Too* (New York: Oxford University Press, 1994), claims that "Liberalism Doesn't Exist" (like pragmatism, in Fish's view, it has no right to offer opinions that have a claim on us since it lacks a foundation, a center, to argue from); and from John Kekes, in *The Morality of Pluralism* (Princeton: Princeton University Press, 1993), who derides the notion that there are "overriding values." From the left, liberals such as Dewey and Rorty (and Arnold) have been attacked

for their adherence to old-fashioned values (Kekes prefers what he calls a "reasonable immorality"; 163); from the right, they have become a convenient target for those opposing tolerance and public-mindedness.

55. Dewey, *Reconstruction in Philosophy*, 197; Trilling, *The Liberal Imagination* (Garden City: Doubleday Anchor Books, n.d.), xii; Rawls, *Political Liberalism* (New York: Columbia University Press, 1993), see chap. 4 ("Overlapping Consensus"), 321 (social union as an orchestra); Dewey, "The Meaning of the Term: Liberalism," *Later Works*, 14: 254. Arnold's forward-looking liberalism is well treated by R. H. Super in *The Time-Spirit of Matthew Arnold* (Ann Arbor: University of Michigan Press, 1970); a welcome recent defense of Dewey's liberalism is Alan Ryan's *John Dewey and the High Tide of American Liberalism* (New York: Norton, 1995). The development of nineteenth-century English liberalism from an individualistic to a more collectivist position is considered by Stefan Collini in *Public Moralists*. J. W. Burrow, in *Whigs and Liberals: Continuity and Change in English Political Thought* (Oxford: Clarendon Press, 1988), stresses the traditional liberal concerns with individuality and diversity. Nancy L. Rosenblum's collection, *Liberalism and the Moral Life* (Cambridge: Harvard University Press, 1989), includes authors like Charles Taylor and Judith Shklar, who consider liberalism's moral purpose. See also Richard Bellamy, ed., *Victorian Liberalism* (London: Routledge, 1990); John Gray, *Liberalisms: Essays in Political Philosophy* (London: Routledge, 1989) and *Post-liberalism: Studies in Political Thought* (New York: Routledge, 1993).

56. Ralph Waldo Emerson, *The Conduct of Life* (1860), in *Selected Writings of Emerson*, ed. Donald McQuade (New York: Modern Library, 1981), 724.

57. Westbrook, *Dewey and Democracy*, 345.

58. Rorty, "Thugs and Theorists," 571; Dewey, *Reconstruction in Philosophy*, 200–201.

59. Dewey, *Human Nature and Conduct* (henceforth cited in text as *HNC*) (New York: Henry Holt and Company, 1922), 279; *A Common Faith* (henceforth cited in text as *ACE*) (New Haven: Yale University Press, 1934), 54; Arnold, *Letters*, ed. Russell, 2:37.

60. Steven C. Rockefeller, in *John Dewey: Religious Faith and Democratic Humanism* (New York: Columbia University Press, 1991), discusses the uses of religion in Dewey's thinking. And see West's advocacy of "Prophetic Pragmatism" (Dewey applied to Christian Marxism) in *American Evasion*, chap. 6. "Symbols control sentiment and thought," Dewey observes in *The Public and its Problems*, "and the new age has no symbols consonant with its activities" (142).

61. "I recollect eulogies of Bacon in Mr. Dewey's works," Mumford complains in *The Golden Days* (1926; reprint, New York: Dover, 1968), "but none of Shakespeare; appreciations of Locke, but not Shelley and Keats and Wordsworth and Blake" (134). Dewey, *Art as Experience* (1934; reprint, New York: Perigree Books, 1980), 346, 105.

62. Dewey, Introduction to *Problems of Men*, in *Later Works*, 15: 156, 169.

Index

Falkland, Lucius Cary, Viscount, 10, 147–49, 173
Farrell, John B., 194n. 11
Fauriel, Claude, 52
Faverty, Frederic E., 181n. 53
Fichte, Johann Gottlieb, 81
Fields, James T., 14
Fish, Stanley, 115, 204n. 54
Flaubert, Gustave, 34, 179n. 28; *Madame Bovary*, 53
Flynn, Thomas, 188n. 62
Fortnightly Review, 30, 183n. 6
Foucault, Michel, 9, 46, 50–51, 66–80, 81, 107, 134, 156, 160–61, 171, 183n. 10, 186n. 45, 187n. 52, 199n. 62, 203n. 37; *Archaeology of Knowledge, The*, 67, 186n. 47, 188n. 60; *Birth of the Clinic, The*, 74; *Care of the Self, The*, 78; *Discipline and Punish*, 73, 74, 75; *Discourse on Language, The*, 68; "Ethic of Care for the Self as a Practice of Freedom, The," 188n. 62; *History of Sexuality, The*, 73, 74, 77; *I. Pierre Rivière. . .* , 68; *Madness and Civilization*, 67, 73; "Maurice Blanchot: The Thought from Outside," 51, 71, 72; "Nietzsche, Genealogy, History," 51, 69, 70; *Order of Things, The*, 73, 74; "Preface to Transgression, A" (on Bataille), 51, 69, 71; *Raymond Roussel*, 51, 71; *Use of Pleasure, The*, 78, 79–80, 188n. 60; "What Is an Author?" 72; "What Is Enlightenment?" 77–78
France: Arnold on, 15–18, 20, 26, 45–66, 81, 130, 150; Henry James on, 15–16, 45, 46
Francis, Saint, 6, 51
Frankfurt School, 120
"Free play of the mind," 12–13, 25, 35, 37, 43, 47, 90, 109, 163, 178n. 11
French Academy (Académie française), 14, 23, 37, 52, 54–55, 62, 183n. 6
French Revolution: Arnold on, 26, 145, 149; Renan on, 61
Freud, Sigmund, 105, 133, 134
"Fusing of horizons," 117–18, 132

Gadamer, Hans-Georg, 2, 5, 9, 10, 78, 105–38, 139, 159, 194n. 10, 194n. 13, 195n. 14, 195n. 18, 198n. 38; "Art and Imitation," 136; *Dialogue and Dialectic*, 2, 112; "Hegel's Dialectic," 118; "Heritage of Hegel, The," 107; *Idea of the Good in Platonic-Aristotelian Philosophy, The*, 113; "On the Contribution of Poetry to the Search for Truth," 136; *Philosophical Apprenticeships*, 110, 111, 114, 194n. 10; "Philosophical Foundations of the Twentieth-Century, The," 133; *Philosophical Hermeneutics*, 5, 108, 117, 124–25, 133, 134; "Plato and the Poets," 112; "Plato's Educational State," 112; "Plato's Unwritten Dialectic," 134; *Reason in the Age of Science*, 107, 137; *Relevance of the Beautiful, The*, 135, 136; "Rhetoric, Hermeneutics, and the Critique of Ideology," 120, 194n. 13; *Truth and Method*, 10, 107–8, 112, 113–20, 121, 124, 128, 134; "Universality of the Hermeneutical Problem," 108, 124–25
Galen, 188n. 62
Gautier, Théophile, 52, 58
George, Stefan, 110, 121
German Higher Critics, 59, 60, 195n. 15
German Romanticism, 8, 106, 107, 112, 113
Germany, Arnold on, 81
God: Arnold on, 94, 95, 102, 131, 177n. 3; death of, 70, 82, 84; Dewey on, 172; William James on, 154, 155; Nietzsche on, 94, 95, 96
Godkin, Edwin L., 14
Goethe, Johann Wolfgang von, 5, 8, 9, 10, 15, 31, 34, 38, 41, 47, 48, 49, 62, 64–65, 78, 83, 84, 86, 89, 90, 92, 98, 99, 100, 112, 122, 131, 136, 143, 148, 150, 154, 172, 175n. 4, 192n. 38; *Wilhelm Meister's Apprenticeship*, 139, 154
Goethe Institute, Paris, 119
Goncourts, Edmond and Jules, 56, 57, 184n. 15
Goodheart, Eugene, 191n. 31